Seppuku

Seppuku

A History of Samurai Suicide

ANDREW RANKIN

KODANSHA INTERNATIONAL

Tokyo · New York · London

Distributed in the United States by Kodansha America, LLC, and in the United Kingdom and Continental Europe by Kodansha Europe Ltd.

Published by Kodansha International Ltd., 17-14 Otowa 1-chome, Bunkyo-ku, Tokyo 112-8652.

ISBN 978-4-7700-3142-6

First edition, 2011
19 18 17 16 15 14 13 12 11   10 9 8 7 6 5 4 3 2 1

Library of Congress Cataloging-in-Publication Data

Rankin, Andrew.
  Seppuku : a history of samurai suicide / Andrew Rankin.
      p. cm.
  Includes bibliographical references and index.
  ISBN 978-4-7700-3142-6
  1. Seppuku. 2. Suicide--Japan--History. I. Title.
  HV6548.J3R36 2011
  394'.880952--dc22
                                          2010041547

www.kodansha-intl.com

CONTENTS

AUTHOR'S NOTE

Japanese names are presented with the family name first, followed by the given name. According to custom, samurai are thereafter identified by their given names. Exceptions are made in a few cases for men of celebrity status whose family names are already familiar.

All translations, from all languages, are my own unless otherwise indicated in the text.

I owe thanks to Professor Karl Friday (University of Georgia), Professor Peter Kornicki (Cambridge), Dr. Mark Morris (Cambridge), and Dr. Dominic Steavu (Heidelberg), each of whom read through a part of the manuscript and made invaluable suggestions for improvement. Cathy Layne, my editor at Kodansha International, did an excellent job of preparing the book for publication and was gentle with her criticisms.

Utagawa Toyokuni III. *Seppuku of Hirai Gonpachi* (Tōkaidō gōjūsan tsugi no uchi: Hirai Gonpachi), ca. 1830. Woodblock print. © The Tsubouchi Memorial Theatre Museum of Waseda University.

INTRODUCTION
Aesthetics of Seppuku

"Behold!" he roared from the castle tower, "I am Prince Morinaga, second son of the divine Emperor Go-Daigo, who traces his lineage through ninety-five generations to the sun goddess Amaterasu. My men have run away. Now I shall destroy myself out of contempt for them—and you! Watch carefully and you will learn how to cut your bellies, for your day will surely come." He removed his armor and hurled it down from the tower. Now all his enemies could see that he was wearing a prince's robes and cloak. As they looked on, he stabbed himself in the stomach, cut cleanly from left to right, and hurled a fistful of his guts against the wall. Dropping to his knees, he inserted the sword into his mouth until the tip of the blade touched his throat. Then he pushed himself forward, and died.[1]

The history of seppuku—Japanese ritual suicide by cutting the stomach, sometimes referred to as hara-kiri—spans a millennium. If the abundant suicides recorded in Japanese war tales are to be believed, the format has been infinitely variable. Defeated warriors slash their stomachs on the battlefield to spite their enemies. There are men who fling their guts into the air or write poems in their own blood. Some disembowel themselves in their rooms and slowly bleed to death. Others are assisted by a comrade or a servant. Whole households commit seppuku together. Friends tearfully dispatch friends.

1. Hasegawa, ed., *Taiheiki*, 1:335.

Fathers behead sons, or vice versa. Brothers stab each other. Lovers tear themselves up at the grave of their beloved. Vassals martyr themselves after the death of their lord. Thwarted assassins turn their swords on themselves. Imperialists slit their bowels in the name of the emperor. Wives stab themselves to shame their husbands. Seppuku can be spontaneous or premeditated, voluntary or obligatory, public or private. It can be solemn ceremony or dramatic theater. Samurai cut their stomachs out of honor, shame, desperation, grief, panic, protest, patriotism, narcissism, revenge, hatred, and love. There are descriptions of seppuku performed by warriors, servants, children, bureaucrats, educators, lawmakers, pirates, poets, princes, and priests. Suicide scenes range in scale from mass self-slayings by hundreds of warriors at a time to the death of a lone swordsman on a cliff top. Samurai disembowel themselves on battlefields, atop castle towers, in mountain caves, in grand mansions, in peasant huts, in jail, at roadsides, at temples, in graveyards, on horseback, and at sea. Through all these colorful variations, the essential idea being presented to us does not change: when it is no longer possible to live proudly, the samurai should endeavor to die proudly, and the proudest samurai death is by seppuku.

Origins

As an enduring sociocultural phenomenon, suicide by cutting the stomach has been known only in Japan. The seppuku ritual is unique to Japanese tradition. Yet it cannot have been an aboriginal Japanese practice. For one thing, the sword came late to Japan. The first examples were imported from Korea and China in the third century AD. Prior to that the Japanese islanders hunted with bows and arrows. Early Chinese explorers who visited the Japanese islands recounted the strange ways of the "Eastern barbarians."[2] They were a hardworking, hard-drinking people, much given to rituals and summary executions, who ate raw fish and rice, and paid homage to Pimiko, their shaman queen. Aesthetically-minded, the Japanese rendered the

2. De Bary, ed., *Sources of Japanese Tradition*, 1:6.

foreign swords less functional by thinning the blades, and may initially have used them only as ceremonial objects. A poem by the Japanese emperor Shōmu (701–756) acknowledges the superiority of swords made in China, where warrior culture had been thriving for a thousand years. Japan's military history cannot be said to begin before the fifth century, when a powerful Japanese force supposedly captured parts of the Korean peninsula. It is in China, not Japan, that we must seek the origins of the swordsman who stabs himself to death.

Chinese warfare was a highly ritualized activity, subject to the constraints of ceremonial laws and divinations. Warriors heading into battle burned offerings to the gods and drank the blood of sacrificial human victims. In victory they decapitated their prisoners and burned the heads before the temple altar. Bloodletting was a noble right. Sacrifice, hunting, and combat were privileges of a military aristocracy. Warfare was less a matter of territorial expansion, more one of aggrandizement. Warriors fought for their ancestors and for their gods. Glory was everything. Not surprisingly, warfare was unending. Chinese histories such as Sima Qian's *Historical Records* (91 BC), which subsequently circulated in Japan, make frequent mention of rebellions, assassinations, massacres, executions, and self-executions. The suicidal strain in Japan's martial ethic can be traced to ancient China: to the chariot-borne warlords of the Western Zhou Dynasty (1050–771 BC), who consecrated their war drums with sacrificial blood and fell on their swords if the battle went against them, and to charismatic heroes such as the rebel general Xiang Yu, who cut his throat on the bank of the Wu River in 202 BC. Away from the battlefield, suicide was an honorable form of martyrdom. A Chinese text from the third century BC reads, "A loyal minister behaves thus: if he can advantage his ruler and profit his state, he will shirk and evade nothing, even killing himself to accompany his ruler in death."[3] But Chinese historians do not dwell on suicide scenes, and death is seldom rhetorical: "He fell on his sword and died"; "He then withdrew and killed himself"; "He then killed himself"; "And so he killed himself"; "And so he swallowed poison

---

3. Lü Buwei, *The Annals of Lü Buwei*, 247. Translated by J. Knoblock and J. Riegel.

and killed himself"; "The three brothers then all wept, drew their swords, and killed themselves."[4]

Another factor encouraging suicide was the deadly absolutism of warfare in early China. This was a matter rooted in pragmatism. Rebels who capitulated one year might rise up again the next. Extermination was the key. The sheer size of the Chinese armies demanded drastic measures. A showdown between the Qin and the Zhao at Chanping in 260 BC is believed to have involved more than a million soldiers. After the battle, the Qin made victory permanent by slaughtering prisoners in their hundreds of thousands. Facing inevitable annihilation, vanquished generals were naturally inclined to turn their swords on themselves.

In time the Chinese purged themselves of this extravagant violence. Laozu condemned warfare as evil. Mencius equated soldiers with criminals. Epic literature of the later Qin and Han dynasties (221 BC–220 AD) did not valorize acts of courage by individual warriors. Military treatises discouraged glory-seeking, and instead stressed an intellectual approach to warfare. Tactics replaced heroics. The self-poisoning princes and self-drowning princesses who feature in Chinese tales of courtly intrigue from this period suggest that suicide was now largely an aristocratic affair. Although obligatory suicide in its bloodless forms endured in China as a mode of capital punishment, voluntary suicide by self-stabbing belongs only to antiquity.

A few episodes in Chinese chronicles stand out for their relevance to our inquiry. One is found in the *The Annals of Lü Buwei*, a massive compendium of histories completed in 239 BC. The work records many suicides, ritualistic and spontaneous, voluntary and obligatory. Warriors fall on their swords, bash their heads against trees, or throw themselves from cliffs. Toward the end of the second book, in a brief chapter dealing with the cannibal barbarians of Di, we read:

> The Di army arrived and found Duke Yi at Rongze. They killed him and ate all his flesh, leaving only his liver. Later,

4. Ibid., 249, 263, 595; Sima Qian, *Historical Records*, 35, 59, 86.

Hong Yan, one of the duke's men, returned home from a mission. He saluted the duke's remains, and offered his report. That done, he cried out to heaven and wept. His tears did not cease until all his grief was spent. Then he exclaimed, "My lord, allow me to serve as your cloak." He cut open his belly, placed the duke's liver inside, and fell down dead.[5]

The date of this incident is given as 660 BC. It is the only stomach-cutting scene in this extremely long text, which includes many other equally bizarre deaths. For that reason it cannot be taken as representing an established myth or tradition. Clearly though, the legend of the loyal warrior who rips open his stomach is being formulated here.

An official Chinese history compiled in the fifth century AD contains this passage:

At the age of eighteen, Rong Liang began employment at the local government office. He was a remarkably handsome young man. His superior, a man named Zhuge Li, took a liking to Rong, and promoted him to the position of scribe. But one of the junior workers spread a rumor about Rong, saying, "Rong is carrying on with one of the maids." To prove his innocence to Zhuge Li, Rong cut open his own stomach and pulled out his entrails.[6]

This is stomach-cutting as an appeal to purity. The logic here is founded on a primitive symbolism: a man with nothing to hide shows his innocence by exposing his insides. The association of purity with wounding had religious provenance. Early self-mutilators included priests and holy men. In the twenty-third chapter of the *Lotus Sutra* a bodhisattva is reborn in the Pure Land after burning himself alive in front of the Buddha. Chinese Buddhists accordingly viewed the

---

5. Lü Buwei, *The Annals of Lü Buwei*, 249–50. Translated by J. Knoblock and J. Riegel. Translation slightly modified.

6. From the *Xiecheng hou hanshu*, quoted in Katō, *Kairiki ranshin*, 67.

body as an obstacle to enlightenment. The flesh must be punished to exorcise the impurities of the world. Chinese monks devised various ingenious methods of *kuxing*, "self-torture." Daoists performed the bloody ritual of *bingjie*, in which a man was liberated from his corporeal prison by means of a sharp blade.

A history of the Tang Dynasty (618–907) records another Chinese stomach-cutting incident, which purportedly occurred in the second half of the seventh century during the reign of Empress Wu. Informed that one of her sons was plotting against her, the empress dispatched one of her advisors, Lai Junchen, to investigate. Lai's predilection for torturing suspects was well known, and when he arrived at the prince's residence no one dared confront him. Then one of the prince's men, An Jingzang, stepped forward to plead his master's innocence.

> An Jingzang faced Lai Junchen and boldly declared, "If my words are not sufficient to convince you, I shall prove the prince's purity by tearing open my chest." Thus saying, he drew his sword and cut open his chest. His internal organs spilled out and his blood gushed to the floor.[7]

As it turns out, this is not a suicide. The text goes on to describe how physicians replaced An's organs and sewed up his wound. He survived, and received high praise for his loyalty from the empress herself.

These episodes from Chinese sources, scattered over centuries, tell us nothing of reality other than that their authors shared a familiarity with the concept of suicide by disembowelment, and that they believed it to be not madness but greatness. As for how the self-disemboweling hero made his way from China to the islands of Japan, his route and the timing of his arrival, nothing at all is known. All we can say with certainty is that the ideal subsequently formalized by the Japanese into the ritual known as seppuku had its roots in ancient Chinese legend. It was not a uniquely Japanese invention.

7. From the *Jiu tangshu*, in ibid., 68–69.

Beauty and Death

Accounts of suicide by stomach-cutting begin to appear in Japanese texts from the eighth century onward, and are a pervasive feature of war chronicles of the thirteenth and fourteenth centuries. None of the Chinese examples given above takes place on a battlefield, and the men who cut their stomachs are not identified as warriors. In contrast, Japanese texts situate stomach-cutting exclusively in a martial context. Seppuku seeks to fuse the noble purity of Chinese aristocrats with the efficient orderliness of military professionals.

> The shogun's forces had surrounded the castle at Tago and cut off all provisions. Soon most of the castle guards were dead from starvation. Lord Chiba Tanenobu, heading the defense, was barely fifteen years of age. He commanded a small force—his entire cavalry consisted of just twenty riders. Realizing that the situation was hopeless, Tanenobu sent his friend Naotoki to the enemy camp with this message: "Let me cut my stomach before Buddha, and the castle is yours."
>
> And so it was agreed. The castle was handed over to the shogun's commanders, and Tanenobu was escorted to a place called Musa where there was a small shrine dedicated to Amida Buddha. There, on August 12, 1455, young Lord Tanenobu courageously cut his stomach at the feet of the Buddha, while priests burned incense and chanted sutras. Tanenobu was beheaded by his friend Naotoki, who likewise cut his own stomach. Each bid his farewell to the world with a poem. Fourteen of the samurai who had fought alongside them also died that day, stabbing each other and laying down side by side, as if to sleep.[8]

This passage is extracted from *The Great Book of Kamakura* (Kamakura ōzōshi), a battle chronicle written around 1490. It is in every

8. Kondō, ed., *Kamakura ōzōshi*, in *Kaitei shiseki shūran*, 5:50.

respect a typical example of how samurai suicide is represented in Japanese war tales. The incident is recounted as historical fact, and the people who first read or heard it no doubt believed it was so. The details are sufficiently precise to suggest a high degree of authenticity; a subsequent paragraph lists the full names of all fourteen dead samurai. The Chiba family and Tago Castle are well documented. We can safely assume that this is not fiction. Yet nor is it unadulterated fact. There is something distinctly unnatural about this report of suicide and executions. A fastidious censor has cleansed the episode of unsightliness. Though sixteen men stab themselves to death, there is no blood, no screaming, no agony. We might say that there is no dying, there is only death. Death as poetry, courage, and comradely love. When heroes such as these decide to die, the text invites us to believe, it is as easy for them as laying down to sleep. This sort of aesthetic cleansing is ubiquitous in samurai texts, and has been a crucial factor in fostering and promoting the seppuku ideal. Had the authors opted for graphic realism, seppuku might have been a very short-lived phenomenon. But if death is made exquisitely poetic, every man can dream of becoming a poem.

Fortunately, we need not rely on medieval war tales for our sources. From later centuries we have reliable and meticulous reports written by surgeons, coroners, ceremonial supervisors, police officers, government officials, and foreign diplomats. That there have been Japanese men who committed suicide by cutting their stomachs cannot reasonably be doubted, though the practice has not been as widespread and frequent as popular literature suggests. What distinguishes the seppuku tradition is not the bare fact of seppuku as a recurring feature of Japan's military history, but the elaborate aesthetic framework that has been constructed around this skeleton of truth. Seppuku is fact augmented by myth and adorned with aesthetic trimmings.

Martial suicide is not, of course, an East Asian monopoly. Suicidal practices have existed among warrior cultures around the world, from the African Ashanti to the Icelandic Vikings. Historians of antiquity recorded martial suicide rituals performed by the Thracians, the Arabians, the Gauls, the Goths, the Turks, and the Abyssinians. Early

Portuguese traders reported mass suicide rituals among the Tamils; after the passing of their king, Tamil warriors tied their hair to branches and sliced through their own necks. Among the Rajputs in northern India, the tradition of riding out from a fallen fortress to die fighting was noble enough to have a name: *saka*. Battlefield suicides were committed by warriors of the Indian Nayar caste, who deliberately tore open the wounds that had been inflicted on them. Hundreds of German Crusaders are said to have fatally stabbed themselves in panic after the accidental death of Barbarossa, swept away in a whirlpool as he attempted to cross the Gőksu River in June 1190. Roman annalists recorded the outpouring of suicidal grief that attended the funeral in AD 69 of Emperor Otho, who killed himself to avert the certain destruction of his army by that of Vitellius. Otho's men had pleaded with him to let them fight to the death. Otho silenced them with the words: "If you truly love me, let me die."[9] He went into his tent and punctured his heart with a dagger.

> As the Praetorian guards carried Otho's body to the funeral pyre they praised his heroic act with tears in their eyes, and kissed his hands and wounded breast. Some stabbed themselves to death by the pyre, not from feelings of remorse, or fear of being punished by Vitellius, but out of pure love for their emperor, and in the hope of following his noble example. Similar suicides were later reported at other camps among soldiers of various ranks.[10]

These episodes are homologous to the mass suicides of defeated Japanese warriors, to suicidal charges by samurai cavalry from besieged castles, and to the samurai tradition of voluntary martyrdom upon the death of one's lord. But the longevity of seppuku is unique, sustained by a process of beautification that turns horrific violence into something poignant and admirable. Mishima Yukio, the novelist

9. Cassius Dio, *Roman History*, 8:217.
10. Tacitus, *The Histories*, 1:243.

whose anachronistic seppuku suicide in 1970 embarrassed Japan and puzzled the world, wrote prolifically about the twin topics of beauty and death. Mishima explains, "In the classical literature of Japan, crimson leaves and cherry trees are metaphors for bloodletting and death. Deeply embedded in our national consciousness, these metaphors have for centuries trained us to apply an aesthetic format to physical fear."[11] Mishima thinks that the aesthetic cleansing we see at work in literary representations of death and suicide has practical consequences reaching beyond the texts, that it is the artistic conviction of bloody-yet-beautiful death which inspires military men toward artful violence.

Thus the history of seppuku is the history of an aesthetic ideal, and of the attempts by generations of would-be heroes to win immortality by realizing this ideal within the context of their life-and-death experience. To survey the myriad representations of samurai suicide in texts of all eras is to slip constantly back and forth between a grim factuality on the one hand and a realm of unworldly beauty on the other, until the boundary between the two disintegrates. Seppuku is as real as moonlight and cherry blossoms, and just as unreal.

Magnificent Failure

Seppuku appears to have formally entered the protocols of Japan's warrior class during the final decades of the Heian period (794–1185), when people were struggling to survive in the face of seemingly endless natural disasters. In his *Account of My Hut* (Hōjōki, 1212), the Buddhist hermit Kamo no Chōmei depicted these terrible times. Death was everywhere. In 1177 a fire decimated much of Kyoto. A monster typhoon in 1180 repeated the damage. A drought in 1181 triggered two years of terrible famine. In 1185 a series of earthquakes wrought more havoc. It was in the wake of these calamities that suicide established itself as the proper way for heroes to make their exit. Nature had rudely demoted men to mere bodies, tossed about and ravaged by the elements. In a spirit of resistance, warriors asserted

11. Mishima, *Zenshū*, 32:572–73.

the power of the body by displays of courageous dying. Ordinary folk
fought to stay alive; often they failed. Dying, at least, was an achievable goal. One of the many Japanese words for suicide is *jiketsu*, self-
determination.[12] A samurai impaled on his own sword, lying in a pool
of blood, with his innards spilling out, is unequivocally, spectacularly,
outrageously dead. But he was not killed by death. He has determined
himself. The heroes of war tales did not succumb to famines or earthquakes. They refused to relinquish death to nature's cruelty. In an
age of chronic involuntary death, theirs were among the few deaths
worthy of celebration.

Warriors dominated the Kamakura period (1185–1333) and
the Muromachi period (1333–1573). These were bloody years. The
power of man and nature alike was asserted through blood, in the
bloody devastation of natural catastrophes, in the bloody humiliations of the defeated, in the bloody spoils of the victors. The warrior was defined by blood. With war a hereditary profession, blood
automatically determined his status and his vocation. His allegiances
and enemies were largely determined by blood, by the terms of blood-
bonds, blood-pacts, and blood-feuds. His courage was measured by
his ability to risk his blood in battle, both literally, by risking his life,
and figuratively, by putting his family's honor on the line. His success
as a warrior depended on his ability to shed blood. His name was
secured in eternity by his readiness to shed his *own* blood, by sui-
cide-charging the enemy or cutting his stomach when circumstances
decreed. He belonged to a social body in which blood was a fundamental dynamic, profoundly influencing the mechanisms of power
while delineating the relation of the individual to the collective.

Amid this vivid omnipresence of blood, abstractions such as courage, honor, and loyalty assumed near-carnal immediacy. The warriors
who, in the war tales, fling their guts into the air or leap from their sad-
dles with their swords in their mouths seem to fight not merely *to* the
death, but *into* death. Driven by a compulsion toward perfection, they

12. The importance of suicide to the Japanese psyche can be gauged from the sheer
number of words for "suicide" in the language: *jisatsu, jiketsu, junshi, chūshi, shishi, shinjū,
shōgai, jigai, jōsatsu,* etc.

are enthusiastic for ruin. The climax of many a combat scene is the
moment when a general, realizing that he cannot win the battle, calls
a sudden halt. His men rally around him, and all speed deliriously
toward death in a suicidal charge or a mass slashing of stomachs.

Let us consider one paradigmatic example. In October 1399
Kyushu warlord Ōuchi Yoshihiro rebelled against the shogun, Ashikaga Yoshimitsu.[13] Details of the incident are preserved in a short
chronicle called the *Record of the Ōei Revolt* (Ōeiki), written around
1410, the alternative title of which betrays the ending: *The Destruction
of Ōuchi Yoshihiro* (Ōuchi Yoshihiro taijiki).

Yoshihiro and his army of five thousand men build a fortress at
the port of Sakai near Osaka. Yoshihiro boasts that a million soldiers
could not penetrate its walls. Meanwhile he is preparing for death. He
writes a will, and sends his personal effects to his mother in Kyushu.
He has a priest explain the last rites to him. His generals suggest various time-saving strategies, but Yoshihiro is impatient to fight. Seeing
his resolve, his generals vow to die with him.

Catastrophe, when it comes, is total. From Kyoto, the shogun calls
on other warlords for assistance. Within a month, thirty thousand riders have arrived at Sakai. Intent on a massacre, the shogun has also
paid a pirate fleet to seal off the coastline. Yoshihiro and his men are
trapped, and face attacks from all sides. They successfully defend the
fortress for three weeks. When the situation turns hopeless, Yoshihiro
rallies his men. He roars at his enemies, "I am Ōuchi Yoshihiro, the
strongest warrior in the world! If any of you think you can kill me,
now is your chance. See if you can take my head to the shogun!"[14] He
hurls himself at the enemy soldiers and is fatally skewered on their
lances. He does not go alone. Scores of his bodyguards launch similar
suicide-charges and are sliced to pieces. Others drop to their knees
and tear open their stomachs or stab each other to death. Mutual self-
slaughter is the apotheosis of their warrior bond. When the attackers
torch the fortress, hundreds more of Yoshihiro's men are burned alive.

13. Yoshimitsu had retired from formal office in 1394, but continued to wield supreme
power until his death in 1408.

14. *Ōeiki*, 74.

"In the morning it was a terrible scene. Smoke was rising from every part of the castle. Every building had been burned to the ground. The sky had turned black and the ground was drenched with the blood of the slaughtered."[15] Later that day the shogun's victorious generals return to Kyoto, taking with them the head of the strongest warrior in the world.

Emile Cioran says of the man of violence, "His occasional efforts to destroy others are merely a roundabout route to his own destruction. Beneath his self-confidence, his braggadocio, lurks a fanatic of disaster."[16] Yoshihiro carries within himself the seeds of his own destruction. His revolt is a military disaster. He has failed utterly. But he has failed magnificently. His catastrophic exit becomes a grandiose assertion of his indomitable energy and pride. In Japan, no stigma or irony attaches to men of this type. Provided that they are consistent, do not flinch, and follow the consequences of their actions all the way to death, their reputations endure.

The Sword

Japan's original warriors were gods. Tradition has it that the first emperor claimed direct descent from the sun goddess and called himself Jimmu, "Divine Warrior." Ceremonial swords have been discovered in Japanese burial mounds of the fifth century AD, and the words inscribed on their blades proclaim their owners as the rulers of heaven and earth. A sword forms one of the three sacred treasures that symbolize the divinely sanctioned authority of the imperial house.

During the centuries of samurai hegemony, the sword retained its sacred authority. It was the meaning and expression of the samurai's existence. A memorable anecdote recorded in a sixteenth-century war history testifies to the exalted status of the samurai sword. At the fall of Sakamoto Castle near Lake Biwa in 1582, the defeated lord, Akechi Hidemitsu, requested a cease-fire in order to save his family's collection of antique swords. His men wrapped the swords in futons and

15. Ibid., 79.
16. Cioran, *The Temptation to Exist*, 34.

lowered them from a window. Once the swords had been whisked to safety, *The Taikō Chronicles* (Taikōki, 1626) tells us, Hidemitsu torched the castle, stabbed to death his wives and children, cut his stomach, and leapt into the flames. The priceless swords joined his enemy's collection.[17] Reports of seppuku rituals often include more information about the history and pedigree of the sword than the condemned man who uses it. A ban imposed on the carrying of swords by samurai in 1876 triggered the largest spate of seppuku suicides seen in Japan for three hundred years. For these men, life had no meaning without the sword.

The ever-present possibility of seppuku imparts to the sword a transcendental dimension. A sword for slaying one's enemies is a tool guided by the swordsman who wields it. Its purpose is defined and limited. It should be respected, treated with care, but it can and must be controlled. It is the property of the swordsman. He possesses it. There are many swords like it, but this one is his. In contrast, a sword used equally to slay enemy, comrade, or the swordsman himself cannot be possessed absolutely in this way. According to the seppuku ideal, every samurai knows that the day might come when he must turn his sword on himself, to commit his own seppuku, or on his comrades, to assist them in theirs. Blood-brothers in battle, each potentially is another's executioner. Seppuku thus obtains a sublime symmetry, since the samurai who lives by the sword not only dies by the sword, *he dies by the same sword with which he has lived*.

It may be objected that suicide, and martial suicide especially, is above all a practical matter. Surely there are more efficient ways to kill oneself with a sword? Here we must briefly consider the logistics of self-stabbing.

Strictly speaking, stomach-cutting is not a mode of suicide, since the wound is not immediately, or even necessarily, fatal. The imperialist zealot Takayama Hikokurō (1747–93) survived for nineteen hours after completely severing his small and large intestines (see p. 158). A surgeon's report on the death of a samurai who committed seppuku

17. Oze, *Taikōki*, 74.

in April 1754 notes that he achieved a stomach cut that was approximately five inches long and one and a half inches deep, yet he continued breathing for fourteen hours (see p.155). Admiral Ōnishi Takijirō (1891–1945), known as the father of the Special Attack ("kamikaze") Squadron, slashed his stomach and stabbed his throat, yet did not expire until fifteen hours later. In each of these cases the cause of death was hemorrhaging.

The medieval war tales show an awareness of these practicalities. Suicide is rarely accomplished only by cutting the stomach. Men stab themselves before cutting their own throats, or, more frequently, before leaping into flames. Bereaved widows stab themselves before leaping into rivers or from cliffs. In every case the stomach cut is a fail-safe. In some scenes, one strike is found to be insufficient; consequently, a cross-shaped double-cut became the standard form. When all else fails, a warrior rests the hilt of his sword on the ground, puts the tip of the blade to his neck or into his mouth, and allows his body weight to do the rest. From the sixteenth century the procedure was made easier by means of a death blow delivered by a colleague or subordinate.

It seems reasonable to ask: If not the stomach, then where? Wrist-cutting is too slow and too passive for heroes. It should be understood that the Japanese short sword is not particularly short. It would not be a simple matter to prick one's heart with such a blade. In any case, the natural angle of the striking arm makes the stomach the inevitable target. A right-handed man will tend to stab himself in his left side, below his ribcage. When both hands are used, the tip of the blade will naturally point to the central lower part of the stomach, not the chest.

Few samurai texts mention pain. The ones that do, such as the account of the seppuku of Minoura Inokichi in 1868 (see p. 178), are horrific. The pain of piercing the abdominal wall is known to be excruciating; that of severing the intestines is, apparently, less so. The degree of pain depends on multiple factors: the depth of the initial stab, the route of the blade across the stomach, the cutting speed, the length and type of sword used, the sharpness of the blade, the age and physical condition of the cutter, and so on. Pain is personal, and experience of it varies greatly between individuals. Tales of warriors cursing their enemies while removing their own guts must be set against accounts of lesser men who barely scratch the skin before letting out a scream. What is clear is that a stomach cut does not immediately incapacitate the cutter, and that the pain, though intense, can be endured at least for a few moments, and by some men for much longer.[18]

Seppuku or Hara-kiri?

The word *hara-kiri* has seldom been used in Japan, where *seppuku* is preferred both in speech and in print. *Hara-kiri* could be translated as "belly-cut" and *seppuku* as "cutting the stomach," though these are imperfect approximations.[19] While *hara-kiri* is sometimes dismissed as a vulgarism, it would be more accurate to say that *seppuku* is a polite euphemism. By employing the Chinese readings of the two characters that form the word, it is a way of saying "cut the stomach" without actually uttering the Japanese words for "stomach" (*hara*) and "cut" (*kiru*). *Seppuku* is the more recent term, making its first appearance early in the fifteenth century. It has been standard terminology since

18. In February 1896 an American surgeon presented a paper to the Philadelphia Academy of Surgery describing his successful treatment of a man who had eviscerated himself with a carving knife. The surgeon, Richard Harte, had been reading A. B. Mitford's *Tales of Old Japan* (1871), and accordingly entitled his paper "A Case of Hara-Kiri which Terminated in Recovery." The patient, a mentally confused butcher, had sliced his stomach from left to right above the navel, making a wound of about nine inches across his abdominal wall. He was discovered standing in a courtyard, twiddling a loop of his large intestine. During surgery, Harte enlarged the wound to control hemorrhaging, removed clots while protecting the exposed bowels with sterilized towels, and stitched up the wound. The stitches were removed after twelve days and the man made a complete recovery. Harte attributed the effectiveness of the treatment to three factors: the promptness of the surgical assistance, the hot weather on that day ("preventing chilling of the exposed abdominal viscera, thereby diminishing the tendency to shock"), and hourly flushing of the abdominal cavity for forty-eight hours after the "hara-kiri." Harte's article is in *Annals of Surgery*, vol. 27, June 1898. For a full medical analysis of the effects of cutting the stomach, see Di Nunno et al., "Suicide by Hara-kiri: A Series of Four Cases," in *The American Journal of Forensic Medicine and Pathology*, March 2001, 68–72.

19. The fact is that no English word satisfactorily conveys the idea of *hara*, which has numerous connotations. Anyone who has studied Japanese martial arts or practiced Zen sitting will be familiar with the emphasis these disciplines place on the abdominal region. The semireligious conviction that the vital center of the human form is in the stomach, not the head, has permeated the Japanese language. A man with a big stomach (*hara ga ōkii*) has a generous nature, while a man with a black stomach (*hara-guroi*) is a scheming villain; your stomach stands up (*hara ga tatsu*) when you get angry, your instinctive sense of time is your "stomach-clock" (*hara-dokei*), and so on.

around 1600. War sagas of the thirteenth and fourteenth centuries generally use the verbal form *hara-kiru*, as in *hara-kitte fukusu* ("he cut his belly and fell down dead"). A common variant is *hara o kakikitta* ("he ripped open his belly"). These expressions are the genesis of the term *hara-kiri*, and predate *seppuku* by at least two hundred years. Many stomachs are cut in the *Chronicle of the Jōkyū Disturbance* (Jōkyūki, 1240) which describes battles fought in the year 1221, but the word *seppuku* is never used; the text refers to battlefield suicide as *jigai* ("self-inflicted [death]"), while using *hara-* formulations to specify the act of stomach-cutting. The *Baishōron*, a military history of 1349, similarly does not use *seppuku*. *Seppuku* gained prominence during the late 1400s, and was the official legal term for self-execution by samurai during the Tokugawa period (1603–1867). Even then, however, *hara-* based structures were preferred in graphic firsthand accounts, with *seppuku* being a more conceptualized term. Distinction between the two sometimes appears arbitrary. For example, Tokugawa execution manuals identify the samurai performing the suicide ritual as the *seppuku-jin* (stomach-cutter), but refer to the sword as the *hara-kiri-ha* (blade for belly-ripping). By the nineteenth century, *seppuku* had become an all-embracing term for samurai suicide, which did not always involve disembowelment; as we shall see, some of the most celebrated "seppuku heroes" did not cut their stomachs at all. The prevalence of the term *hara-kiri* is a result of its appearance in early accounts of Japan written by foreigners, to whom this word was more easily comprehensible than *seppuku*. While *seppuku* was used in the neutral language of government proclamations and judicial records, *hara-kiri* often featured in sensational titles of literary and dramatic works. In the Kabuki repertoire there is *Nagamachi onna no hara-kiri* (The woman of Nagamachi who ripped her belly, 1712), and the famous suicide scene in *The Treasury of Loyal Retainers* (Chūshingura, 1748) is known as *Kanpei hara-kiri no ba* (Kanpei's belly-ripping scene). Yamaoka Shunmei, the first Japanese scholar to examine the samurai suicide tradition, entitled his 1770 essay *Hara-kiri kō* (Thoughts on belly-ripping). A twentieth-century study of suicide among samurai women by popular historian Mitamura Engyo is entitled *Daimyō no onna hara-kiri* (Belly-ripping wives of the feudal lords, 1925). A parliamentary dispute of January 1937, in which an exasperated politician suggested that the Minister of War might do the nation a favor by cutting his stomach, was promptly dubbed the *hara-kiri mondō*: "the belly-rip altercation." Today the word *hara-kiri* is so exotic that some Japanese even assume it to be an import, a misreading by foreigners of the *seppuku* characters.

Bushido

After the reorganization of the samurai fiefdoms under a single governing administration at the start of the seventeenth century, there were few opportunities for men to carve their names into history through exhibitions of suicidal heroism in combat. During the prolonged peace of the Tokugawa period the martial ethos of the Muromachi-period warriors inevitably waned. Tokugawa authorities saved seppuku from desuetude by incorporating it into the rules of conduct for samurai, commonly known today as Bushido.[20]

Although *bushidō* translates as "the way of the warrior," the concept was largely concocted by scholars, authors, and pedagogues who had never experienced war. To the traditional martial requisites of courage and fearlessness they bonded humility and loyalty, virtues which, frankly, are not often on display in the medieval war chronicles. Tokugawa educational manuals such as *Basics of the Martial Way* (Budō shoshinshū, 1720) and *The Warrior's Code* (Bushikun, 1725), and anthologies of military anecdotes such as *Tales of Jōzan* (Jōzan kidan,1739), aimed to foster a new breed of samurai, one who combined the indestructible machismo of the Muromachi warriors with the docile servility of a peacetime bureaucrat. Many of the most celebrated samurai myths can be traced to these texts. Here we encounter the titanic stoicism of Bisaku, ten-year-old son of a commander killed at the battle of Osaka Castle in 1614. When soldiers solemnly returned his father's head to him, Bisaku is said to have stunned them with this response: "If a samurai loses his head, it should go on a spike at

20. For a sensible evaluation of the thorny concept of Bushido, see Hurst, "Death, Honor, and Loyalty."

his enemy's camp. Why is my father's head here? Did he die like a dog?" Only after assurances that his father had died fighting did Bisaku accept his head.[21] Then there is Shibata "the Jar-Breaker" Katsuie (1522–83), whose response to a starvation siege was to smash the jars containing his army's dwindling supply of water. We are told that Katsuie roused his men with the words, "Better a quick death in battle than a slow one from thirst!"[22] Bushido is a cluster of attributes derived from such semifictional sources. Tokugawa thinkers tranquilized the martial ethic of the Muromachi warriors, straining it of its morbidity while injecting healthier concepts such as righteousness and fortitude. But, in theory at least, death remained the denominator. In 1723 Muro Kyūsō, a Confucian scholar, wrote, "Righteousness is the mental act of cutting through reason, just as a tailor cuts material for a garment. It is the act of not accepting that which you should not accept, of not saying what you should not say, of living when you should live and dying when you should die."[23] The truth about man is revealed in the moment and manner of his death, in the how and why of his dying.

The purpose of articulating these issues was to impart identity and structure to the lives of the samurai during the years of peace, while validating their division from and authority over the common folk. There were many codes of conduct, not one, since scholars often disagreed on the stipulations. But there was a consensus that stoicism toward death was an essential samurai quality. Ordinary men, supposedly, are unhinged by death, their pretensions and insincerities shorn away by the imminence of the abyss.[24] The samurai, towering above the ordinary, should be unchanged and unmoved. He must remain the same man he has always been, right up to and through the instant of death. When a samurai dies, no essential thing is destroyed. Birth and death are merely the pulse of his undying samurai spirit. Hence Tokugawa leaders elected to retain the seppuku ritual as a daunting

21. *Dai Nihon shiryō*, no. 12, 16:979.

22. Yuasa, *Jōzan kidan*, 34.

23. Muro, *Kenkaroku*, 135.

24. One Kabuki comedy, *Yasaku's Sickle-suicide* (Yasaku no kama-bara), depicts what happens when a pretentious commoner tries to cut his stomach. The result is blood-spattered slapstick. In Atsumi, ed., *Nihon gikyoku zenshū*, vol. 15.

epitome of the samurai-commoner divide. It is essential to a proper understanding of seppuku to recognize that it was a symbolic privilege of an elite class, and never a means of humiliation or degradation. Commoners were chopped, burned, or crucified. The samurai determined himself.

The most extreme interpretation of Bushido is that of Yamamoto Tsunetomo (1659–1719), a samurai of the Hizen domain (now Saga Prefecture) in northwest Kyushu. After the death of his lord in 1700, Tsunetomo renounced the world, adopted the Buddhist name Jōchō, and entered a hermitage. *Hagakure*, a collection of dicta from his last seven years, was not widely read until the modern era and therefore cannot be accorded historical significance. But as a treasury of seppuku anecdotes—and fantasies—it is without equal.

Jōchō's system is one of suicidal fatalism, the coordinates of which are servitude and martyrdom. Jōchō's vassal-hero dies when he has completed his function, when he can function no longer, or when functioning entails dying. *Hagakure* illuminates the nature of servitude with a parable. The residence of a certain lord caught fire, and was soon burning beyond control. Of all his possessions, the lord bemoaned most the loss of a unique scroll charting his family's lineage, which was said to be the most beautiful of its kind in Japan. Hearing this, one of his men stepped forward. "My lord, I know I have never been of much use to you. I have waited for the day when I might truly be of service. Now seems to be that day." With these words, he rushed into the burning building. He did not come back. When the fire was finally extinguished, they found his charred corpse. He had slit open his stomach and placed the scroll inside; it was stained but intact. "Thenceforth," writes Jōchō, "it was known as the Scroll of Blood."[25] This fanciful tale defines his vision of samurai perfection. In a non-samurai version the hero would have leapt from the flames in the nick of time, with the priceless document tucked safely inside his shirt and the inferno crumbling behind him.[26] The two heroes'

25. Jōchō, *Hagakure*, 3:129–30.

26. On the big screen today these scenes are invariably shown in slow motion. This deceleration is duplicitous, as it is intended to conceal from us what the "hero" is really

heroics point in opposite directions: one leaps away from death, the other leaps toward it.

Before and during World War II, Japanese intellectuals made orthodoxy of Jōchō's fanaticism in order to strengthen the nation's resolve. The historian Wada Katsunori, writing as the pilots of the Special Attack Squadron slammed their planes into US warships in the Pacific, echoed *Hagakure* when defining Bushido's suicidal indifference:

> The attitude to Life and Death espoused in Bushido is not one that can be grasped by logic or learning. It is founded entirely on a necessity arising from within the Self, an explosion of inner life. Therefore, all the activity of Life is there—tough, yet flexible to the core, while at the same time containing a rich humaneness. Bushido teaches men to master the art of being decisive, for not to die when you ought to die is more shameful than death itself.[27]

How can voluntary death be an "explosion of inner life"? In *The End of Faith*, his hatchet job on faith-based religion, Sam Harris takes it as self-evident that only a mind that has been brainwashed by religious dogma could willingly destroy itself (and others) for glory.[28] One might counter that only a mind that has been brainwashed by secular logic could fail to appreciate how infinitely more thrilling it is to be a suicidal terrorist than a survivalist goatherd. The philosopher Slavoj Žižek has suggested that a suicide bomber about to hit the explode button may experience a more acute sense of being *alive* than a soldier operating an unmanned missile via a computer screen thousands of miles away.[29] The distinction is between rational calculation and rapturous intoxication. It is something that many of us sense intuitively. What young hero yearns for long life? The dream of dying

---

doing: sprinting away from danger as fast as his legs can carry him. Jōchō will not tolerate such duplicity.

27. Wada, *Seppuku*, 91–92.

28. Harris, *The End of Faith*, 31–33, 123–27.

29. Žižek, *Welcome to the Desert of the Real*, 88.

at one's peak, of self-destructing for some higher cause, or for the sake
of beautiful death itself, holds a natural and powerful appeal for the
male ego. A fierce lust for death simmers beneath all manifestations of
fanaticism. Religious extremism and suicide cults harness this death-
drive; they do not create it. That perfect death makes life complete is
an ancient truism, exalted in Norse sagas, Indian myths, and Greek
tragedies. Lust for death is as old as life. Dreaming of apocalypse is
only human. Cioran, haunted by suicidal impulses, writes:

> I would like to explode, flow, crumble into dust, and my
> disintegration would be my masterpiece. I would like to
> melt in the world and for the world to melt orgasmically
> in me and thus in our delirium to engender an apocalyptic
> dream.[30]

Cioran's desire to transcend his subjectivity carries him ineluctably
toward death. Few samurai writers have acknowledged their death-lust
with such candor. Jōchō tells us, "Dreams are the truest expression of
a man's soul. I myself have often dreamed of dying in combat, or of
tearing open my belly."[31] Mishima Yukio lived his whole life dreaming of death, and articulated his dreams in fiction. In *Runaway Horses*
(Honba, 1969), his novel of imperialist assassins in the 1930s, there
is a harrowing moment where the ringleader of the assassins' group, a
student named Isao, seeks an interview with a lieutenant in the imperial army. Isao lists his complaints against the corrupt financier he
is plotting to murder. But the lieutenant sees through this pose, and
carefully coaxes from Isao a confession of blinding honesty.

> The lieutenant seemed to be rehearsing his next question
> in his mind. "Very well then," he said, "let me ask you
> this: what do you desire more than anything else?"
>   Stuttering slightly, Isao gave a daring reply: "To

---

30. Cioran, *On the Heights of Despair*, 57.
31. Jōchō, *Hagakure*, 2:92–93.

climb . . . to climb to the top of a cliff at sunrise . . . pay
homage to the rising sun . . . look down over the sparkling
sea, and . . . . and at the foot of a noble pine tree I
want to stab myself to death."[32]

Mishima's characters seldom have difficulty expressing themselves,
but it is apt that Isao stammers here. In struggling to confess something that cannot be expressed in words, he is not pellucid to himself.
The allure of death is that it is unknowable. Isao strides on, unstoppable, infatuated with the destiny he has chosen. The last lines of the
last page find him at a cliff's edge. There is no sea, there is no pine
tree, but the blood of his victim is fresh on his sword. Isao plunges
the blade into his stomach and tears himself open. Furious, agoniz-
ing, exquisite fulfillment is the concluding experience of his life. In an
instant, suicide completes him, "as the blazing orb of the sun soared
up and exploded behind his eyelids."[33]

If it makes sense to speak of an art of dying, some of the death scenes
presented in this book can be regarded as small masterpieces. The ceremonial suicide of Lord Kikkawa Tsuneie, who disemboweled himself
in the grounds of Shinkyōji Temple; the deaths of the three Shimizu
brothers on the lake at Takamatsu; the mass suicide of the boy soldiers
of the White Tiger Unit on the hillside overlooking Wakamatsu Castle;
the ritual martrydom of General Nogi Maresuke as the imperial guns
sounded a salute for the late emperor Meiji. In their different ways,
these men destroy themselves in the belief that death will complete
their world—and their posthumous reputations. The same principle
is embodied in the primordial myths, the war tales, and the Bushido
fables, and elaborated in the nihilistic visions of Jōchō, who concludes
by quoting an ancient poem: "Everything in this world is false; the
only sincerity is in death."[34]

32. *Honba*. In Mishima, *Zenshū*, 13:520–21.
33. Ibid., 819.
34. Jōchō, *Hagakure*, 3:122.

History of Seppuku to 1600

Ikkasai Yoshitoshi. *Seppuku of Reizei Takatoyo* (Reizei Hangan Takatoyo), 1868. Copy of woodblock print held by Tokyo Historiographical Institute.

Ancient Texts

In 713, shortly after the establishment of Japan's first permanent capital in Nara, each of the nation's provinces was commanded to compile a geographical catalog called a *fudoki*, literally a "record of wind and earth." This was to be a detailed survey of the topography, crops, wildlife, and produce of that province, along with explanations of place-names and local customs. Of the sixty-six catalogs presented to the state council, all but five have long been lost. One of those five, the *Harima fudoki*, compiled by the authorities of Harima in the south-western part of what is today Hyōgo Prefecture, contains the following cryptic description of an area of barren marshland:

> The goddess Aomi came to this place in search of her hus-
> band, the god Hananami. Unable to find him, she flew
> into a bitter rage, slashed her belly [*hara wo saki*] with a
> sword, and threw herself into the marsh. The marsh too
> lost its bowels, for no carp or other fish have been found
> there since. Thus it became known as the Belly-slash
> [*Harasaki*] Marsh.[1]

This is the first mention of stomach-cutting in Japanese literature. It stands entirely alone. Neither the *Records of Ancient Matters* (Kojiki, 712), nor the *Chronicles of Japan* (Nihon shoki, 720), Japan's oldest surviving documents, contains a similar reference, and we must fast-

---

1. Uegaki, ed., *Harima fudoki*, 117–18.

forward four centuries for the next example. Although the wording is specific—Aomi does not slash her wrist or throat, or stab herself through the heart—these lines do not suggest a common practice. The extraordinary manner of her suicide is the reason for its mention. It is unclear whether she stabs herself as an expression of her rage, or as a preparatory measure for drowning. Whichever it is, the anonymous author of these lines is plainly articulating a correspondence between suicidal fury and stomach-cutting that must have taken root as early as the sixth or seventh century.

Tales of Times Now Past (Konjaku monogatari), a collection of fables and legends compiled around 1140, contains several episodes featuring a charismatic thief nicknamed Hakamadare. Described as "a great leader of cunning thieves," Hakamadare was based on an actual bandit chieftain named Fujiwara Yasusuke, who terrorized the countryside around Kyoto toward the end of the tenth century. No fewer than fifteen imperial warrants were issued for his arrest. His crimes, flight, and capture are related in grittier detail in a later anthology, *More Old Tales* (Zoku-kojidan, 1219). Yasusuke is hunted by a posse of marshals who finally corner him in his mountain hideout. This is how the tale ends:

> Now there was no escape for Yasusuke. Drawing his sword, he tore open his belly [*hara wo sashikirite*] and pulled out his guts. The marshals pounced, and Yasusuke was confined in the jailhouse, where he was treated by a doctor but died the next day.[2]

Yasusuke was notorious enough in his day to earn himself a brief entry in *Nihon kiryaku*, a comprehensive history of Japan completed by court scholars early in the eleventh century. There he is described as a "leader of thieves" who "killed himself [*jigai*] in prison."[3] The date of his death is given as August 7, 988, almost three hundred years after the *Harima fudoki*.

2. Harima, ed., *Zoku-kojidan*, 127–28.
3. *Nihon kiryaku*, 164.

Although imperial histories of the tenth and eleventh centuries recount suicides of various sorts—hanging, drowning, self-strangulation, throat-cutting—no other references to stomach-cutting have been found in early Japanese texts.

Minamoto no Tametomo (Died April 1170)

The fact that the first two hara-kiri on record are those of a deranged wife (albeit a divine one) and a murderous criminal posed problems for historians keen to pinpoint the origin of the practice in Japan's martial tradition. This was the view of Ise Sadatake, a scholar in the employ of the shogun, writing in the 1770s:

> Although we find many examples of suicide in the *Chronicles of Japan* and subsequent histories, these are all achieved by poisoning, or hanging, or by fire; there is not one that involves cutting the stomach. There was no stomach-cutting in ancient times. The first case is found in *The Tale of the Hōgen Rebellion*, which tells us how the mighty warrior Minamoto no Tametomo, at the age of twenty-eight, ripped his belly while his back was pressed against a pillar in his house. This is the genesis of stomach-cutting as a display of martial valor.[4]

Here, suicide "by fire" is a reference to those warriors who were said to have leaped into the flames of their burning fortresses rather than face capture. As in China, poisoning was for a time the standard method of execution for persons of high rank. Among numerous examples, the *Chronicles of Japan* records how, in 729, Senior Minister of State Nagaya no Ōkimi was condemned to death for treason; the emperor also ordered the destruction of Nagaya's family. Nagaya, his wife, and his children drank poison; his infant grandchild was strangled to death. The practice of obligatory suicide faded with the rise

4. Ise, *Anzai zuihitsu*, 2:292.

of the Fujiwara family, courtiers who controlled Japan from the late 700s. The death penalty was officially abolished in 810. Thereafter, traitors and troublemakers were banished.

The Tale of the Hōgen Rebellion (Hōgen monogatari, ca. 1230) describes a bloody revolt of 1156. The death of Emperor Toba that year triggered a power struggle between the retired emperor Sutoku and his half brother, the incoming emperor Go-Shirakawa. Sutoku, backed by a majority of the Fujiwaras, attempted to capture the throne by force from Go-Shirakawa, whose principal support came from the Taira family. Sutoku's coup, known as the Hōgen Rebellion, was crushed in just one day, and he was exiled to the island of Shikoku. The quarrel between the two families of courtiers would eventually lead to the decline of their power and the rise of a military regime.

Minamoto no Tametomo (1139–70) is the hero of the *Hōgen Rebellion*. This seems odd, since he is a disagreeable character who fights on the losing side and ultimately kills himself. In a Greek epic or Norse saga he would be the villain, or perhaps the villain's henchman. His strengths are his martial prowess (he is the greatest bowman in the land), his loyalty, and his doggedness. He does not think much, and when he does he thinks about death and glory.

As depicted in the tale, Tametomo is a wild child. His father, a Kyoto police commissioner, soon has enough of him and sends him away to Kyushu, the heart of warrior country. Perhaps he hoped that the boy's stormy temperament would attract less attention there, or that the Kyushu warriors would knock some humility into him. If so, the plan backfired. By the time Tametomo returns to Kyoto at the age of nineteen, he has lost count of how many men he has killed. He is variously described as "coarse," "ferocious," "demon-like," and "monstrous." In context the words are not entirely disparaging. Clearly this is not a man who swoons at the scent of plum blossoms.

Lending his support to the Sutokus and the Fujiwaras, Tametomo advises raiding the Taira camp. The courtiers overrule him, electing to sit tight and wait for reinforcements. This turns out to be a fatal mistake. It is the Taira who raid the Sutoku camp, six hundred soldiers attacking at dawn. Tametomo defends the camp almost single-handedly, picking off the attackers one by one with his arrows. In the most thrilling scene, two brothers on horseback charge a gate defended by Tametomo. He lets fly a single arrow. It slices clean through the first brother and buries itself in the armor of the second, whereupon the men behind them decide to try a different gate. The battle is lost only when the Tairas set fire to the palace.

Tametomo escapes, and goes into hiding in the hills south of Lake Biwa. Lack of food and a bout of typhoid fever force him down into one of the villages, where someone recognizes him and alerts the authorities. Thirty soldiers ambush him while he is taking a bath—the only time they know he will be unarmed. Stark naked, he resists arrest by swinging at them with a wooden pole, but is overpowered and taken back to the capital. Crowds fill the streets to catch a glimpse of him. Emperor Go-Shirakawa orders his guards to slit the sinews in Tametomo's arms, in the hope of putting an end to his archery career, and banishes him to Ōshima, a volcanic island off the coast of Izu.

Tametomo is soon causing more trouble for the islanders than the volcano. He marries the daughter of a government official, and then refuses to pay taxes. When he discovers that his father-in-law is secretly paying tax on his behalf, he chops off the man's fingers. He gathers a band of fighting men and asserts control over Ōshima and six other islands. In the spring of 1170, Tametomo's twelfth year in exile, reports reach Go-Shirakawa that he is plotting an uprising. A flotilla of twenty warships, carrying five hundred horsemen, is immediately dispatched to Ōshima.

As the warships come into view, Tametomo's men wonder if they are merchant ships. Tametomo's instinct tells him otherwise: he knows they are coming to kill him. For the first time, we see a humane side of him:

> "A man cannot be a warrior without killing. I, Tametomo, have fought in over twenty battles, and do not know myself how many men I have killed. But I can say for certain that I never killed an unworthy opponent. I do not kill deer or fish, and for more than twenty years I have

devoted myself to the Bodhisattva Jizō, guardian of men's souls in Hell. For misdeeds in a former life, I was doomed to be a warrior; for my misdeeds in this life, I shall suffer more in the next. I hereby repent my crimes, and submit myself to the infinite mercy of Buddha."[5]

Tametomo has resolved to die. He tells his men to flee and regretfully prepares to slaughter his three children. But when his wife sees him fatally stab their son, she whisks the other two children away and heads for the hills.

The great archer cannot resist shooting one last arrow. He selects one with a special turnip-shaped head and lets it loose over the approaching ships, which are barely within range. The arrow pierces the hull of the leading ship, and exits from the other side. Water leaks in from both holes. The ship starts to sink, and the men on board go with it, clutching desperately at the oars, or climbing to safety aboard the other ships. For Tametomo, it is the greatest bull's-eye of his career: "In the days of Hōgen I killed two warriors with one arrow. Now with a single arrow I have killed many. All praise to Buddha!"[6] He goes inside, and, supporting his back against a pillar, rips open his stomach.

The soldiers cannot understand why they are not being showered with arrows. They land on an empty beach, and cautiously approach the house. When they find Tametomo motionless against the pillar, at first no one dares to go forward. One, a man named Kagekado, moves in from behind and realizes that Tametomo is dead. Kagekado takes aim and decapitates him with one blow. The head is taken to the capital for inspection by the emperor, and that is the end of Minamoto no Tametomo. "From time past to time present, never was there a hero so wild in spirit . . ."[7]

The *Hōgen Rebellion* is hardly the sort of text that can be accepted as credible history. Its importance lies in the prodigious influence of the myth it brought into being. By later standards the suicide scene is

5. Kishitani, ed., *Hōgen monogatari*, 116.
6. Ibid., 117.
7. Ibid., 119.

clumsy: warrior heroes of subsequent generations will take care not to be decapitated by an enemy soldier lest his name be immortalized alongside theirs, as happens here. Nonetheless, Minamoto no Tametomo is a towering archetype whose name echoes through samurai literature, reappearing time and time again in the war cries of warriors charging into battle and in valedictory speeches of men condemned to die. Every samurai wants to be a Tametomo—or so we are encouraged to believe.

Medieval War Tales

War tales such as the *Hōgen Rebellion* were originally popularized in oral versions recited by professional storytellers who accompanied themselves on the *biwa* (a fretted lute). Printed texts often went through many revisions. The oldest extant version of the *Hōgen Rebellion* dates from the early 1300s, the last was compiled in the late 1500s. While the only stomach-cutting scene in the earlier texts is Tametomo's, later versions feature stomach-cutting horsemen, guards, and attendants of all sorts. A popular sixteenth-century version contains a scene where, following the murder of an infant prince, four grieving nursemaids cut their bellies; seeing this, two guards also stab one another to death. The text comments that, while it was not unusual for warriors to cut their stomachs in battle, suicides such as these were unprecedented. In another episode found only in this later version, a senior attendant who has just seen his young master beheaded delivers a stirring suicide speech before drawing his short sword and cutting a line across his stomach.

Through such revisions and rewrites, additions, and embellishments, heroes were made more heroic. *The Tale of the Heike* (Heike monogatari), which follows the conflict between the Minamoto and Taira families of the 1180s, exists in over eighty versions, the first of which seems to have been written around 1220. *The Tale of Yoshitsune* (Gikeiki), the story of the Minamoto hero who finally destroyed the Taira forces at Dannoura in 1185, was probably not written down until late in the fourteenth century. Like the *Hōgen Rebellion*, these texts cannot be treated as historical records. While some are more overtly

literary than others, all mix fact with fiction. The clerics and scribes
who initially wrote them down based their narratives on existing tales,
stories told by professional reciters, and perhaps also on accounts provided by warriors who claimed to have been involved in the events
described. It is in these tales that the legend of seppuku takes root.
Over the course of roughly a hundred years, we see stomach-cutting
evolve from an accepted method of suicide to the expected method.
The Tale of the Soga (Soga monogatari), a semihistorical account of
warrior vengeance, was probably composed in the early 1300s; it does
not contain a single suicide. *The Tale of the Heike* contains just five
instances. Seppuku deaths proliferate in the *Baishōron* of 1349. By the
time we come to the epic war chronicle known as the *Taiheiki*, written
between 1371 and 1402, a mass suicide by defeated soldiers is the
conclusion to almost every battle scene, and the narrative emphasis
on these moments leaves us in no doubt that stomach-cutting had
become an essential component of the immortal warrior dream.

The most carefully depicted suicide in *The Tale of the Heike* is that
of Minamoto no Yorimasa at the Battle of Uji River on May 26, 1180.
The text describes how Yorimasa, then seventy-six years old, retreats
with a handful of followers into the grounds of Byōdōin Temple. He is
wounded in the knee, and has just seen his son cut down in the battle.
Unlike Tametomo, Yorimasa is an educated man, and before suicide
he pauses to recite an impromptu poem. Disembowelment does not
immediately occur to him. He first asks one of his men, Watanabe
Tonau, to decapitate him, but Tonau refuses. "How can I kill my own
master? No, I will behead you after you are dead."[8] Using his long
sword, Yorimasa cuts open his stomach and dies face down on the
grass, still impaled on the sword. A tearful Tonau cuts off Yorimasa's
head, ties it to a stone, and hurls it into the river.

Other early cases are rather messier. On November 3, 1186, Satō
Tadanobu, loyal to Minamoto general Yoshitsune, was cornered by
enemy soldiers in a house in Kyoto. In the account in *The Tale of
Yoshitsune*, Tadanobu decides to kill himself before he is captured and

8. Itiko, ed., *Heike monogatari*, 331.

forced, by torture, to reveal Yoshitsune's whereabouts. He breaks out
through the roof of the house and calls to his pursuers, "Now you'll
see a tough man cut his belly! I'll kill myself before any of you can
take my head, and my death will be a model for all who come after
me."[9] Tadanobu recites some Buddhist verses, then drops to his knees
and turns his sword on himself. First he cuts across his ribcage from
left to right. Then, removing the sword, he drives it into his chest and
cuts downwards. Perplexed to find himself still alive, he pulls out his
intestines and flings them to the ground, but still does not die. He
runs himself through once more, much deeper this time, until the hilt
of his sword meets his ribs. He does not even lose consciousness. In
desperation he struggles to his feet, inserts the tip of the blade into his
mouth as far as the back of his throat, and throws himself face-first to
the ground. This achieves the desired effect.

The enemy commanders are overawed. They cannot conceive of
a more heroic death. Tadanobu's death sets a new standard: a cross-
shaped cut across the stomach and removal of the intestines, preceded
by a challenge and a prayer, and concluding with a fatal wound to the
head, all in full view of witnesses. His brave display has a powerful
posthumous effect. After exhibiting Tadanobu's head on a spike, the
enemy leaders take it down after just three days, rather than leaving it
there to rot, which was more usual. They have realized that they are
advertising a hero.

Minamoto no Yoshitsune (1159–89), the general whom Tadanobu
protects by dying, is one of Japan's most popular heroes. Described
in *The Tale of Yoshitsune* as a pale-faced young man of small stature,
his dynamism and tactical brilliance recall the young Napoleon. But
after Yoshitsune's triumph over the Taira at Dannoura, his jealous
brother Yoritomo turned against him, and Yoshitsune was forced
to spend the last four years of his short life on the run. His adven-
tures during these fugitive years have been celebrated for centuries
in Noh, Kabuki, and Bunraku dramas. Yoshitsune-mania broke the
bounds of conventional narrative and headed into the fantastical.

9. Kajihara, ed., *Gikeiki*, 336–37.

Sixteenth-century prose narratives about Yoshitsune have him learning martial arts from goblins, and, after death, riding down to the underworld to build himself a castle in hell.

According to *The Tale of Yoshitsune*, the hero and a handful of his most devoted men make their last stand on June 15, 1189. Overwhelmed by sheer numbers—as with Tametomo, five hundred cavalry have been sent against him—Yoshitsune tells his servant, Kanefusa, that this is the end of the road:

> "The time has come for me to kill myself. How do you think I should do it?"
>
> Kanefusa replied that people were still speaking highly of Tadanobu's suicide in Kyoto.
>
> "Very well," said Yoshitsune. "Then I shall use the same method. I think a wide cut will be best."[10]

Yoshitsune produces an eight-inch dagger he has hidden beneath his armor, and stabs himself below his left nipple: "He plunged the blade in so deep that it nearly protruded from his back. Then he ripped the wound in three directions. After pulling out a small portion of his innards, he wiped the dagger on his sleeve and draped his cloak over the wound."[11] A telling detail here is Yoshitsune's question to Kanefusa: "How do you think I should do it?" It is inconceivable that a military man of Yoshitsune's rank would not have known the proper procedure for suicide if such a procedure had been established; the text strongly suggests that it had not. Yoshitsune makes a single incision high on his stomach, and stretches it—apparently without retracting the blade—in three directions. He then calmly cleans his blade, rests his sword on his lap, and waits for death to come.

Yoshitsune's wife berates her husband for not killing her first: "Why must you humiliate me by forcing me to stay alive?"[12] Yoshitsune's eyes close, his shoulders droop, and he dies. After shedding a few

10. Ibid., 490.
11. Ibid., 491.
12. Ibid., 492.

tears, his wife begs the other soldiers to kill her. Holding her down with his left hand, Kanefusa slits her stomach from right to left, and she expires with the name of Amida Buddha on her lips. Although this moment is unique in the war tales—there is no other instance of a man cutting a woman's stomach—women are generally a strong presence in many of the suicide scenes. Typically, wives urge their husbands to do the right thing and die, or assist them directly by creating a diversion or locking doors.

In 1192 Yoritomo established a new military government, known as the *bakufu*, in Kamakura. After Yoritomo's death, his widow and her family, the Hōjōs, seized control. In 1221 they defeated the imperial army in Kyoto and consolidated their power nationwide. The Hōjō family, who (ironically) were descended from the Taira, controlled Japan from the city of Kamakura for the next hundred years. Their rule saw the gradual ascendance of a warrior aristocracy. These men were essentially equestrian archers, trained in "the Way of the Bow and the Horse." During the thirteenth century the Hōjōs kept the peace, while successfully defending Japan against two Mongol invasions. But in 1333, forces backed by Emperor Go-Daigo overthrew the bakufu government and restored imperial power. The political machinations of Go-Daigo form the backdrop for the next generation of warrior sagas.

The longest of these is the *Taiheiki*. Although a literal translation of the word *Taiheiki* means "Record of the Great Peace," anyone who reads a few chapters of this work will query its title; "Record of the Great Bloodbath" would be more apt. The narrative guides us through fifty years of relentless insurgency, peaking midway with the sacking of Kamakura in 1333, and continuing into the turbulent early years of the Ashikaga shogunate. We are in the midst of a death-lust epidemic. A popular battle cry, repeated throughout the narrative, is "Let each man fight until the hilt of his sword breaks, and let each slit his belly at the end!" No one is afraid to die, and many seem impatient to get on with it:

> When he realized that no reinforcements would be arriv-
> ing, Lord Nakatoki gathered his warriors in the grounds of
> the temple, four hundred and thirty-two men in total.

"Men! Even in the knowledge of certain defeat, you have stood by me to the end. For this, I salute you. My gratitude to you is deep indeed, and I have no words to express it. Now I shall kill myself for your sakes, to repay in death the trust you have shown me in life. I may be a man of no special importance, but I bear the name of Hōjō, and the Minamoto will offer you a thousand fortunes for my head. Take it, and deliver it to them, that you may atone for your offenses and pledge new allegiance to them." As soon as he had uttered these words, he removed his armor until he was naked above the waist, slashed his stomach in the shape of a cross, and fell down dead.

Lord Nakatoki's chief councilor, Kasuya Muneaki, spoke up, as his tears dripped onto his armor:

"O bitter fate, that you should go before me! I thought to take my life first, and prepare a path for you on the other side. Now I have witnessed your death in this world, but I will not break our bond. Wait for me, I shall follow you to the world beyond!" Taking the sword, which was buried to its hilt in his lord's corpse, he made two cuts in his own belly and fell forward, dying with his arms wrapped around Lord Nakatoki's knees.

The four hundred and thirty-two warriors tore off their armor and ripped their bellies simultaneously. Rivers of blood gushed forth. Corpses were strewn about the temple like so many slabs of meat in a slaughterhouse.[13]

Most terrible was the self-massacre at Kamakura that terminated the Hōjō regency in July 1333. According to the *Taiheiki*, after the army of Nitta Yoshisada broke into the castle town, nearly nine hundred defenders slit their bellies. Thousands of civilians also committed

---

13. Hasegawa, ed., *Taiheiki*, 1:470–74. Mass suicides also feature in Chinese war tales of the same era. In 1279, for example, eight hundred Sung princes and warriors were said to have massacred themselves with the young emperor Bing rather than submit to the Mongol invaders.

suicide in one way or another, mostly by fire, many by stabbing themselves. Those who choose life are portrayed as rascals:

> The battle cries of Yoshisada's soldiers could already be heard outside as Lord Kunitoki prepared to address his men for the last time. Now only two hundred warriors remained; they assembled in the courtyard, each one ready to die with his lord. Kunitoki ordered them to keep Yoshisada at bay for as long as they could with volleys of arrows, until he had finished preparing for suicide. His men bowed and hurried out.
>
> Kunitoki recited a sutra, kneeling beside the body of his son, Toshitoki, who had already cut his stomach. The only retainer still with him was an old man named Kanono Shigemitsu. To him, Kunitoki gave special instructions.
>
> "Wait until I have cut my stomach, then set fire to the house. I will not give my enemies the satisfaction of taking my head."
>
> As his master reached the fifth part of the sutra, Shigemitsu went to check on the gate. He returned at once saying, "My lord, our bowmen are slain and the enemy is upon us! You must take your life without haste!"
>
> "So be it," said Kunitoki, and with the sutra scroll in one hand and his sword in the other, he cut a cross into his stomach and lay down on the same pillow as his son.
>
> But an evil spirit had planted an idea in Shigemitsu's mind. He did not burn the house. Instead he stripped the armor from his two dead masters, took their swords and daggers, and all the gold and silver in the house. He holed himself up in Engakuji Temple, gleefully counting his loot:
>
> "With all this treasure, my life will be sweet indeed!"
>
> But the gods made sure that justice was done, for the incident reached the ears of Yoshisada's commanders. They wasted no time in tracking down the thief, and

Shigemitsu's head was soon gracing the tip of a spike. No one mourned his death.[14]

Notwithstanding the unremitting carnage, the *Taiheiki* eschews graphic description of suicide scenes. Usually we are told only that soldiers "cut their stomachs," and death is invariably, often implausibly, instantaneous. One suspects that the text is using the terms *seppuku* and *jigai* (suicide) generically, and that the men are not only stabbing themselves but also stabbing each other, cutting their own throats, falling on their swords, and making every effort to finish each other off as efficiently as possible. This convention of omitting specific details of self-stabbings was adopted by most subsequent military chroniclers.

Despite its numerous scenes of mass suicide, the *Taiheiki* usually reserves suicidal glory for outstanding individuals. Only generals and their most faithful vassals and bodyguards—who may sometimes number in the hundreds—voluntarily die together. Rank-and-file foot soldiers, on the other hand, have a tendency to flee for the lives when the battle turns against them. The willingness to cut one's stomach is a mark of especially strong character, a tragic and noble gesture beyond the range of the common man.

The *Taiheiki* also indicates that the practice of administering a death blow to a stomach-cutter by removing his head had not yet become standard. Inspection of enemy heads (*kubi-jikken*) was a time-honored post-battle ritual. Decapitation consequently had shameful connotations. We can presume also that the absence of a prisoner-taking tradition encouraged suicide. Defeated soldiers were often slaughtered. Those of high rank were usually gibbeted. "If I am captured they will exhibit my corpse!" is a constant refrain in the *Taiheiki*. Informed that ten thousand imperial riders are advancing on his castle, Lord Nagoya Tokiari cries out, "What point is there in fighting, when we are so few in number? If we fall into enemy hands, future generations will mock our names." Tokiari, his brothers, and his cousins place their weeping

14. Ibid., 1:516–17.

wives and children in a boat and send them out to sea. After watching them drown, Tokiari and his men—seventy-nine in all—set fire to the castle, slash their bellies, and throw themselves into the flames.[15]

By far the most common form of stomach-cutting in this tale is *jūmonji*, two crossed cuts. There is little explanation as to how the warriors accomplished this. Slightly later texts state that the first cut was usually horizontal, across the abdomen, and the second was vertical, cutting upwards from, or downwards to, the navel. If the horrible deaths in these tales can be taken as reflecting any aspect of reality, then there are several conceivable reasons for the predominance of the crossed cut.[16] First and foremost, warriors would surely have discovered that a single cut was seldom fatal; a second deep cut, piercing the solar plexus, was required. If enemy soldiers were watching, all the better: a double cut would double the effect. It may also be relevant that the word *jūmonji* was frequently used in the *Taiheiki* to describe sword fights themselves, in regard to swinging a blade in a cross-like motion or slicing with crisscrossing cuts: "He charged into the fray, swinging his blade in a cross-like motion"; "They hacked their way through the enemy's front line, slicing with crisscrossing chops"; "Fountains of blood erupted as he slashed his enemies mercilessly with crossed cuts." Or perhaps the glorification of cross-cutting in literature provoked its occurrence in reality. Whatever the derivation, cross-cutting remained the ideal ever after. Samurai of later centuries who had a point to prove would remember the heroes of the *Taiheiki* and likewise tear themselves open in jūmonji.

Mass suicides peak at this point, both in the text and in history. Solo suicides dominate the later chapters. These include the first to be performed on horseback, as troops of Musashino Shingen fled from a devastating raid on their camp outside Kyoto in March 1353:

> General Musashino made it as far Nijō. But then he saw
> [his commanders] Abu and Okino turn, and heard them

15. Ibid., 1:212–14.
16. That jūmonji is not sheer fantasy is proven by samurai of the 1800s, whose bloody self-mutilations were carefully documented by doctors and police detectives.

call to him: "Sir, you cannot outrun the enemy! Kill yourself while you can!" Still in his saddle, the general ripped
open his stomach and fell headfirst to his death. Instantly,
the enemy surged forward to take his head.[17]

At the battle for Yoshino Castle in February 1332, things have gone
badly for Prince Morinaga, son of Emperor Go-Daigo. With arrows
embedded in his armor, and "bleeding waterfalls of blood" from his
wounds, the prince is preparing for suicide. Hundreds of his men are
ready to follow him. One of his generals, Murakami Yoshiteru, suggests a way out. If the prince will exchange armor with him, Yoshiteru explains, he will climb one of the castle turrets and disembowel
himself in full view of the enemy; this will allow the prince time to
escape. Prince Morinaga is moved to tears. The two men swap clothes,
and Yoshiteru climbs the turret above the castle gates. He waits until
the prince is out of sight before showing himself to the attacking
troops:

> "Behold!" he roared from the castle tower, "I am Prince
> Morinaga, second son of the divine Emperor Go-Daigo,
> who traces his lineage through ninety-five generations to
> the sun goddess Amaterasu. My men have run away. Now
> I shall destroy myself out of contempt for them—and you!
> Watch carefully and you will learn how to cut your bellies,
> for your day will surely come." He removed his armor and
> hurled it down from the tower. Now all his enemies could
> see that he was wearing a prince's robes and cloak. As they
> looked on, he stabbed himself in the stomach, cut cleanly
> from left to right, and hurled a fistful of his guts against
> the wall. Dropping to his knees, he inserted the sword into
> his mouth until the tip of the blade touched his throat.
> Then he pushed himself forward, and died.[18]

17. Hasegawa, ed., *Taiheiki*, 4:32–33.
18. Ibid., 1:335.

A catalog of such self-sacrificial heroics, the *Taiheiki* became immensely popular. It was the epic that everyone knew well, and its influence was far-reaching. Samurai of subsequent eras measured themselves by its standards. It is one of the texts that taught Japan's warriors how to die.

The war tales are not unanimously positive about suicide. Some contain episodes where bands of over-zealous soldiers, unaware that reinforcements are about to arrive, throw away the battle by removing themselves from it prematurely. Warriors are sometimes shown arguing over whether to gut themselves or die fighting. Commanders about to perform seppuku leave instructions for their subordinates not to copy them. For instance, the *Baishōron* quotes a letter from General Shōni Sadatsune (1272–1336) to his son, purportedly written on the day that Sadatsune killed himself:

> The time has come for me to lay down my life for the shogun. Son, after I am dead, do not bother with the usual mourning rites. You and those who survive must unite, stand fast, and give the shogun many more years of loyal service. Consider this your duty to Buddha, and do not waste your years chanting sutras in the name of your dead father, for I will not hear them.[19]

The same work contains several passages that explicitly criticize suicide-mania. At the fall of Kamakura, a Hōjō general named Sadanao finds himself stranded on the beachfront with the remnants of his cavalry. They see flames rising over the castle and know that all is lost. Some of the riders dismount and rip their bellies on the sand. Sadanao sneers:

> "Look at them, the bravest cowards in Japan! Real courage is when you're one against a thousand and still you charge in for the kill. That's how you put your name in history.

19. Yashiro, ed., *Baishōron*, 100.

> Men, this will be our last battle. So let's do what warriors
> are meant to do—charge, kill, and die!"[20]

Sadanao and his cavalry race headlong into the center of the imperial army, trampling and killing hundreds before being hacked to
pieces themselves.

The *Baishōron* makes frequent use of the term *uchijini-jigai*, meaning "to die fighting or by one's own hand," the implication being
that these have equal validity. But the remarks attributed to Sadanao
here indicate a divergence of opinion in regard to this point. Similarly, the *Record of the Ōei Revolt* (1410) ends with a hot-tempered
"suicide debate" among the rebel commanders. Ōuchi Hiroshige is
entrenched at the castle town of Sakai. When nine hundred of the
shogun's cavalry charge the castle, Hiroshige, with five hundred, goes
out to meet them. He is easily pushed back, and soon he is left with
only two hundred riders. As they regroup, a cry goes up: "It's hopeless! We can't win!" They dismount and prepare to cut their bellies.
But an old retainer named Hirai urges Hiroshige to stop: "What need
is there for you to die like this? Negotiate, and seek terms for surrender." Hiroshige refuses: "Should we bargain for our lives just because
the fight has gone against us? Shame on any warrior who taints his
family's name!" Hirai manages to calm him down, and eventually
persuades him to remove his helmet and give himself up. Another
commander scoffs at this: "One minute they're your mortal enemies,
and the next you try to make peace? What nonsense is that? To hell
with surrendering!" He and his men hurl themselves into the enemy
ranks and die fighting.[21] Not everyone is so intrepid. In *The Ōnin War*
(Ōninki, 1467), one commander tells his men, "Here's an idea. We'll
pretend that we've cut our bellies, then sneak back into position. Let
the enemy think that they have the advantage. Then we can attack
and catch them off guard."[22] The gritty complexities of these scenes
surely indicate authenticity. It would appear that excessive enthusiasm

20. Ibid., 103.
21. *Ōeiki*, 75–78.
22. Shimamura, ed., *Ōninki*, 372.

for stomach-cutting was cause for consternation among some samurai commanders.

Mass suicides on the scale of those at Kamakura were not seen again. But the intensity of battlefield suicides continues to rise in war tales of the fifteenth century. Examples are thrillingly documented in *The Tale of Akamatsu* (Akamatsu monogatari, ca. 1475). From the late 1420s, Akamatsu Mitsusuke (1381–1441), a powerful warrior of Harima Province, was locked in a bad-tempered dispute over land titles with Ashikaga Yoshinori, the sixth shogun. On July 12, 1441, the shogun's forty-seventh birthday, Mitsusuke settled their dispute once and for all by inviting Yoshinori to a celebratory banquet and having him decapitated during pre-dinner drinks. *The Tale of Akamatsu* describes the assassination and consequent mayhem.

Mitsusuke and his men dig in at Harima and await the mighty army they know will be sent to obliterate them. Death is assured; the only question is how. The fighting unfolds in a delirium of animalistic butchery. Riders knocked from their mounts make no attempt to defend themselves; they tear open their stomachs and scatter their intestines over the heads of their enemies. Castle archers who have used up all their arrows hurl their guts from the turrets. Whereas in the *Taiheiki* and earlier tales, the drama—a defiant speech, a tearful farewell, a mutual promise to meet in the netherworld, a scrawl in blood on a temple pillar—precedes the death, here the death itself has become the drama, as the fighters strive for mid- or post-belly-rip displays of transcendental endurance. No longer an act born of panic or despair, seppuku has become self-empowerment, and every delayed death is an intimation of immortality. Jūmonji is now the norm, and a warrior who fails to manage that risks being written off as a coward. The only poignant moment in *The Tale of Akamatsu* is where Mitsusuke, who has announced his intention to cut his stomach, has to dissuade his hot-headed teenage son from doing the same: "If you kill yourself here with me, who will bear the name of our ancestors into the future? You are young, leave death for later! Forget about the netherworld, and devote your energies to *this* world. Be patient, and your time will come." Reluctantly, the young man makes his escape with a consort of bodyguards, but is

soon betrayed to enemy forces. Before tearing his bowels he composes a
death poem to be delivered to his sweetheart. On reading it, we are told,
she is overcome with grief and kills herself by leaping into a creek.[23]

Back at the castle, where the shogun's forces are massing, Mitsusuke demands a status report from his most loyal retainer, Asaka, the
very man whose sword had severed the shogun's head. Asaka tells him
that all is lost.

> "Then it is settled," replied Lord Akamatsu. Facing east,
> he put his palms together and prayed to the sun goddess
> Amaterasu, and asked Hachiman, the god of war, to give
> him strength. Turning to the west, he prayed for forgive-
> ness and begged Amida for mercy and peace in the after-
> life. Then he ended his sixty-one years by ripping open his
> stomach. His band of loyal followers, sixty-nine men in
> all, likewise expired with their swords in their bellies.[24]

In the *Taiheiki* this would be the last line of the episode. Here,
however, a more flamboyant display is being formulated. Asaka burns
the corpses, and is just about to join them in the flames when pride
suggests a better idea:

> Asaka put on his cherry-patterned kimono and tied it with
> a silver cord. He climbed to the top of the south-facing
> tower and bellowed at the top of his voice:
> "I am Asaka, loyal retainer of Lord Akamatsu! For years
> I have served him faithfully. I have fought in many battles,
> and my sword has done plenty of damage. Your shogun
> will verify that for you—if he ever finds his head! Any of
> you down there think you can match me?"[25]

Asaka postpones following his lord to the netherworld and takes the

23. Yashiro, ed., *Akamatsu monogatari*, 173–74.
24. Ibid., 175.
25. Ibid., 175–76.

time to dress for death. The dream of perfection in suicide has temporarily superceded feudal devotion. A challenger named Nomura comes forward and lets fly an arrow that pierces the butt end of Asaka's spear. More arrows sink into the castle defense turret. With a devilish scream, Asaka leaps down from the tower and slays riders left and right as he makes his way toward Nomura, who dismounts in preparation. When Asaka kills Nomura after an implausibly long duel, the attackers lose heart. For a moment they withdraw. Asaka scrambles back to the castle and taunts them one last time:

> "Weaklings! Watch me cut my stomach, and I will show you how it is done!" He ripped open his belly, pulled out his guts, and hurled them down from the tower. But Asaka was too tough to die quickly. He went to his lord's chamber and set a fire. After slitting his own throat, he lay down in the flames with the body of his lord as his pillow.
>
> The attackers rushed forward and smashed their way inside. Retainers of Lord Yamana, captain of the Left Cavalry, jumped into the fire and retrieved the heads of Akamatsu and Asaka, but no one could say which was which.[26]

As before, lord and vassal are united in death. But Asaka has done more than avoid capture. The narrative encourages us to believe that, as far as posterity is concerned, the one who commits suicide is the victor here. Asaka dominates, evades, and ultimately prevails by killing himself courageously, and by disposing of his own remains through self-cremation. His glorious death is a glorious victory, and his enemies are left fumbling through his ashes.

Seppuku as Execution

It was not long before suicide was itself subsumed into the field of strategy. Fifteenth-century battle histories show military commanders

26. Ibid., 178–79.

pressuring their enemy counterparts to cut their stomachs as soon as possible. The earliest recorded example of this sort of "forced" seppuku is found in an account of the Eikyō War of 1438. After the (natural) death of the fifth shogun, Yoshikazu, in 1425, Ashikaga Mochiuji (1398–1439), lord of Kamakura, saw himself as rightful successor. Over the following years he repeatedly provoked the new shogun, Yoshinori, who did his best to avert a direct confrontation. But Mochiuji's temperament was not well-suited to compromise. A letter promising to devote one hundred million years to annihilating Yoshinori, dated March 18, 1434 and written in Mochiuji's own blood, has been preserved. By 1438 Yoshinori had had enough, and sent a massive attack force to Kamakura. Hopelessly outnumbered, Mochiuji sought sanctuary in the Zen temple of Engakuji. The attackers cut off his escape while Yoshinori deliberated on Mochiuji's fate. Here is the relevant passage in *The Eikyō War* (Eikyōki), which is believed to have been written very soon after the events it describes:

> Intermediaries pleaded with the shogun to spare Mochiuji's life, assuring him that Mochiuji would never again be permitted to interfere in political matters. But the decision handed down from Kyoto was unequivocal: "Mochiuji has strayed from the path once too often. If he is not severely punished there will be more trouble in the future and more disturbances across the land." On February 10, 1439, the shogun's troops moved in, swarming around the temple and urging Mochiuji to kill himself.[27]

Mochiuji's bodyguards rushed out to fight, and were slaughtered to the last man while Mochiuji committed suicide. That left the problem of what to do with Mochiuji's son. It took the shogun and his advisors two weeks to make up their minds:

27. Kondō, ed., *Eikyōki*, in *Kaitei shiseki shūran*, 12:738.

Though young master Yoshihisa was but nine years of age, it was decided that he must die. On February 28, men were dispatched to Hōkokuji Temple to inform him of his fate. Very calmly, the young master burned incense before the altar and recited the *nenbutsu* ten times. He drew his dagger and cut himself open from his left side, falling forward as he expired. It was a most tragic and pitiful sight. Those who had been sent to deliver the boy unto death returned with their kimono sleeves pressed to their tear-soaked cheeks.[28]

The sooner a potential troublemaker could be persuaded to cut his stomach, the sooner things could return to normal. This was seppuku as crisis management. Ironically, however, mutineers could similarly use seppuku to their advantage. Persuading one's lord to cut his stomach was easier on the conscience than killing him. No one wanted the label of "lord-murderer." An example can be seen in the removal of Ōuchi Yoshitaka, lord of Yamaguchi Province, whose men hounded him to suicide in 1551. After the untimely death of his son and heir, Yoshitaka had lost interest in running his fiefdoms. He whiled away his days reading poetry and playing *kemari*, an ancient form of soccer. Eventually, one of his commanders, Sue Harukata, felt bold enough to attempt a coup, and raised a rebel force of five thousand men. Thousands of Yoshitaka's own troops deserted, while those of his vassals who did not participate in the coup gave tacit support by doing nothing. The only one of Yoshitaka's top men to remain loyal to him was Reizei Takatoyo (1531–51), a warrior-poet of some renown whose family had served Yoshitaka's for generations. Takatoyo had repeatedly warned Yoshitaka about the possibility of a coup. Now, with a dwindling number of guards, the pair escaped to Taineiji Temple at Nagato, where they were quickly surrounded by Harukata's army. But Harukata did not order an attack. Instead he sent a team of negotiators, who humbly implored Yoshitaka to cut his stomach. After a

28. Ibid., 12:738–39.

brief standoff, Yoshitaka capitulated. To the attacking troops a tearful Takatoyo announced: "Lord Ōuchi will now cut his stomach. No
one must enter!" Yoshitaka, who had taken great care over his death
poem, slit his stomach with one stroke. Takatoyo struck off his head.
Nine other retainers also cut their stomachs. As the last one alive,
Takatoyo burned the bodies. According to the only account we have
of the incident, which was written a full century later, he went outside
where the enemy could see him and cut his stomach in a cross shape.
He removed his guts, flung them about him, and stabbed himself in
the throat.[29]

In this way, suicide was increasingly a product of careful arbitration
and tactical ingenuity, rather than an autonomous outburst of defiance.
The trend was consolidated in the mid-1500s, as warrior households
incorporated obligatory stomach-cutting into their official punishments. This appears to have had no immediate affect on the symbolic
importance of suicide. *Facts Concerning Shōrin* (Shōrin yawa), an anonymous military history of Echigo Province compiled in the 1590s, lists
these punishments for samurai in ascending order of severity:

1. House arrest.
2. Disbandment of guards and attendants.
3. Confiscation of property.
4. Banishment.
5. Death [by seppuku].
6. Confiscation of family swords [i.e., forfeiture of samurai
   status].[30]

---

29. Kagawa, *Intoku taiheiki*, 2:43–46. The same passage relates a bizarre case of a samurai attempting to compose his death poem *after* slitting his belly. Hiraga Takayasu, guardian
of Kashirazaki Castle in Hiroshima, killed himself during a siege in 1551. After cutting
horizontally across his stomach, Takayasu seems to have become delusional. To the astonishment of his men, while blood gushed from the wound, Takayasu begin to reminisce
about his childhood days. After rambling on for a minute or so, he asked for a piece of
paper in order to write down his poem. When his men politely reminded him of the matter at hand, Takayasu came to his senses and punctured his heart. His retainers explained
away the episode as a manly demonstration of "spiritual calmness in the face of death."
    30. Kondō, ed., *Shōrin yawa*, in *Kaitei shiseki shūran*, 14:286.

Thus death was preferable to dishonor. The same document describes a case that illustrates exactly how these rules were applied. In 1560 a samurai named Nagao Uemon somehow incurred the wrath of Uesugi Kenshin, lord of Echigo. Uemon was subject to punishments (2), (3), and (6) above. In other words, he lost everything and was demoted to peasant status. His family appealed, requesting that his sentence be "reduced" to seppuku. Their appeal was successful. Uemon's swords were returned and he was permitted to disembowel himself, leaving family honor (and the family property) intact. Incidentally, it was common practice in Echigo to dispense with swords altogether when slaughtering prisoners of war. Mass strangulations were preferred. Those who allowed themselves to be captured alive had forfeited the right to die by the sword.

In Kumamoto during the 1590s, Lord Katō Kiyomasa liberally incorporated seppuku as a punishment for various offences in his rules of conduct: "Reckless sword fighting is strictly forbidden. A samurai who thinks that drawing his sword entitles him to kill is mentally defective. Anyone who indulges in reckless swordplay outside of training will be ordered to cut his stomach."[31] Furthermore, Kiyomasa introduced an all-embracing "three-strike rule" that made seppuku the punishment for three consecutive offenses, including even minor breaches of etiquette. Not surprisingly, Kiyomasa's samurai were renowned for their impeccable conduct.

In war tales dating from the middle of the fifteenth century onward there are instances where defeated enemy commanders are granted the honor of ripping their bellies *after* hostilities have ceased, sometimes several days after. In a logical inversion of the principle that a warrior's readiness to eviscerate himself epitomized his loyalty, a prisoner's refusal to submit could be rewarded with permission to eviscerate himself. This privilege was an exceptional one, and seems to have depended largely on the behavior of the captured commander. A bit of charisma went a long way. On June 28, 1570, armies of Oda Nobunaga and Asakura Yoshikage clashed on the fields of Anegawa.

31. Kondō, ed., *Kiyomasaki*, in *Kaitei shiseki shūran*, 15:664.

Nobunaga's men captured one of Yoshikage's commanders, a samurai named Kanemaki, and brought him before their leader. Nobunaga offered to spare Kanemaki's life if he would pledge allegiance. Kanemaki scoffed, "If I could not die fighting for my lord, how could I let his enemy spare my life? Cut off my head, and be quick about it!" As one of Nobunaga's guards stepped forward to oblige, Kanemaki thundered, "Am I a common foot soldier? Let me cut my stomach first!" They gave him a sword and allowed him to stab himself before they chopped off his head.[32]

We have this account of the forced suicide of Tsuchimochi Chikashige, lord of Matsuo, following his capture during a battle fought in April 1578:

> Chikashige was handed over to a group of samurai from Urabe. They wondered what to do with him. One said that the only way to treat an enemy captive was to chop off his head. A few were willing to spare his life. They quoted the proverb "You don't clip a withering weed." Others argued that execution was unavoidable. In the end they agreed that it would be best to make him cut his stomach.[33]

In his *Tales of Jōzan* (1739), Yuasa Jōzan relates the story of a young samurai named Obata Sukerokurō, who was captured alive during the great battle of Sekigahara in 1600. Threatened with torture, Sukerokurō refused to divulge his commander's whereabouts: "Torture me if you wish, break my bones—I will tell you nothing." Impressed by the young man's proud manner, his enemies set him free. But Sukerokurō, shamed by this unusually lenient treatment, went to a temple and cut his stomach.[34]

Samurai status in itself was no guarantee of exemption from conventional beheading. Only those who were deemed to have conducted themselves according to samurai ideals were given special treatment.

32. Yamamoto, *Seppuku*, 29.
33. *Ōtomo kōhaiki*, 1:278.
34. Yuasa, *Jōzan kidan*, 24.

Autumn of 1594 saw the execution of Ishikawa Goemon, heir to a
wealthy samurai family of the Miyoshi domain. Goemon was no Zen
warrior. Since stealing the family treasure at the age of sixteen he had
lived a life of crime, terrorizing the roads around Kyoto with a gang of
drunken thugs. After capture, his men were crucified at Sanjōgawara,
watching from their crosses while Goemon was boiled alive in a caul-
dron of oil.[35]

The ubiquity of obligatory seppuku in public life is evident in the
following extract from a letter written by Gaspar Vilela, a Spanish
missionary who arrived in Japan around 1550. The letter is dated
October 28, 1557.

> When the king passes sentence of death on one of his
> subjects, a messenger delivers to the condemned the date
> on which he must die. The man thus condemned does
> not abscond, or attempt to flee. He deems himself permit-
> ted to end his life by imperial command, and regards it
> an unparalleled honor. At the specified time, he puts on
> his finest robes, and with his dagger stabs himself in the
> chest. He cuts down to his stomach, then makes a second
> cut from side to side, so as to form the shape of a cross;
> and thus he dies. Those who dispatch themselves in this
> manner are not branded as traitors; indeed their heirs and
> their families receive much reward.[36]

As a Catholic, Vilela was horrified at the official sanctioning of suicide. His conclusion: "For such monstrous acts they will surely fall into
hell. They are completely blind to this, and put honor above all else."
Cultural differences in attitudes to death were most notable during
the religious purges that began in 1618. Several thousand missionaries, friars, and native Catholic converts were executed. Condemned to
straightforward decapitation or drowning, in some cases the Christians

---

35. Avila, *Nihon ōkokuki*, 226–27.
36. *Jesus kaishi Nihon tsūshin*, 1:120–21.

marched to their deaths with displays of defiance, by linking arms, dancing, and singing hymns. Inflamed by this, the executioners revised their methods. They tied the martyrs' ankles with rope and suspended them upside down with their heads buried in the ground, having first slit their temples to allow a smooth drip of blood. Death, after unimaginable agonies, could take days. There was no more singing.[37]

Kaishaku

Mass suicides by warriors, so prominent in chronicles of the Kamakura period (1185–1333), are rare in war literature of the Sengoku period (1467–1568). It is unusual for more than two men to kill themselves at the same time. Even when a dozen retainers rip themselves up, they do so in ones and twos. The paramount objective of bodyguards and chief retainers was to ensure that no enemy sword touched the body of their lord or general. For a lord to be taken alive was, of course, a disgrace, both for him and his vassals. Thus we see cases of retainers suicidally throwing themselves upon the enemy so as to allow their lord time to cut his stomach. A history of the Shigas, a military family in Oita, includes a terse account of the battle for Tsunaharu Castle, fought in 1586. The castle was defended by Lord Shiga Akitaka. Here is the description of his suicide:

> It was hopeless. Lord Shiga pulled back to Jōrakuji Temple as his men tried to keep the enemy at bay. Many men were trampled in the chaos. While the men around him stalled the attackers with volleys of arrows, Lord Shiga was able to cut his stomach. Six of his best men lost their lives at this time.[38]

It was still normal for a vassal who decapitated his superior to kill himself immediately afterwards, though protocols were not clear.

37. There were, however, remarkably few apostasies.
38. *Nanzan Shiga kishō*, 742.

Some confusion is evident in the death of Lord Azai Hisamasa, who killed himself at Odani Castle on September 23, 1573. Under attack from the massive army of Oda Nobunaga, Hisamasa was "ready to rip his bowels and make his castle his pillow," as an official chronicler describes it. He poured himself three cups of saké from a bamboo flask he carried in his belt. He slashed his stomach and was immediately beheaded by one of his vassals. His men were determined to die too. However, "fearing that it would be improper for them to die in the same room, they hurried down to a lower part of the building." The samurai who had beheaded Hisamasa stabbed himself in the chest and was beheaded by a third, who also cut himself open.[39]

Amid chaotic scenes of this sort, a new word makes its appearance. The derivation of the term *kaishaku* is not known. Some scholars believe it might be a misreading of *baishaku*, an old word meaning something like "kind assistance." In the *Taiheiki* and other medieval chronicles, *kaishaku* denotes someone who assists in general matters not specifically related to the suicide ritual. No special term yet existed for compassionate decapitation, though the phenomenon itself was familiar enough. For instance, the *Jōkyū Disturbance* of 1240 has "They cut off the head of the man who had stabbed himself [*jigai no kubi wo kiru*]."[40] The word *kaishaku* appears frequently from the 1500s, when the ritualization of seppuku was almost complete. An early example comes in the *Records of the Two Hosokawa Families* (Hosokawa ryōkeki, 1573), a history of the Hosokawa family, for centuries one of Japan's most influential military households. In an account of the seppuku of Miyoshi Yukinaga at Chionji Temple in Kyoto in 1519, the text informs us that "a retainer named Jinshirō acted as kaishaku and then slit his own belly."[41] Until the latter half of the sixteenth century, to serve as kaishaku was simultaneously to submit to a death sentence: a samurai whose sword had touched the body of his lord could not honorably continue to live.

39. Kondō, ed., *Azai sandaiki*, in *Kaitei shiseki shūran*, 6:274–75.
40. Matsubayashi, ed., *Jōkyūki*, 228.
41. *Hosokawa ryōkeki*, 590.

Nishina Morinobu (Died March 2, 1582)

Nishina Morinobu (1557–82) was the fifth son of Takeda Shingen (1521–73), lord of Kai (now Yamanashi Prefecture). The Takedas were descended from Emperor Seiwa on the Minamoto side, a lineage that kindled passionate ambitions. Shingen was born a troublemaker. His childhood tutor, a Zen priest, was said to have tossed the boy from a balcony (and into a carp pond) for his insolence. For his battleground exploits Shingen earned himself the nickname "the Tiger of Kai," and by the age of fifty had expanded the Takeda domain to include Shinano and Suruga, as well as parts of Hida and Kozuke. In 1573 he led his army toward Kyoto with the intention of challenging Oda Nobunaga (1534–82), who was attempting to subjugate quarreling domains and unite Japan under a single military hegemony. Shingen might have succeeded had he not succumbed to tuberculosis during the campaign. (Residents of Yamanashi prefer a rival theory that he was picked off by an enemy sniper.) Shingen's abortive attempt to destroy Nobunaga is one of the great "what-ifs" of Japanese history.

After the Tiger's death, the Takedas came under pressure from all sides. In 1579, Morinobu took over as commander of Takatō, a castle of great strategic importance and the Takedas' last point of defense against attack from the east. So many of the Takedas' allies had deserted or betrayed them that a vast army loyal to Nobunaga, and led by his son Nobutada, was able to reach the region of Takatō without shedding one drop of blood. On the first day of March in 1582, fifty thousand troops under Nobutada's command surrounded Takatō Castle, which was defended by fewer than three thousand of Morinobu's men.

Morinobu and Nobutada were both twenty-five years old, and each claimed his father to be Japan's greatest military commander. Aside from the long-standing power struggle between their families, there was bad blood between the young men on a personal level. As a teenager Nobutada had briefly been engaged, through an optimistic arrangement aimed at keeping the peace, to Morinobu's sister, but had contemptuously refused to marry her. It was an insult that Morinobu had not forgotten.

Nobutada saw no need to lay siege to the castle in the usual manner; with such a superior force there could be no doubt about the outcome. This enabled some Takatō civilians to escape. Among them was Morinobu's eight-year-old son, escorted by three bodyguards and carrying a portrait of his grandfather for identification.[42] Hoping for a quick result, Nobutada sent a priest to deliver his terms for surrender. Morinobu was not one for cutting deals. The priest was sent back, minus his nose and ears. Outraged by this, Nobutada ordered a dawn attack, dividing his army in three groups so as to assault the castle simultaneously from three sides. His instruction to his generals was: "Kill everyone."[43]

The attackers began maneuvering in the dark at around four in the morning. With rivers to east and west, and rocky hills behind, Takatō was not easily approached. It took two hours for the cavalry to reach their attack positions. When he learned that an assault was imminent, Morinobu gave an incredible order: he would lead his men outside and charge the enemy head-on.

The fight that followed has endured as Japan's Thermopylae. What should have been a brisk massacre turned into a prolonged and frenzied battle. Morinobu charged out westward at the head of four hundred riders, with his standard, a silver gourd, in full view. Every surviving account of the battle stresses the ferocity of this charge. The Takatō samurai fought with the invincibility of men who know they are doomed. To the astonishment of Nobutada's generals, their own troops were pushed back. Two hours later, they had not retaken this ground. Cavalry approaching the front and east gates were stopped in their tracks by jettisoned rocks and heavy logs, and by fire from arquebuses (Portuguese-made matchlock rifles). Nobutada was enraged at his commanders' failure to penetrate the castle defenses. He abandoned his vantage point and led a thousand riders around the eastern

42. The boy made it all the way to Chiba Prefecture, where his descendants live today. The portrait of Shingen is a treasured family heirloom.

43. Ōta, *Shinchō kōki*, 2:357.

side to attack Takatō from the rear. By this time Morinobu had been shot in the thigh and was no longer able to ride. He returned to the castle and began fighting on foot. As dead bodies piled up around the castle barriers, Nobutada's infantry used them as cover. Each attacking wave that tired or retreated was replaced by fresh troops. Again and again the Takatō samurai charged out to drive the enemy away, but by mid-afternoon they were exhausted. When the attackers broke through the west gate, the castle guards pulled back to the second circle and removed their *sashimono* (flags attached to the backs of their armor) to prepare for close-quarter combat. Hundreds were slaughtered as the attackers poured in from all sides. Seeing that the guards were overwhelmed, civilians joined the fight. Women and old folk fought with spears taken from the dead. Children fired arrows from hidden positions. It was hopeless, and the attackers were already collecting heads. Nobutada and his troops entered via the east gate, climbing over corpses. Morinobu, left with only thirty men, desperately fought on near the main tower. At four in the afternoon he threw down his sword. He climbed onto the roof of the tower, removed his armor, and drew his dagger. Stabbing himself in his left side, he cut a line across his stomach, and made a second cut upwards from his groin. Still on his feet, he reached into the wound, pulled out a handful of intestines, and threw them against the castle wall while screaming a curse on the Oda family. His legs gave way and he collapsed. When his men saw this, they fell on their swords or stabbed each other to death. There were no survivors.[44]

The resilience of the Takatō defenders was praised in battle reports by the enemy commanders, an unprecedented distinction. After Morinobu's head had been delivered to Oda Nobunaga for inspection, his body was buried with full honors at Keisen Temple.

Little else is known about Nishina Morinobu. A family document notes his resemblance to his father. An early chronicle describes him as "intelligent and quiet, but tough."[45] There seems no reason to

44. Ibid., 358–60; Kasuga, *Nishina Morinobu*, 196–208; Kaisōsho Kankōkai, ed., *Kōranki*, 295–99.

45. Kasuga, *Nishina Morinobu*, 15.

doubt that assessment. He is said to have married the girl he loved, and declined to keep concubines. That is about all. But his last stand has become legend. While other Takeda generals deserted one after another, he alone stood fast, knowing that to do so would mean destruction. His suicide—a complete jūmonji, after a full day's combat, at the brink of defeat but still undefeated—is regarded by many as the perfect warrior death. Takatō Castle still stands today, and locals are fond of saying that the extraordinary purplish tint of the cherry blossoms there is caused by the blood of its heroic defenders seeping in through the roots. Even Morinobu's dying curse hit its target: within months, both Odas were dead. On June 21, Nobunaga perished in flames during a treacherous attack by one of his own generals, Akechi Mitsuhide, at Honnōji Temple. Nobutada died a few weeks later, while defending Nijō Castle against Mitsuhide's rebel army.

Shimizu Muneharu (Died June 23, 1582)

Late in the night of June 21, 1582, a messenger delivered the news of Nobunaga's death to Hashiba Hideyoshi (1537–98), one of Nobunaga's finest generals, whose army was encamped near the castle town of Takamatsu in Bitchū. Bitchū was one of several important provinces in western Japan controlled by Mōri Terumoto, a warlord who rivaled Nobunaga in wealth and ambition. In April of that year, at Nobunaga's command, Hideyoshi had invaded Bitchū and laid siege to Takamatsu.

Hideyoshi's siege of Takamatsu is a gem of samurai history known to every Japanese schoolboy. Takamatsu was thought to be impenetrable. Mountains enclosed it from north and east, and the great Ashimori River ran along its western side; in addition, the castle was moated on three sides and defended by five thousand guards under the command of Shimizu Muneharu (1537–82), a loyal retainer of Mōri. Muneharu's military career was a catalog of triumphs. Even with twenty thousand troops under his command, Hideyoshi knew better than to attempt a direct assault.

His solution was inspired. The rainy season had come early that

year, and the Ashimori was already rising. Hideyoshi ordered water
from the river to be redirected toward the castle. Thousands of local
peasants were hired to assist Hideyoshi's soldiers in the construction
of an elaborate series of dams and viaducts. As heavy rains continued, more water seeped down from the mountains. Takamatsu began
to flood. Muneharu's men tried repeatedly to destroy the dams. But
Hideyoshi, always one step ahead, had prepared rafts and comman-
deered fishing boats from which his bowmen showered the defenders
with arrows. A nighttime breakout from the castle by an elite ninja
team, under orders to contact Mōri and persuade him to send immediate reinforcements, was easily detected and suppressed. Muneharu was
completely cut off. After three weeks of flooding, conditions became
impossible. Castle guards were wading though muddy water. Snakes
and rats infested the town. Provisions had almost run out, and people
were beginning to starve. Envoys from Hideyoshi urged Muneharu
to surrender, stressing the impossibility of his situation. On June 22,
Muneharu dispatched a messenger to Hideyoshi: "Indeed we are lost.
I implore you to spare my people. My life you can have."[46]

What Muneharu did not know was that his head had already been
on the bargaining table for some time. Mōri was in fact leading his
army toward Takamatsu, all the while exchanging couriers with Hideyoshi to discuss terms for a settlement. Ignorant of Nobunaga's assassination and fearing total extermination, Mōri had offered three of his
fiefdoms to Hideyoshi in return for peace. Hideyoshi had accepted.
Muneharu's suicide would be the requisite gesture of defeat.

Shimizu Muneharu was forty-five, and had been lord of Takamatsu
for nearly twenty years. The title had come to him unexpectedly. He
was the middle brother of three, and became head of the family only
after his older brother, Gessei, took the tonsure and became a lay
monk. Gessei lived in Takamatsu with his brothers, devoting himself
to religious worship and taking no part in military matters. However,
according to *The Taikō Chronicles*, a history of Hideyoshi's campaigns,
when Gessei learned that Muneharu was to commit suicide, he

46. Nakajima, *Chūgoku heiranki*, 270.

insisted that they both die together; as the oldest brother, by rights the fate ought to have been his alone.

Arrangements were quickly made. Hideyoshi agreed to provide a boat to take Muneharu from the castle gate. A second boat, carrying Hideyoshi's representatives, would meet Muneharu in the center of the "lake"—the expanse of water around the castle that was the result of weeks of flooding. There, facing Hideyoshi's camp, Muneharu was to cut his stomach in the boat. As a sign of respect for Muneharu's service and sacrifice, Mōri ordered one of his top men, Sechika Nobuyoshi, to commit suicide alongside Muneharu.

To prevent sympathy suicides among his own men, Muneharu did his best to keep his death sentence secret. Initially he informed only his brothers and a few close retainers. To his young son he penned some "Notes for Correct Behavior," which, within a few lines, convey the warmth and humor of the man:

> Be grateful, charitable, and honest.
> Work hard and trust to Heaven.
> Rise early and obey your superiors.
> Be efficient in regard to accounts, weapons, and
>   construction.
> Fight all corruption and excess.
> Don't confuse your mind with women and wine.[47]

Muneharu's son-in-law, Nakajima Motoyuki, had commanded a valiant defense of the castle's second circle. He later wrote a record of what transpired that day, in which we learn that he pleaded for a place in the boat alongside his father-in-law, but Muneharu refused him, insisting that he stay alive to care for his wife and children. In addition to Gessei, Muneharu's younger brother, Nanba, also requested a place in the boat. Since Muneharu could not dissuade him, it was agreed that all three brothers would die together. Motoyuki also

---

47. Kondō, ed., *Shimizu Chōzaemon-no-jō Taira Muneharu yurai oboegaki*, in *Kaitei shiseki shūran*, 15:309.

offers a poignant anecdote about one of Muneharu's veteran retainers, an old samurai named Shirai Haruyoshi. That evening Haruyoshi sent a page asking Muneharu to meet him in the castle tower. "My lord," said Haruyoshi when Muneharu arrived, "it is not difficult to cut one's stomach—look." He opened his robes to reveal two deep crossed cuts he had gouged into his stomach. Motoyuki tells us that Muneharu shed tears as he beheaded his old friend.[48]

At ten o'clock on the following morning, Muneharu, Gessei, Nanba, and Nobuyoshi, accompanied by two priests, climbed aboard the boat that was waiting for them as arranged. All were dressed in white death robes with Buddhist mantras written on the backs. Their boatman was a samurai named Kōichi, who was also to act as their executioner.

The entire population of Takamatsu turned out to see them off. There were hysterical scenes. People thronged into the main courtyard, sobbing and howling. From the castle walls Muneharu's men shouted out their unswerving devotion: "We shall never forget your lordship's kindness!" "Future generations shall hear your name!" "We will let no one speak ill of you!"[49] Some men rushed into the water after the boat. They included Gessei's groom and one of Muneharu's servants, all of whom Muneharu had ordered to remain alive and serve Mōri. When they saw that they would be left behind, they drew their swords and stabbed each other to death. As the boat pulled away, the people of Takamatsu fell silent and bowed their heads in reverence.

The rains had stopped during the night, and the surface of the lake was completely still. When the boat reached the designated spot, Hideyoshi's men were waiting for them. Oze Hoan, Hideyoshi's official historian, has left us an account of what happened next.

"I am Horio Mosuke," came a shout, "Chief retainer of Lord Hashiba Hideyoshi." The boats drew alongside each other. "Lord Hashiba thanks you for keeping your word, and offers you his deepest respect. It has been a long siege. You must be very tired."[50] Mosuke offered Muneharu

48. Nakajima, *Chūgoku heiranki*, 275.
49. Ibid., 276.
50. Oze, *Taikōki*, 60–61.

and his men some food and a bottle of saké. With Hideyoshi's army on the northern hills and Mōri's to the south, the eyes of sixty thousand men were focused on them—the largest crowd for any seppuku in history, before or since. They drank a few glasses each ("not so much as to get drunk"[51]) while Gessei sang a Buddhist song.

Being the oldest brother, Gessei was the first to die. "Gessei removed his upper robes, and with a cry of 'Ya!' he ripped his stomach in a cross shape," Oze tells us.[52] Kōichi struck off Gessei's head. Muneharu saluted the two armies, and, after reciting his farewell poem, cut his stomach. Oze depicts an exquisite scene, the surface of the lake glittering like a mirror, a team of ducks passing across the sky. According to Motoyuki, neither Muneharu nor Gessei allowed the slightest indication of pain to enter their expressions. Next to go was Nanba, then Nobuyoshi. With great solemnity Kōichi placed the four heads in specially prepared boxes and handed them to Mosuke. The ceremony over, Hideyoshi's troops began moving out. By noon they had vanished from Takamatsu.

Such is the story as reported in contemporary accounts. Yet, while the plethora of accurate details points to a high degree of historicity, it is difficult not to suspect that the death scene has been subjected to significant beautification. Consider what we are being invited to believe: that a swordsman standing in a small makeshift boat, which was floating in what could have been only a few feet of water and contained several other men, was able to move about the boat and decapitate the men one by one, immediately after they had cut their stomachs, without the slightest upset or complication. The story would be more credible if it were admitted that the men climbed out of the boat in order to perform their suicide rituals. But mundane details of that sort work against the aesthetic ideal. Contemporary chroniclers considered it mean or disrespectful to insist on drab realism when recounting a heroic seppuku. Only perfect death is worth memorializing. Hence the bloody end of the Shimizu brothers is fastidiously

51. Ibid., 61.
52. Ibid., 61.

sanitized and presented to us as an unblemished moment of shimmering poetic beauty. Fact is safely encased in myth.

From Takamatsu, Hideyoshi returned to Kyoto where his army massacred Mitsuhide's rebels to avenge the death of Nobunaga. Mitsuhide's death fell somewhat short of the heroic ideal. He and a small band of survivors fled from the battlefield, only to be set upon by bandits as they attempted to escape into the mountains. Mitsuhide's head, riddled with bamboo splinters and battered almost beyond recognition, eventually turned up and was delivered to Kyoto. Hideyoshi had it impaled on a spike at Honnōji Temple, the original scene of Mitsuhide's treachery.

Shibata Katsuie (Died June 14, 1583)

Hashiba Hideyoshi was unusual in having no hereditary title. His family was not of samurai stock, and he had first entered Oda Nobunaga's service as a lowly sandal-bearer. He joined the army and rose through the ranks with extraordinary rapidity. By his midthirties Hideyoshi had three fiefdoms to his name, reward for his success in subjugating Nobunaga's enemies. Hideyoshi combined military brilliance with a natural aptitude for negotiation and persuasion. He was lenient toward enemies who capitulated quickly, ruthless toward those who resisted; he would insist that defeated enemy generals cut their stomachs, and often had their families crucified as well. Nobunaga nicknamed him "the Monkey," though that may have been less for his slippery cleverness than for his physical appearance. (Hideyoshi was a small, wiry man with unappealing features; he is also said to have had an extra thumb on his right hand.) Once he had maneuvered himself into a secure position as Nobunaga's successor, Hideyoshi changed his family name to the more aristocratic-sounding "Toyotomi" and never looked back.

During one of his final campaigns for Nobunaga, Hideyoshi uncharacteristically waived his insistence on his opponent's suicide. This was after his six-month siege of Tottori Castle in 1581, which had reduced its inhabitants to cannibalism. Hideyoshi was so impressed by the fortitude of the defending commander, Kikkawa Tsuneie (1547–98), that he offered to spare his life by permitting a pair of Tsuneie's captains to cut their stomachs in his place. Tsuneie was too proud to accept. His quip to his men over their last bottle of saké together, although probably apocryphal, is a seppuku classic: "I've never practiced this. I hope I don't let you down." He did not.[53]

Another victim of the unstoppable Hideyoshi in those hectic months following Nobunaga's assassination was Shibata Katsuie (1522–83), a formidable warrior from the northern province of Fukui. Katsuie was a different type of man to Morinobu and Muneharu. He was not highly educated, and though an efficient administrator, in politics he had a reputation for heavy-handedness. Fighting was all that he knew. As a military leader he was ironfisted, daring, and relentless. In an era of fearless men he was greatly feared. During his younger years his enemies dubbed him "the Demon," which says it all.

Katsuie was initially a retainer of Oda Nobuyuki, Nobunaga's younger brother, a man whose ambitions consistently outweighed his abilities. After the death of their father there was friction between the two brothers. In August 1556 Nobuyuki had mounted a challenge to Nobunaga. But Nobunaga crushed Nobuyuki's rebel army, in which Katsuie commanded one thousand troops. This was the first defeat of Katsuie's career. Nobuyuki, too frightened to surrender to his brother, asked their mother to act as intermediary. Nobunaga's terms: Nobuyuki and Katsuie must come to him with shaved heads—traditionally symbolizing contrition—and prostrate themselves before him. They did so, and were spared. Katsuie recognized Nobunaga's greatness, and from that day pledged lifelong allegiance. But Nobuyuki was soon seeking allies for a fresh coup. When he tried to persuade Katsuie to rejoin him, Katsuie informed Nobunaga, who resolved to get rid of his brother once and for all. Nobunaga accomplished this with characteristic ingenuity, pretending that he had succumbed to a serious illness. Hearing this, Nobuyuki dropped his guard and hurried to visit his "dying" brother—

53. Segawa, comp., *Kikkawa Tsuneie-kō jiseki*, 24. For a description of Tsuneie's suicide, see p. 220.

not to do so would have been self-incriminating. Upon arrival he was arrested and forced to disembowel himself at Nobunaga's feet.

With Hideyoshi and now Katsuie as his generals, Nobunaga stormed from province to province, subduing all resisters. Katsuie's finest hour came in 1570, when he successfully defended Chōkōji Castle in Ōmi (now Shiga Prefecture) against the army of Rokkaku Yoshikata, one of a number of powerful warlords in that region who were attempting to stop Nobunaga. Intimidated by Katsuie's reputation, Yoshikata took the safe route and opted to impose a starvation siege rather than launch a direct assault. Four thousand of Yoshikata's troops took positions around Chōkōji and destroyed its aqueduct. Since the castle had no internal water supply, this strategy quickly took effect. Yoshikata sent men posing as messengers to the castle under the pretense of offering terms for a peaceful settlement; their true intention was to spy on conditions inside the castle. Realizing this, Katsuie concealed the water shortage by welcoming them with plenty of drinks and allowing them to wash their hands. Once things became desperate, he gathered his men and had the last water reserves brought out. Only three large jars were left. He told his men to drink their fill and then smashed the jars, shouting, "Better a quick death in battle than a slow one from thirst!" At dawn they surged out of Chōkōji and beat Yoshikata into retreat, collecting eight hundred enemy heads. For this performance Katsuie earned himself another nickname, "the Jar-Breaker."[54] In all he fought over twenty battles for Nobunaga, winning every one.

At the age of sixty Katsuie married O-ichi, the widow of his former enemy Asai Nagamasa, late lord of Ōmi. O-ichi, twenty-five years younger than Katsuie, was "the most radiant beauty this side of heaven" according to a contemporary report.[55] (The complexities of samurai feuding during this period may be surmised from the fact that she was a younger sister of Nobunaga, who was also responsible for her widowhood: Nagamasa had been driven to seppuku when Nobunaga's army, commanded by Hideyoshi, invaded Ōmi in the

54. Yuasa, *Jōzan kidan*, 39.
55. Kondō, ed., *Sofu monogatari*, in *Kaitei shiseki shūran*, 13:327.

summer of 1573.) O-ichi's intelligence and strength of character also won compliments. Nobunaga liked to say that his sister would have made a great general. The newlyweds grew devoted to one another, and became something of a celebrity couple.

Katsuie now had more fiefdoms than any of Nobunaga's retainers, though signs of tension between him and Hideyoshi were already noticeable, as Katsuie became increasingly threatened by Hideyoshi's meteoric rise. In the early 1580s, while Hideyoshi was expanding Nobunaga's domain in the south, Katsuie tore his way through the province of Kaga near the western coast, delivering the heads of nineteen Kaga warlords for Nobunaga's inspection. At the time of Nobunaga's assassination, Katsuie was battling hard against the recalcitrant Uesugi clan in the snowy hills of Etchū (now Toyama Prefecture) while Hideyoshi slowly strangled Takamatsu. In June 1582 they met face-to-face at a crisis council of Nobunaga's top generals. One of the aims of the meeting was to determine Nobunaga's successor. Katsuie pledged his support for Nobunaga's third son, Nobutaka. Hideyoshi, however, backed Nobunaga's grandson, Hidenobu. Though the generals managed to agree on the division of some of Nobunaga's fiefs, they could not resolve the succession issue. Hideyoshi and Katsuie consequently left the meeting on sour terms.

It was not long before they clashed. By the end of that year, Katsuie had organized a league of generals loyal to Nobutaka. On learning this, Hideyoshi immediately raced a small army northward, hoping to engage Katsuie before he had time to mobilize his forces. Crossing difficult terrain at astonishing speed, Hideyoshi's army reached Katsuie's camp at Shizugatake on June 12. Caught off guard, Katsuie's soldiers scattered. Katsuie retreated over the hills to his home castle at Kitanosho. Hideyoshi waited for reinforcements, and arrived at Kitanosho two days later with twenty thousand troops.

According to an account of the incident compiled later by his retainers, Katsuie, who had not fired so much as an arrow in Hideyoshi's direction, had decided to die even before Hideyoshi arrived. The implication is that Katsuie chose death over submission. The same document claims that Katsuie implored O-ichi to escape, and to take her three daughters (by her first husband) with her. O-ichi refused. The girls were sent out, escorted by three guards. O-ichi had decided to die alongside Katsuie.

For her fidelity, O-ichi has been hailed as a model warrior's wife. But her decision was swayed by something more than marital devotion. It was well known that Hideyoshi wanted her for himself. He was said to have been smitten with love when he first laid eyes on her. Unfortunately for him, that was just after he had crucified her nine-year-old son in the wake of his victory at Ōmi. Life with Hideyoshi would have been an abomination for O-ichi. She resolved to die with the Demon rather than marry the Monkey.

Katsuie and O-ichi killed themselves on the evening of June 14. We have several conflicting accounts of the event. A document prepared by Katsuie's retainers states only that "Lady O-ichi looked on as Lord Katsuie killed himself, and then she too ended her life."[56] Oze's version has Katsuie climbing to the top of the castle tower and announcing his decision to cut his stomach to his men, who shed tears. They then enjoy a farewell banquet together, and drink plenty of saké before Katsuie and his wife retire to the fifth floor of the tower. Ladies-in-waiting weep and wail as they chant sutras for their mistress. As Katsuie and O-ichi are preparing themselves for death, they hear the call of a cuckoo. Hence their death poems: "Is it the cuckoo that beckons us to part on this shimmering summer eve?" (O-ichi) and "On this summer eve of fleeting dreams, let the cuckoo offer our names to the clouds!" (Katsuie).[57] No specific details of their suicides are given. Hideyoshi, in a boastful letter to one of his senior commanders notifying him of the victory at Kitanosho, claimed that Katsuie had "stabbed his wife, children, and other members of his family, and then cut his stomach, together with over eighty retainers."[58]

According to the report by Katsuie's surviving retainers—surely the most reliable source—once Katsuie's death was confirmed, his men set fire to the tower. Some men leaped into the flames. An unidenti-

56. Adachi, ed., *Shibata Katsuie-kō shimatsuki*, 66.
57. Oze, *Taikōki*, 154.
58. Suzuki, *Toyotomi Hideyoshi*, 65–66.

fied number of ladies-in-waiting cut their throats or perished in the fire. Around forty samurai committed suicide by stabbing each other or disemboweling themselves, while others charged from the burning castle and hurled themselves against their attackers. Hideyoshi spared the lives of all who surrendered.[59]

O-ichi's three daughters made it safely to Hideyoshi's camp. A few years later he took one of them, Chacha, as his lifelong concubine. As was noted at the time, of the three girls, she resembled her mother most markedly.

Sen no Rikyū (Died April 21, 1591)

Hideyoshi's surging power seems to have induced a similarly surging paranoia. He became extremely distrustful, seeing traitors and assassins on all sides. Since ritual suicide could be performed in private at the house of the condemned, without arrest or formal process, and without the slightest delay, it was ideal for deleting undesirables. All it took was one messenger, and the target was gutted and headless before his supporters could come to his defense. Most tragic among Hideyoshi's many victims was his tea master Sen no Rikyū (1522–91), who was forced to commit suicide at the age of sixty-nine.

Legend has it that Oda Nobunaga himself started the craze for tea among warriors. An attractive tea house and a collection of first-class utensils became status symbols among the military community. A curious episode from this time reveals the importance attached to tea. Matsunaga Hisahide, a despotic warlord based in Yamato Province, had long been a thorn in Nobunaga's side. In November 1577, after a failed attempt to stall the progress of Nobunaga's forces, Hisahide retreated to his castle at Shigizen (now part of Nara Prefecture). Nobunaga surrounded Shigizen with twenty thousand troops, but did not immediately attack. Hisahide owned a famous tea bowl with a design of spiders, which Nobunaga wanted for his own collection. Nobunaga offered to spare Hisahide's life in exchange for the bowl.

59. Adachi, ed., *Shibata Katsuie-kō shimatsuki*, 66–68.

Hisahide replied that he would rather smash it and kill himself. Nobunaga upped the pressure by having Hisahide's sons crucified in Kyoto.
Hisahide retaliated by smashing the priceless spider bowl and ripping
open his stomach. In accordance with his instructions, his retainers
coated Hisahide's severed head with gunpowder, set fire to the castle,
and threw his head into the flames. Hisahide has gone down in popular folklore as the first samurai to die by *bakushi*: blowing himself up.[60]
Hisahide, who had tyrannized the province for years, was so unpopular with the people of Shigizen that they celebrated his explosion with
three days of drinking and dancing.[61]

The source of Rikyū's troubles with Hideyoshi is unclear. According
to one theory, problems began with, of all things, a disagreement over
tea aesthetics. Rikyū's philosophy of humble simplicity did not sit well
with Hideyoshi's megalomania. A number of oft-quoted anecdotes
illustrate the rift between them. In one, with the morning glories in
full bloom Rikyū suggested an afternoon of tea and flower apprecia-
tion. Hideyoshi arrived, expecting a garden of resplendent blossoms.
There were none: Rikyū had arranged a single flower in the alcove.
After a series of similar mishaps, Hideyoshi grew impatient with the
old sage. (Incidentally, Hideyoshi's notion of an ideal tea room can be
enjoyed today at Osaka Castle, where his Golden Tea Room has been
reconstructed. Gilded from top to bottom in gold leaf, and with a set
of gold utensils, it is arguably the most uninviting tea room in Japan.)

According to another theory, someone informed Hideyoshi that,
two years previously, Rikyū had installed a grand statue of himself
above the entrance to Daitokuji Temple, a clear indication of his spi-
raling hubris. In fact it was a small wooden carving of Rikyū; the temple priests had added it to other carvings displayed in the gatehouse

60. This accolade should properly go to Morozumi Masakiyo (?–1561), a general of the
Takedas, who obliterated himself by deliberately leaping onto a land mine to avoid capture
and disgrace after a battle. Masakiyo's head survived the blast intact. It was jettisoned into
the air, and was momentarily seized by enemy forces before being retrieved by Masakiyo's
retainers. The *Kōyō Military Chronicles* (Kōyō gunkan), a history of the Takeda family, records
the frantic scramble for Masakiyo's head. Three centuries later, the artist Utagawa Kuniyoshi
(1792–1861) idealized Masakiyo's unusual suicide in a striking woodblock print.

61. For Matsunaga Hisahide's suicide see Kaionji, *Akunin retsuden*, 360–61.

as a token of their gratitude after Rikyū paid for the gate's renovation with his own money. Hideyoshi, by now a firecracker with a very short fuse, was a frequent visitor to Daitokuji. He was not amused to learn that he had been passing beneath the old man's clogs. He had the statue removed and nailed to a cross at Modori Bridge in Kyoto. Rikyū was banished to Sakai, his home town.

Rikyū was a popular figure, and numerous nobles and lords attempted to intervene on his behalf. Hideyoshi sent a rider to Sakai demanding an apology. None was forthcoming. Furious, Hideyoshi ordered Rikyū back to Kyoto and sent troops to cordon off the streets around his residence. Two days later, on the morning of April 28, Hideyoshi's representatives arrived with the official sentence: Rikyū must cut his stomach. The men had brought a lacquer box filled with salt, in which they would carry Rikyū's head back to Hideyoshi.

There are many accounts of Rikyū's suicide, some of them highly implausible. The most reliable document is probably the *Sen no Rikyū yuishogaki*, a biography of Rikyū written in 1653, more than sixty years after his death, and based in part on interviews with students of his students. According to this document, when Hideyoshi's men announced the death sentence to Rikyū, he bowed and calmly offered them tea. There were six guards and three official witnesses. Hideyoshi had ordered one of the three witnesses, a man named Maita Awajino, to serve as kaishaku. Hideyoshi had chosen Awajino for this task out of pure malice: Awajino was a former pupil of Rikyū's. After all had drunk their cups of tea, Rikyū wrote down two death poems. The men handed him a sword, and Rikyū slit his stomach with a single cut. Awajino decapitated him successfully.[62] The men then carried the head back to Hideyoshi, who refused to inspect it. Instead, he ordered that it be exhibited at the Modori Bridge, traditionally a site for public executions of notorious criminals. Large crowds are said to have gathered every day to see Rikyū's head.

---

62. The account of Rikyū's death in the *Sen no Rikyū yuishogaki* is quoted in Kuwata, *Sen no Rikyū kenkyū*, 253–56. The document claims that Hideyoshi initially intended to have Rikyū crucified, but commuted the sentence to seppuku under pressure from Rikyū's supporters.

Toyotomi Hidetsugu (Died August 20, 1595)

Despite a flock of concubines, Hideyoshi was still childless when he turned fifty in 1586. He had adopted seven boys from various warrior families, but feared succession troubles. The only candidate was his sister's son, Hidetsugu. In October of 1591, Hideyoshi formally adopted Hidetsugu, then twenty-three, as his son, and two months later transferred to him the title of Regent.

Hidetsugu (1568–95) was a controversial figure. Hagiographers did their best to beautify him by highlighting his aesthetic accomplishments, his love of tea and poetry. But there was no disguising his chief interest. As one early chronicler ominously puts it, "His Lordship delighted in cutting things."[63]

Hideyoshi had amassed a collection of two hundred fine swords, gifted by allies or plundered from enemies, and entrusted them to his nephew, who was an excellent swordsman. Swords need testing. Hidetsugu's method was to ride out into the countryside and test them at random on peasants, travelers, and pilgrims. These expeditions became known as Hidetsugu's *sengiri*, his "one thousand chops."[64] He had an execution arena set up within the grounds of his own residence so that he could practice decapitation; new swords were broken in by hacking limbs off the corpses. He kept his rifles in good working order by taking potshots at farmers in the paddy fields. A story of Hidetsugu slitting open the belly of a pregnant woman so that he could see what babies looked like before they were born became notorious. That might have been a fabrication, but Hidetsugu's prodigious sadism was also noted in letters of the Portuguese missionaries, at least one of whom was on personal terms with him. It is also a fact that by the age of twenty-five Hidetsugu had become known as "the Slayer" (*sesshō*), a pun on his official title (*sesshō kanpaku*: Regent and Chancellor).

Just two years after Hidetsugu's promotion to regent, one of Hideyoshi's concubines became pregnant. It was Chacha, the daughter of O-ichi, whom Hideyoshi had hounded to death with her husband

63. *Honchō tsugan*, ca. 1670, quoted in Ōkuma, *Seppuku no rekishi*, 87.
64. Ōta, *Taikō gunki*, 151.

Shibata Katsuie ten years earlier. Chacha gave birth to a healthy baby boy in the autumn of 1593.[65] At fifty-seven, Hideyoshi had a son. Hidetsugu worried that his own position was under threat, and that Hideyoshi would try to make the child his heir. That is exactly what happened. Hideyoshi decided he had no more use for his nephew, and wanted him out of the way. In August 1595 Hidetsugu was accused of treason and ordered to present himself at Fushimi, the three-moated castle Hideyoshi had rebuilt in Osaka. Surprisingly perhaps, Hideyoshi did not immediately order his nephew to commit seppuku. Instead he stripped him of his rank and sent him into exile, after forcing him to sign a pledge of loyalty. Hidetsugu headed for Mt. Kōya, a Buddhist sanctuary in the mountains of Wakayama, taking three hundred samurai with him. That was too many for Hideyoshi's liking. He insisted that the number be reduced to twelve. A tense few days followed. On the afternoon of August 20, a rider from Hideyoshi arrived at Kōyasan with the order that everyone expected: it was time for Hidetsugu to die.

The suicide ceremony was performed that evening at Kōyasan's Kongōbuji Temple, in the Willow Room, named for the paintings of willows in four seasons that cover its walls. Four of Hidetsugu's young admirers agreed to die with him: a monk named Ryūseidō, and three samurai boys, all aged seventeen. These included Fuwa Mansaku, whose extraordinary good looks had already made him famous. (It was said that one old samurai had been so struck with the boy's beauty that he offered his life for a night with him; Mansaku accepted, and the samurai, true to his word, cut his stomach the next morning.) Hidetsugu selected five of his best swords, a different one for each man. Rather than dying first, as would have been customary, he elected to die last after beheading the other four. This was to be his final sword-practice. Hideyoshi sent a local magnate, Fukushima

65. This was in fact the second child Chacha had borne to Hideyoshi. The first, also a boy, died in infancy in 1591. It was after the death of this boy that Hideyoshi, resigning himself to being childless, had transferred power to Hidetsugu. In view of Hideyoshi's failure to produce children with any of his other concubines, and his advanced age at the time of the births, there has inevitably been speculation that he was not the father of Chacha's sons.

Masanori, to supervise the executions. Fearing that groups loyal to Hidetsugu might attempt a rescue, Masanori arrived with three thousand guards, who took up positions around the temple. Oze Hoan gives this account of the proceedings:

> Lord Hidetsugu began by presenting young Yamamoto with a sword made by Kuniyoshi.[66] The boy examined it, then cut into his left side and dragged the blade to the right. "Now!" he cried, and his head shot off to the front. Next to go was Sanjūro, using a rare blade said to have been made by Kuniyoshi's son. He studied it carefully before ripping himself wide open in two crossed lines; and off went his head. Third was Mansaku, who spoke movingly of his regret that it had come to this, that he must scar the body given to him by his beloved parents. "May they forgive me," he said, "for it is loyalty that compels me." Having inspected the blade, another excellent piece from the Kuniyoshi school, he plunged it into himself with great resolve. Next was the monk Ryūseidō, who expressed a modest request to choose the man who would behead him. But Lord Hidetsugu argued against this, saying the result would be the same; and so it was, for Ryūseidō's head was soon separated from his neck. Fifth and last was Lord Hidetsugu himself, with a blade of the Kamakura period made by the hand of Okazaki Gorō. For a moment he gazed at it in silence. Then, with a mighty shout, he opened up his bowels, and was seen to by his man Sasabe, using a fine sword of Uemitsu.[67]

The Slayer was dead at the age of twenty-seven. But the killing did not stop there. A further twenty men, who were connected to Hidetsugu in one way or another, committed suicide over the next few days. Hideyoshi had signed a death warrant for Kimura Shigekore,

66. Kuniyoshi (?–1267), an outstanding sword maker of the Kamakura period.
67. Oze, *Taikōki*, 501–2.

one of Hidetsugu's top retainers, who was obliged to cut his stomach in the garden of Daimonji Temple in Osaka. Hideyoshi also ordered the seppuku of Shigekore's son, the decapitation of his wife and concubines, and the crucifixion of his daughters. Other suicides appear to have been voluntary:

> Awano Hidemochi, loyal servant to Lord Hidetsugu, made his way to the eastern side of the capital, where, on the road that leads to the Awata Shrine, he killed himself by gouging a cross into his stomach. As he did so, he shouted out, "My lord was no traitor!"[68]

Oze's account suggests that married couples preferred to perform their suicide rituals separately. For example, Shirai Norihide, Hidetsugu's chief councilor, is reported as having killed himself at the Daiun-in, a temple in central Kyoto, while on the same day Norihide's wife cut her throat at the nearby Konrenji Temple. It can be imagined that priests did not relish these occasions. They certainly did not provide their services free of charge. We are informed that one samurai "humbly offered thirty gold pieces as he begged for permission to stain the temple with his blood."[69] People who could not afford an expensive ceremony within the temple grounds often killed themselves outside the temple gates, as appears to have been the case with Hidemochi above.

Hidetsugu also had a sizeable retinue of wives and concubines, and three children. On Hideyoshi's orders they were rounded up and taken to Kyoto. Thirty-one females of various ages, the youngest only twelve, were charged with treason. On the morning of September 5, they were taken in carts to Sanjōgawara, where Hidetsugu was on display, and were executed one by one at the foot of the spike that carried his head. A Portuguese Jesuit who witnessed the scene left this description:

68. Ibid., 506.
69. Ibid., 503.

When the carts were come to the place of execution . . .
[Hidetsugu's] three children were first murdered, and then
all the other Ladies in rank one after another were taken
out of the cart and . . . their own heads were stricken off.
All their bodies by order from Hideyoshi were thrown
into a pit . . . over which he caused to be built a little cha-
pel with a tomb in it with this inscription: *The Tomb of the
Traitors*.[70]

Three years later, Hideyoshi passed away. Over the next decade,
Chacha did her best to ensure that his powers passed to her son, who
by his mid-teens had grown to the size of a sumo wrestler (thereby
seeming to resolve the issue of whether or not he was Hideyoshi's).
But by then the shogun, Tokugawa Ieyasu, had decided to liquidate
Hideyoshi's family, and besieged their forces in Osaka. Chacha and her
son committed ritual suicide together at Osaka Castle on June 4, 1615.

70. From a letter by Louis Frois, October 1595, quoted in Berry, *Hideyoshi*, 219.

The Seppuku Ritual

Kurahashi Shōsen. A detail from the work *Seppuku of Ōishi Kuranosuke* (Ōishi Kuranosuke seppuku no zu), 18th century.

Seppuku Ritual Protocols

As we have seen, for the early warriors there was no ritual: men slit their stomachs on the spot before inevitable capture or defeat. The earliest guidelines were written down in the 1520s, though none of these texts has survived. Later manuals largely comprise instructions for the kaishaku and his assistants. The most comprehensive are *Concerning Stomach-cutting and Decapitation* (Seppuku kaishaku no shi-dai)and *Main Points of Stomach-cutting* (Seppuku mokuroku), which date from the early 1700s. Yamaoka Shunmei's *Thoughts on Belly-ripping* (Hara-kiri kō, 1772) is an investigation into the suicide tradition, written by a samurai scholar. From the nineteenth century we have Kudō Yukihiro's *Records of Suicide by Sword* (Jijin-roku, 1840), Usami Tomoharu's *Rules for Stomach-cutting* (Seppuku kuketsu, ca. 1840), and the anonymous *Decapitation Method* (Kaishaku no shikihō, ca. 1830). Kudō's treatise is the "Rare Japanese Manuscript" translated in synopsis by A. B. Mitford in his *Tales of Old Japan* (1871). All are very similar in content, and differ only in regard to emphasis. In addition, Sobue Tsunetsugu's *Remarks on Stomach-cutting and Decapitation* (Seppuku kaishaku den, 1633) offers practical tips based on experience. The guide below broadly follows the sequence of the *Main Points of Stomach-cutting*, which appears to have had the widest circulation, while synthesizing material from all seven of the texts mentioned above. Relevant examples from various sources are appended at the end of each section.

Announcing the Sentence

The messenger or colleague who delivers the sentence of seppuku should keep his announcement brief, and speak in a firm voice. He should choose his words carefully, so as to inspire courage in the condemned man, and must not say anything that might cause him to panic. If the condemned offers a reply, listen to him without being swayed by his manner or words. If he requests writing materials, it is best to make an excuse and decline: if he is a reasonable man, he will already have said his piece during his confinement. His swords should be confiscated from the moment of his incarceration. It is customary to deliver the sentence to him at night and execute him the following morning, though he should be considered dead from the moment the sentence has been read to him.

Choosing the Location

The seppuku ritual can be performed in the grounds of a temple, in the house where the condemned man is being held, or in jail. While the wishes of the condemned himself may be taken into consideration, the choice of venue is not a matter for him to decide; it should be determined by those in charge, in accordance with his rank, offense, mental state, and his behavior during his confinement. Lords and their direct retainers may perform the ritual inside the palace. Senior samurai may cut their bellies outside, usually in the garden. Samurai of lower ranks should cut their bellies at the place of their confinement. To force a man to kill himself in the house of a superior is demeaning; only those whose offenses are of a serious criminal nature should be treated in this way.

In March 1646 Kurita Uemon, a samurai of the Aizu domain, was refused permission to perform seppuku at Dairyūji Temple. Uemon had murdered a fellow samurai in a vendetta attack, but when his superiors interrogated him about his motive he offered no explanation, saying only that he had a long-standing grudge against the victim. Uemon's request to die at Dairyūji was therefore denied, and he was ordered to cut his stomach without ceremony in the house where he was being confined.[1]

A letter in the records of the Kaga domain for March 1708 concerns the seppuku arrangements for one Sugimoto Kujurō. Kujurō, the teen-age son of a low-ranking swordsman, had killed another boy during a fight over a game of Go. The samurai in whose residence Kujurō had been ordered to commit suicide complained in writing to his superi-ors. His point was that, since the fight was a fair one, the incident did not warrant the charge of criminality implied by ordering Kujurō to perform his seppuku in the house of a superior. The samurai regis-tered his strong displeasure, declined to confiscate the boy's swords, and refused to supervise any future suicides. Kujurō was eventually granted permission to disembowel himself in a tent erected especially for that purpose in the samurai's garden.[2]

Preparing the Location

For samurai of the lowest ranks, little preparation is required; if the execution is to be performed outside, a hole for the head may be dug in the ground. For higher ranks, a path of mats is laid out leading to the seppuku area. It is preferable that the site is dimly lit, to make the spectacle less unpleasant for those observing. Incense should be burned to conceal the stench.

A base of at least three tatami mats is laid, with another mat on top. Red rugs may also be provided to hide blood.

For higher ranks, a leather carpet is laid in the garden inside a picket fence, forming an enclosure of about thirty-six square feet, with entrances at the south and north sides. White curtains are hung from the sides of the enclosure, and candles are positioned around the mats. The condemned enters from the north entrance, and sits fac-ing the witnesses. The assistants need not face the witnesses, though they should take care not to completely turn their backs. The sword, head-basket, bucket of water, and other items being used should be concealed behind a screen at the rear.

1. Yamamoto, *Seppuku*, 65–66.
2. Heki, ed., *Kaga-han shiryō*, 5:786–94.

Swords

A short sword of eight or nine *sun* (roughly ten inches) is used for cutting the stomach. The blade is removed from the hilt, and the base of the blade is wrapped with paper or cloth; twenty-eight windings are customary.

A long sword from the collection of the condemned is normally used for decapitation. However, a short sword can also be used; in this case it is customary to use only one hand when striking with the short sword. It is highly irregular for the kaishaku to use his own sword, and most will resist this if suggested. Even if the condemned requests that the kaishaku use a sword of his own, it is not wrong to borrow one secretly from elsewhere. If the condemned is of high rank, the hilt of the sword used to behead him is wrapped with white thread. All details relating to swords should be confirmed in advance.

Robes

Robes appropriate for the seppuku ceremony should always be kept ready in a samurai household. Assuming that he is of sufficiently high standing, the condemned wears ceremonial attire (*kami-shimo*). While many choose to wear light blue, there are no particular restrictions on color. Garments should be worn somewhat more loosely than usual to facilitate movement and to expose the neck. The kaishaku also wears kami-shimo. When the condemned man is of very high rank, the kaishaku should wear white robes.

Shaving of the Head and Bathing

The condemned man should bathe, freshly shave the bare part of his head, and tie his hair into a tight topknot. A samurai about to commit seppuku should not wash his face with hot water, since this increases bleeding. It is advisable to apply rouge to the cheeks: a samurai should be the color of cherry blossoms, even in death.

Witnesses

If time permits, the official witnesses should confirm their attendance in writing beforehand. The chief witness may ask to interview the kaishaku before the ceremony. On entering the house, the witnesses need not remove or reverse their swords. Tea and sweetmeats are offered to the witnesses, but it is customary to decline.

Family and Relatives
The condemned may be permitted to write letters to family and friends, and a will. His letters should be checked for inflammatory content. Family members do not attend the ceremony.

The Kaishaku
The condemned may nominate a friend or colleague to act as his kaishaku. For executions performed in prison, the jailer acts as kaishaku.

A samurai should always keep in mind that he may be called upon to act as kaishaku, and must prepare himself spiritually and technically for the task. Young men should not be employed as kaishaku unless they are exceptionally skillful swordsmen. To be asked to perform kaishaku should be regarded as an honor, not a burden, and the kaishaku must comport himself with dignity. Any mistake by the kaishaku is a breach of decorum: every samurai must be able to cut off a man's head.

The role of the kaishaku is not only to decapitate, but to ensure that all aspects of the execution proceed smoothly. Errors envisaged during the execution itself include excessive spattering of blood, resistance or unruly behavior by the condemned, and problems with the head (for example, rolling too far forward, or in an unintended direction).

It is customary for the kaishaku to say to the condemned: "Sir, I have been designated as your assistant. Rest assured I shall not fail you." The intention of this greeting is to keep the condemned in a calm state of mind. The condemned might ask at what point the kaishaku intends to strike. Whatever the situation, it is best to reply, "I will strike when you cut your stomach." This is to maintain the honor of the condemned.

In his *Hagakure*, Jōchō approvingly quotes this letter, which was written by Yamamoto Gonnojō to his friend Sawabe Heizaemon in

November 1682 in response to Heizaemon's request that Gonnojō act as his kaishaku the following day:

> I sympathize with your predicament and agree to act as your kaishaku. Initially I wondered whether I should decline, but if the ritual must be performed tomorrow there is no time for hesitation. I humbly accept the task. I am honored that you have chosen me, over many others you could have considered. Rest assured that all will be as it should. Despite the late hour, I will come to your house tonight to go over the details.[3]

For a long time, Jōchō adds, swordsmen considered it unfortunate to be requested to act as kaishaku, since a job well done earned no fame, while a mistake brought lifelong disgrace.

Assistant Kaishaku

The duties of the kaishaku may be delegated among several assistants. One brings out the tray and the sword for the condemned, another cuts off the head, and a third displays it to the witnesses. While all these tasks can be performed adequately by one man, it is preferable for him to have at least one assistant. Assistants should be unarmed. Their role is to support the smooth progression of the execution in any way they can.

Presenting the Sword

The condemned is not obliged to make a formal greeting to the kaishaku or his assistants. It is possible that the condemned might ask the kaishaku for his name, and offer a polite expression of trust in his abilities. The assistants place the tray (*sanbō*) and sword (*wakizashi*) before the condemned; this should be done in complete silence. The tray must be far enough away from him that he needs to lean forward to take the sword. A distance of about three feet is usual.

3. Jōchō, *Hagakure*, 2:167.

Cutting the Stomach

The condemned takes his seat, and bows in silence to the witnesses. He removes his upper garment, the right side first, then the left. He takes the sword in his left hand, then also with his right. He puts the tip to the left side of his belly, and then switches the grip to his right hand. Now with his left hand he strokes his stomach three times, an inch or so above or below his navel. He thrusts the blade into his left side and drags it to the right. It is best to make a shallow incision and slice across quickly: no deeper than roughly one inch and no wider than six inches. Cutting should be directed by the right hand, with the left for support. As for the correct grip, while many assume that the right fist should be palm-up, so that the thumb is farthest from the belly, greater strength is in fact achieved with the fist inverted, so that the thumb is nearest the belly.

Rules for Stomach-cutting recommends a nine-step procedure:

1. Pull the table closer.
2. Pick up the sword.
3. Press the tip of the blade to the left side of the abdomen.
4. Cut above the navel.
5. Force the blade across to the right side.
6. Turn the angle of the blade ninety degrees.
7. Make a downward cut.
8. Using both hands if necessary, force the blade down to below the navel.
9. [Remove the blade and] rest the sword on the right knee.

Decapitation

Once the condemned is in position, the kaishaku should stand to the rear left, taking care to hold his sword at such an angle that it is not visible to the condemned: this is a matter of courtesy. The kaishaku assumes striking position as the condemned removes his arms from his kimono. If necessary, the kaishaku should adjust his right sleeve for ease of motion.

The precise moment of striking is a matter for the kaishaku's discretion. He is not obliged to consult the condemned beforehand on this point. Even if the condemned requests a consultation, the kaishaku is not bound by any prior agreement: it is not the function of the kaishaku to indulge the condemned. The best moments to strike are:

1. When the condemned reaches for the sword.
2. When he points the blade to his belly.
3. When he makes the initial incision.

To delay any longer is to risk things becoming messy. The kaishaku should imagine a line where the nape of the condemned man's neck connects to his right shoulder, and aim for that line. The kaishaku needs to bear in mind many factors to ensure that things go smoothly. In cold weather the kaishaku should keep his hands and feet warm. In hot weather he should wipe the sweat from his palms. He must closely watch the eyes and feet of the condemned, and judge the distance carefully. The kaishaku must not lose his composure.

The condemned is not expected to speak during the ceremony, though some men cannot resist the urge. If the condemned utters any hostile or offensive words, the kaishaku should decapitate him immediately. No matter how the condemned behaves, the kaishaku must not be intimidated, remaining alert but always calm. He must summon up his courage, and act as a samurai should.

Some expert kaishaku prefer to strike from a semi-kneeling position. But the striking stance should not be a matter of great concern. The kaishaku should cut the best way he knows how. The only important thing is that he removes the head.

The first blow might not sever the head completely. If the man is dead, but his head is not properly severed, the kaishaku must strike again. Depending on the rank of the condemned, it is acceptable for the kaishaku to grab his topknot for this second strike. If he is wounded but not dead, the kaishaku can push him down and stab him. If he panics, resists, or writhes about, the other assistants should hold him down firmly for the kaishaku to strike again, or they can use their own swords. The head can then easily be removed. If the kaishaku's sword happens to get stuck in the wound, he should cut in a sawing motion until the head is off. He can use his short sword for this if necessary.

If the first strike is successful, the body should fall forward. If it remains upright, or slumps to either side, the kaishaku is permitted to pull the legs from under the body so that it falls to the front. After the head is cleanly off, the kaishaku should check the legs and feet for movement; if they are still moving, he should make another thrust through the neck.

In 1643 a rebel leader named Katayama was executed in the grounds of Aizu Wakamatsu Castle. The execution was attended by Katō Akinari, lord of Aizu, who supervised proceedings from behind a bamboo blind. When Katayama was brought forward and made to kneel, he fixed his glare on the blind. The kaishaku, a samurai named Kinzaemon, ordered Katayama to face the front. Katayama shouted back at him: "Impudent serf!" The moment the words were out of Katayama's mouth, Kinzaemon lopped off his head.[4]

Handling the Head
The lips and eyelids of a freshly severed head are liable to quiver for a few seconds. The kaishaku should not be unnerved by this; it is quite normal.

Without altering his grip on his sword, the kaishaku should drop to one knee and wipe the blade with a piece of paper that he has tucked inside the sash of his kimono beforehand. He should return his sword to its scabbard, adjust his sleeves, and step back. His assistants should then pick up the head and show it to the witness. In the absence of assistants, the job of showing the head to the witnesses falls to the kaishaku. He should switch his sword to his left hand, and with his

4. Kudō, *Jijin-roku*, 55.

right hand pick up the head. It is not improper for him to support the head with the blade of his sword while exhibiting it to the witnesses. A more respectful method is for the kaishaku to put down the sword, place a strip of paper on the palm of his left hand, and place the head on this paper. A samurai's severed head should be picked up by grasping its topknot. It is exhibited first in right profile, then in left. If the head is bald, the kaishaku may use his scabbard pin to pierce the left ear of the head, and lift it in that manner. Exhibition of the head is necessarily a delicate matter, and must be conducted with due regard for the standing and reputation of the samurai who has been beheaded. If the kaishaku is in any doubt, he should consult his superiors or the official witnesses in advance.

The head may be placed in a box made especially for that purpose. This is an honor reserved only for those of high rank. It is more conventional to cover the head with a white cloth. The kaishaku should cover the head as soon as possible after inspection. A samurai's head must not be exhibited to persons of inferior rank—this is most disrespectful.

In *Miscellany of Military Studies* (Bugaku shūsui, 1853), an exhaustive guidebook offering the samurai advice on everything from saddling his horse to beating his servants, it is suggested that blood can be cleaned from the sword by wiping the blade with a paste obtained by burning straw *hakama* (samurai trousers) and mixing water into the ash. This ash can also be sprinkled onto the neck of a severed head in order to clot the blood prior to inspection.[5]

Exit and Conclusion
The witnesses should inspect the head and confirm that execution has been carried out. The corpse is cleared away, the witnesses rise and exit in silence, and the ceremony ends.

5. Hoshino, *Bugaku shūsui*, 268.

Types of Seppuku

Ichimonji (One horizontal cut)

Although this became standard in the Tokugawa period (1603–1867), it was not originally so. Many early cases of *ichimonji* are actually aborted jūmonji, where a warrior intending to make two cuts runs out of steam after the first. A notable ichimonji from the Muromachi period is that of Yakushiji Yoichi, also known as Motokazu, who assassinated the head of the Hosokawa family during a succession feud in 1504. Motokazu was confined in Ichigen-in, the Kyoto temple he had built in his own honor. The *ichi* and *kazu* of his names, and also the *ichi* in the name of the temple he had named after himself, are different readings of the character representing "one," which is written with a single horizontal brush stroke. According to an account in the Hosokawa records, Motokazu spoke these words before stabbing himself: "As you all know, I have a fondness for straight lines. My name is Yakushiji Yoichi, some call me Motokazu, and I named this temple Ichigen-in. I shall therefore cut my stomach in one straight line."[6] And so he did. The inference here must be that a single horizontal cut was still unusual at that time.

The *Sendō War Chronicles* (Sendō gunki) of the late sixteenth century describe one particularly novel modification of ichimonji. Instead of cutting across his abdomen, the samurai Tagawa Hachirō is said to have run himself through sideways with his long sword, pushing the hilt against his right side so that the blade protruded from his left. Grabbing the hilt with both hands he twisted it sharply round to his left side, thereby dividing himself into two pieces.[7]

When performing ichimonji, there is a tendency for the blade to rise as its crosses the body, resulting in a diagonal cut. Many cases of this are recorded, most of them before 1600, when stomach-cutting was often performed spontaneously and at high speed. Uesugi Mochinari, who killed himself at the mountain temple of Dokuzenji in 1439, is

6. *Hosokawa ryōkeki*, 582.
7. *Sendō gunki*, 27.

said to have cut "from his left side upwards to his right nipple."[8] A diagonal cut does not appear to have been regarded as incorrect or inferior.

Jūmonji (Two crossed cuts)

The classic seppuku format. The horizontal cut is made first, usually well below the navel. A vertical cut is added from just above the groin. (In some cases the second cut is made downwards from the solar plexus.) The first cut is preferably a shallow one, so as to prevent the intestines from spilling out too early.

Variations include *kagi-jūmonji* (cutting with the left hand from the left side diagonally downwards toward the crotch, then switching hands and cutting up to the right), and *migi-jūmonji* (cutting lightly across from left to right, then turning the blade and cutting diagonally left back to the left nipple). According to a sixteenth-century document known as the *Kō Battle Records* (Kōranki), a samurai named Oyamada Masasada, who died in the battle of Takatō Castle in April 1582, killed himself with a single vertical cut from his navel to his chest.[9]

Hachimonji (Two upright cuts)

In the *Taiheiki*, a warrior named Kasuya Muneaki cuts his belly in the shape of the Chinese character for "8" (八) by making two inwardly tilting vertical strokes, read as "hachi" in Japanese.[10]

Sanmonji (Three horizontal cuts)

Ever since Yoshitsune, greatest hero of them all, ripped his stomach in three directions, those who manage three or more cuts have been regarded with awe. *Remarks on Stomach-cutting and Decapitation* advises beginning well below the navel and working upwards from there.

In *Records of Suicide by Sword*, Kudō Yukihiro mentions a rare four-stroke seppuku by an unnamed samurai who killed himself after the death of his lord. According to Kudō, the samurai made a long horizontal cut across his lower abdomen and added three vertical ones above

---

8. Kondō, ed., *Eikyōki*, in *Kaitei shiseki shūran*, 12:737.
9. Kaisōsho Kankōkai, ed., *Kōranki*, 298.
10. Hasegawa, ed., *Taiheiki*, 1:472.

that, forming the Chinese character for "mountain" (山, *yama*, from the name of his castle). Algernon Mitford, attaché to the British legation in Tokyo from 1866 to 1870, reported the case of a twenty-year-old samurai from Chōshū who stabbed himself three times horizontally and twice vertically before driving the blade through his throat.

Oi-bara

Literally "following with the belly," this term was first used in the 1500s to categorize the deaths of men who killed themselves immediately after acting as kaishaku for their superiors. A retainer who had beheaded his own lord, albeit at his lord's request, could not continue to live with honor. After 1600 the term was more loosely applied to any samurai who committed suicide upon the death of his lord.

Tachi-bara

A stomach-cut performed in standing position. Minamoto no Tametomo was standing when he cut his stomach on Ōshima island, while leaning against a wooden pillar to hold himself steady. The blade penetrated through his body and became embedded in the pillar, holding him upright after death. Nishina Morinobu was supposedly still on his feet when he cut his stomach at the battle of Takatō Castle. A rare example of *tachi-bara* off the battlefield was that of Kumatani Daizen, chief retainer to Hidetsugu, who was said to have performed jūmonji in standing position.[11]

The papers of the Sanada military household in Nagano record the death in 1658 of an old samurai of the Matsushiro domain named Suzuki Tadashige, who killed himself after the death of his lord. When Tadashige was a boy, his father had disemboweled himself on his feet after being duped by rebels who had successfully lured him away from his fort. Tadashige wanted to die in the same manner as his father. However, after discussing it with his kaishaku and assistants, Tadashige, who was in his mid-eighties, was persuaded to stab himself in sitting position.

11. Oze, *Taikōki*, 503–4.

Kanshi

Literally "a remonstrative death," *kanshi* is a suicide committed in protest at another's actions. Use of this term is not limited to seppuku. An early instance of a remonstrative seppuku, recorded by Ōta Gyūichi in his biography of Oda Nobunaga, was the death of Hirate Masahide on February 25, 1553. A former general, in his sixties Masahide served as personal tutor to the young Nobunaga, whose teenage bad-boy antics are legendary in Japan. After a characteristic outburst by Nobunaga at his father's funeral—he arrived late, on horseback, refused to dismount, threw a fistful of incense at the altar, and galloped off—Masahide ripped himself open. He left a letter imploring the youngster to mend his ways. A chronicle from 1600 gives these as Masahide's last words: "I have failed to serve my purpose. What reason is there for me to continue living?" His death fulfilled its objective. Nobunaga expressed remorse, erected a temple in Masahide's honor, and generally mended his ways.[12]

Kama-bara

Belly-rip using a sickle (*kama*). The term has no basis in reality; it comes from the theater. The Kabuki comedy *Yasaku's Sickle-suicide* (Yasaku no kama-bara, 1791)[13] recounts the gory fate of a peasant named Yasaku whose brother has been adopted into a samurai family. After shooting a nobleman, Yasaku hope to impress his brother by killing himself in the samurai manner. However, being of peasant stock he has no sword. He decides to use a sickle instead, but cannot muster the courage to stab himself. After numerous false starts he abandons the idea, only to trip and fall onto the sickle, gouging himself in the stomach. His brother finds him, and comes to his rescue the only way a samurai knows how—by cutting off his head.

12. Ōta, *Shinchō kōki*, 1:29.
13. *Irowa kana yonjū-nana kun Yasaku no kama-bara*. In Atsumi, ed., *Nihon gikyoku zenshū*, vol 15.

Kage-bara

This term, which means "concealed belly-rip," is used when a samurai secretly cuts his stomach, covers the wound with his robes, and subsequently reveals it to dramatic effect. While *kage-bara* is principally used in regard to suicide scenes in Kabuki plays, the death of Shirai Haruyoshi, the old retainer of Shimizu Muneharu who dramatically ripped his stomach the night before Muneharu's execution, seems to fit the category. Even more ostentatious was the suicide of the Tōhoku warlord Yajima Mitsuyasu, whose army was defeated in 1593. In response to a formal request from Mitsuyasu, the victors pulled back to give him time to prepare for death. With a cry of "My preparations are complete!" Mitsuyasu is said to have come into view displaying the sword he had plunged through his torso; the blade protruded from the middle of his back. Assured that all eyes were on him, he opened the wound into a cross-shape, reached inside, and extracted a handful of intestines. When he bellowed, "Now cut off my head!" one of his guards rushed forward and beheaded him.[14]

Seppuku as Murder

A samurai cuts his stomach in the vindictive hope that this will incriminate another or obligate him to do the same. In other words, murder by suicide. There is no specific Japanese term for this concept, and, like kage-bara, it probably derives from fictional sources. References crop up in reports of homosexual squabbles during the seventeenth century, most commonly in cases where a jilted lover contrives to cause the death of a rival.

No one has matched the feat of Toshima Nobumitsu, who committed murder, followed by suicide and another murder *simultaneously*, in the west circle of Edo Castle on August 10, 1628. As castle guards attempted to arrest Nobumitsu for his first murder, one of them bear-hugged him from behind. Nobumitsu plunged his short sword through himself and the guard, and ripped two stomachs at once.[15]

14. Kondō, ed., *Ōu eikei gunki*, in *Kaitei shiseki shūran*, 8:522–23.
15. Ōkuma, *Seppuku no rekishi*, 161–62.

Suicide

Lastly, a few cases of stomach-cutting were plain suicides, due to depression, loneliness, or poverty. Even under such circumstances, the samurai ideal was to die with dignity. In the autumn of 1685 a young swordsman disemboweled himself in the garden of Kōgonji, a Zen temple of the Rinzai sect in Hyōgō Prefecture. The priest who discovered him recalled seeing him near the temple on the previous day. The following letter was found beside his body, along with a death poem and some coins he had placed on a paper fan:

> I am from a distant province. Last year I left my home town and began my wanderings. Now I find myself here, at your temple. I have no kin, no ties, nothing to detain me any longer in this world. The only clothes I own are those I wear now. I have left what small change I have, in the hope that you will do me the service of disposing of my remains. Please accept my apologies for troubling you with this matter.
>
> Your humble servant,
> Hashi Seishin
> October 2, 1685.[16]

---

16. Nakayasu, *Seppuku: Rekishi to bungei*, 45.

History of Seppuku after 1600

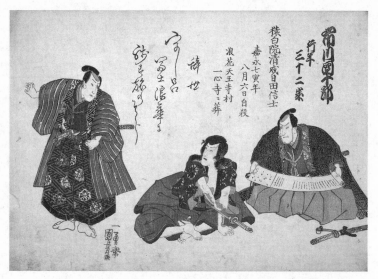

Utagawa Kuniyoshi. *Kanpei's Belly-ripping Scene* from the Kabuki play *The Treasury of Loyal Retainers* (Chūshingura), ca. 1850. © National Diet Library, Tokyo.

Junshi Martyrdom

The military government established by Tokugawa Ieyasu in 1603 launched a new era of political unification. While each feudal domain retained its own bureaucracy, the lords swore their allegiance to Ieyasu. Before long, internecine conflict had become a thing of the past. Now there were few opportunities to secure immortality by fighting to the death beside one's lord or slashing one's bowels over his corpse. The seventeenth century consequently saw the popularization of a new phenomenon known as *junshi*—martyrdom by self-disembowelment after the *natural* death of one's lord.

Although the precipitous rise of junshi seems to have taken most people by surprise, in spirit the practice dated back to antiquity. Strictly speaking, junshi denotes martyrdom (by sword or otherwise) after the death (natural or otherwise) of one's lord or master. Early histories such as the *Chronicles of Japan* and *Records of Ancient Matters* contain various stories of martyrdom, though none by self-stabbing. The original martyrs were not volunteers. In ancient Japan, as in ancient China, a lord's dependents were sometimes killed and buried alongside their chieftain to ensure his safe passage into the next world. The tradition was supposedly prohibited in Japan after the death of Empress Hihasu in AD 3, when a councilor named Nomi no Sukune suggested to the imperial court that, instead of burying three hundred *live* attendants in her tomb, it might be more economical to use clay replicas instead. Voluntary or near-voluntary martyrdoms of one kind or another feature in accounts of later imperial dynasties. The *Chronicles of Japan* quotes this proclamation from the year 646:

When a man dies, there have been cases of people sacrific-
ing themselves by strangulation, or of strangling others
by way of sacrifice . . . Let all such old customs be entirely
discontinued.[1]

Nonetheless, an entry for 649 relating to the suicide of one
Kurayamada no Maro informs us that: "his wife and children, to the
number of eight persons, sacrificed themselves with him."[2] Countless
other instances are recorded down the centuries. From the servant of fifth-
century Prince Kurohiko, who followed his master into death by embrac-
ing his burning body, to the Kamakura warriors who fatally stabbed
themselves at their generals' feet, the central idea was unchanged: a lifetime of loyal service is ideally concluded with a loyal death.

Spontaneous martyrdoms after a lord's suicide or death in battle
increased during the feudal wars of the 1500s. Suicides after a lord's
natural demise, on the other hand, were rare—but then so were natural demises. The first case of junshi in this sense is found in the *Record
of the Meitoku Rebellion* (Meitokuki, ca.1394), which describes how an
attendant of Lord Hosokawa Yoriyuki fatally stabbed himself after
Yoriyuki's death (from pneumonia) in March 1392:

He carved a cross into his stomach, thrust the blade through
his throat, and lay down with his hands clasped together.
All who saw him were moved to tears. "From olden times
many men have died fighting alongside their lord on the
battlefield, or by cutting their bellies after seeing him fall,"
they said, "but for a man to cut his stomach like this, out
of grief over his lord's natural passing, and thus follow him
along the path to death, is surely unheard of."[3]

Since junshi was an expression of loving devotion, the usual
protocols did not always apply. Samurai who committed junshi

1. Aston, *Nihongi*, 2:220.
2. Ibid., 2:234.
3. Tomikura, ed., *Meitokuki*, 154.

often went to extraordinary lengths to increase their suffering. This they achieved by delaying or declining decapitation, or by choosing unusual modes of suicide. The emotional pain of losing a benefactor needed to be mirrored in the physical pain of death. There was a long Japanese tradition of affirming devotion through shared pain and cutting. Lovers shared identical tattoos. Comrades in arms swore blood oaths or scarred each other's forearms and shins. Junshi can be regarded as the logical extremity of this tradition.

Let us now examine some examples.

The *Shimazu yorokki*, a history of the Shimazu family compiled around 1670, records a peculiar instance of junshi that supposedly occurred in 1571. After the death of Shimazu Takahisa, lord of Satsuma, his vassal Hirata Sumisada is said to have committed junshi by joining Takahisa in his coffin before it was pushed out to sea. As the water seeped in, Sumisada's teeth could be heard grating against the wood. (A visit to his tombstone at Matsubara Temple is traditionally believed to strengthen teeth.) In his later years Takahisa had retired from warmongering and devoted himself to Buddhism. This may be the reason why Sumisada chose not to die by sword.

The papers of the Nakamura family, retainers to the shogun, record the grisly suicides of two teenage boys after the sudden death of Nakamura Kazutada, who was nineteen, in 1609:

> On the morning of May 13 [the day after Kazutada's death], Tarui Kageyu and Hattori Wakasa cut their stomachs at Kannōji Temple. They burned incense sticks before the statue of the Buddha, and then proceeded to the room where they would die. Cushions were laid out, and daggers were wrapped with ceremonial paper. The two bid farewell to their friends and sat down to write their death poems. [. . .] Wakasa was the first to go; he took the dagger and boldly stabbed himself in the stomach. "I shall follow you, my friend!" cried Kageyu, and with a shout he beheaded the other, who was still impaled on the dagger. Kageyu dropped to his knees and shredded his belly with

two crossed cuts. A comrade stepped forward to behead
him, but Kageyu refused assistance. He dragged the sword
from the pit of his stomach to each side, pushing the blade
in deep. Howling with pain, somehow he struggled to his
feet. Using both hands, he drove the blade further downward and fell forward to the floor, still alive. The swordsman, who was poised to decapitate him, now saw his
chance, and struck; but he missed, and only trimmed the
boy's topknot. Kageyu, lying facedown, pushed himself up
and offered his neck. The job was done, and he was dead.[4]

Kageyu and Wakasa were buried along with Kazutada at Kannōji Temple.

In the spring of 1607, two of Ieyasu's sons, Tadayoshi and
Hideyasu, died of illness within weeks of each other. Two of Tadayoshi's friends cut open their bowels; a third, who was in banishment on
a remote island, returned to Edo and killed himself at Zōjōji Temple.
Likewise, two of Hideyasu's samurai followed him into death, and
the man who decapitated them promptly killed himself. These deaths,
six in all, caused a sensation. Ieyasu let it be known that he was displeased.[5] The suicides won wide admiration all the same, and triggered a junshi boom that continued for half a century. Now there was
a way for warriors to prove their caliber with their swords in peacetime. Buddhist leaders found no fault with the practice, and temples
began to give pride of place to the gravestones of junshi martyrs.

Junshi was not an option for everyone. It was a prerogative of those
who had received special favors from the deceased lord. Those favors
might be very special indeed. A strong homoeroticism often cemented
the bonds between samurai, and many of the seppuku incidents from
these years appear to have centered on intense masculine friendships.
These were not always straightforwardly sexual, and could just as
easily be charged by the passions that hide behind love unrequited or
unconfessed. Initially, the junshi trend was led by distraught young

---

4. Kondō, ed., *Nakamura Kazuujiki*, in *Kaitei shiseki shūran*, 14:104.
5. Nakayasu, *Seppuku: Hisōbi no sekai*, 102.

lovers, as appears to have been the case in the Nakamura incident above, and by elderly retainers who had served the deceased lord their entire lives. If a high-ranking retainer committed junshi, several of his own retainers might kill themselves in turn. This was known as *mata-junshi*: martyrdom at one remove. The death of a lord could trigger a series of suicides at ever-decreasing levels, in something akin to a seppuku domino effect. After the death of Date Masamune, lord of Sendai, in 1636, sixteen of his direct retainers martyred themselves. Five of their samurai committed mata-junshi. Three boys followed those five, and two of the men who had acted as kaishaku also killed themselves. It became customary for those closest to the deceased to die within hours of his passing, while others delayed until the following day. Ieyasu's grandson Iemitsu died on the afternoon of June 8, 1651, after twenty-eight years as shogun. Three of his closest friends, including his longtime lover Hotta Masamori, killed themselves before nightfall. Iemitsu's death was officially announced the following morning, whereupon twelve other samurai of various ranks cut their stomachs. An official document notes that there was some disagreement among these men as to who was eligible for martyrdom. One senior retainer was criticized by colleagues for *not* killing himself.[6]

Where circumstances permitted, most martyrs chose to perform the death ritual on sacred land. Monks of the temples diligently recorded the personal information of those who came to kill themselves. For instance, Nagataki Temple in Mino (southern Gifu Prefecture) lists deaths among retainers of the Matsudaira family in this manner:

April 15, 1645
Lord Matsudaira, of Kanazawa Castle in Kashū, died suddenly. Two of his men followed him into death.

August 1, 1645
Lord Matsudaira, of Fukui Castle in Echizen, passed away from illness at the age of forty-eight. Seven followed.[7]

---

6. Fujii, ed., *Edo bakufu nikki*, 25:69–74.
7. Nakayasu, *Seppuku: Rekishi to bungei*, 41.

The names, ages, and stipends of those who followed are recorded, along with their death poems. The samurai domains kept their own records, which included an explanation of each man's motivation in choosing martyrdom. Junshi mania began to cause consternation. It was obviously detrimental for any domain to have its best men ripping themselves up in droves. Nonetheless, some argued that junshi served a practical purpose, pointing out that the continued presence of veterans who had been close to the deceased lord often made things awkward for his successor. And while the sudden exit of a dozen good men temporarily weakened a domain's power structure, it did no damage at all to its reputation, since a high incidence of junshi was seen as testament to the constancy and fearlessness of its men.

There was probably some truth in this notion. Certainly, the brave stoicism of the samurai martyrs contrasts sharply with the chaotic suicide culture that prevailed in China at the same time. While junshi was a manifestation of ardent fealty, suicides of Chinese retainers were generally grudging or non-voluntary. When the peasant army of Li Zicheng captured Beijing in 1644, Emperor Chongzhen told his sons to flee, but ordered his wife, daughters, and mandarins to kill themselves. Some complied by strangling each other; many refused. When one of his daughters respectfully declined to be set on fire, Chongzhen chopped off her arm. His guards deserted and left him for the rebels. Abandoned and desperate, the last Ming emperor fled into the imperial garden where, after an ungracious tirade against his worthless subjects, he hanged himself from a tree, assisted by a trusty eunuch. One searches the samurai archives in vain for anything approaching this pitiful fiasco[8]. Centuries earlier, the poet Po Chu-i had defined the precariousness of Chinese servitude in an epigram: "In the morning my lord offers me patronage, in the evening he offers me death."[9]

But Japan's military rulers realized that they must curb the tide of overzealous martyrdom. Ieyasu officially expressed disapproval of the

---

8. Spence and Willis, eds., *From Ming to Ch'ing*, 50.

9. Kondō, ed., *Eikyōki*, in *Katei shinseki shūran*, 12:777

practice in his *Laws for the Military Houses* (Buke shohatto), first read to the court in 1615, and when he passed away a year later, none of his retainers followed him. After Ieyasu's death, however, the junshi craze regained momentum. Junshi was most rampant in Kyushu. After the death of Shimazu Yoshihiro, lord of Satsuma, on July 21, 1619, there were fears of crippling junshi losses. Yoshihiro had lived eighty-four years, and even his oldest retainers had spent their entire lives in his service. Moreover, Yoshihiro was greatly loved and respected. As a military commander he had endeared himself to his men by refusing to direct the battle from afar, as was customary, preferring the thrill of charging into the action alongside them, even in his late sixties. Yoshihiro suffered a long period of ill health before passing away. This had given aspiring martyrs ample time to make their arrangements. In the hope of averting what was perceived as an impending suicide epidemic, leaders announced that the family of any man who killed himself would be punished by the confiscation of their property. Thirteen of Yoshihiro's samurai ignored this warning.

Yoshihiro had spent his last years in seclusion in the town of Kajiki. His body was to be returned from Kajiki to the Shimazu family tomb at Tokushige Temple (in today's Hioki city) one month after his death. Several of the thirteen samurai who agreed to end their lives with his had fought under his command during Hideyoshi's Korean campaigns, and at the great battle of Sekigahara. They planned their deaths together; some had already bought their gravestones. Six of the men performed their suicides at Kajiki, while the other seven waited for Yoshihiro's body to arrive at Tokushige Temple. All were open about their intentions, and spent their last days paying their respects to friends and benefactors. Yoshihiro's body was to be buried at Tokushige on August 16. One of the seven samurai who planned to die that day, Yamaji Tanekiyo, was up before first light, planting seeds in his family's vegetable patch. A stream of last-minute well-wishers arrived throughout the morning, delaying his departure. On his way to the appointed place, Tanekiyo encountered spectators who were already on their way back: he was late for his own suicide. He decided to go no further. He sat down under a pine tree, pointed to a distinctively shaped rock nearby, and announced that it would do as his gravestone. He opened his bowels and died at that spot, which is now a miniature shrine. The lands of all thirteen samurai were duly confiscated. It was not until a decade later that Satsuma leaders finally relented, and allowed the men's bodies to be interred at Tokushige.[10]

According to historical records of Kurume, another Kyushu domain, four chief retainers of Lord Arima Tadayori committed suicide after his death in 1655. They were joined by a low-ranking samurai named Horie Iemon, whose only claim to fame was his chronic ugliness, which was said to have been breathtaking. When Iemon's family tried to dissuade him from killing himself, Iemon gave his reason as follows. A young girl had once openly laughed at his face in the presence of Tadayori. Iemon immediately dropped to his knees and prepared to stab himself, out of shame at having embarrassed his lord. According to Iemon, Tadayori kindly calmed him down: "His Lordship saved my life that day, and now I shall give it back to him." Iemon performed his seppuku that evening.[11]

Instances of junshi appear to have been less frequent in the capital. Only one man killed himself after the death of the second Tokugawa shogun, Hidetada, son of Ieyasu, in March 1632. This was Morikawa Shigetoshi, a childhood friend of Hidetada. Unusually, Shigetoshi left a suicide note:

> There is nothing I could do that would adequately express my gratitude for the kindness and guidance Lord Hidetada has offered me at every stage of my career. It breaks my heart to leave behind my children when they are so young. What can I say? Some things are even more important. I had hoped to compose a death poem, but I fear there is no time. I must hurry to meet my lord.[12]

10. Miki, *Shimazu Yoshihiro no subete*, 235–42.
11. *Kurume jinbutsu-shi*, 435.
12. Quoted in Yamamoto, *Junshi no kōzō*, 41.

Tokugawa Yoshinao, another of Ieyasu's sons, died of palsy in May 1650 at the age of fifty. His death was followed by five junshi suicides, which were followed in turn by four more. Yoshinao had been bedridden for months. His martyrs were determined to go out in fine style and had planned their deaths carefully. It is recorded that one of them, a young swordsman named Suzuki Shigeyuki, achieved a rare X-shaped rip. He inserted the blade just below his left nipple and cut all the way down to his right hip. He removed the blade, switching hands as he did so, reinserted it below his right nipple, and made a long intersecting cut down to the opposite side. He remained on his feet throughout and did not make a sound. Everyone agreed it was a remarkable performance.[13]

Samurai leaders were alarmed at the increasingly high rank of those opting for junshi suicides. When nine samurai ripped their bellies after the death of Matsudaira Tadamune, lord of Mutsu, in July 1657, they included some of his most experienced councilors, men who handled the domain's financial and administrative affairs. Six retainers loyal to these men killed themselves the next day, a total of fifteen martyrs. For Mutsu, a small domain of only three hundred samurai, these were heavy losses.

Anti-junshi reformers had their work cut out. How do you pressure a man who is ready to cut himself open? The solution came from the domain of Saga in Kyushu. When Nabeshima Tadanao, son of the Saga lord, died of smallpox at the age of twenty-two, four of his closest friends committed junshi. A fifth, Ezoe Kinbē, did not. Kinbē went into self-imposed exile, practicing asceticism on Mt. Kōya. He returned to Saga a year later, and, on the anniversary of Tadanao's death, he slit his stomach at the temple where his friend was buried. When Tadanao's son assumed the leadership of the Saga domain in 1661 he remembered the fate of his father's friends and announced a junshi ban, which he called *oi-bara kinshirei* (literally, "a ban on following with the stomach"). In a characteristic twist of samurai logic, the ban on seppuku martyrdom was enforced by a threat of seppuku

---

13. Furukawa, *Junshi: Higeki no iseki*, 126–28.

death sentences. From then on, the brothers, sons, and nephews of any man who did not comply would be forced to cut their stomachs. One of the Saga samurai affected by this was Yamamoto Tsunetomo, who served as a retainer to Tadanao's grandson, Mitsushige. Forbidden from committing junshi upon Mitsushige's death, Tsunetomo entered a hermitage, took the Buddhist name Jōchō, and spent his remaining years dreaming of disembowelment.

The effectiveness of the Saga countermeasures impressed the fourth Tokugawa shogun, Ietsuna, who reinforced the prescription against junshi two years later in an amendment to the *Laws for the Military Houses*, released in June 1663:

> Junshi has long been criticized as wrong and wasteful. Despite this, in the absence of an official ban, many persist in this practice. As of today, lords will be expected to express their firm disapproval to any of their retainers who may be motivated in such a direction. Should any instance occur in breach of the present warning, the lord concerned will be deemed culpable on grounds of negligence, as will his heir, on grounds of incompetence, for having failed to prevent the suicide.[14]

Many samurai still did not accept this. In particular, provincial domains objected to interference from Edo; they recognized no authority but that of their own lord. Traditionalists viewed the ban as an attack on martial values. The junshi ideal was encapsulated in a proverb: "A true samurai cannot serve two lords." Several Kyushu chieftains who tried to implement the ban faced mass desertions by samurai protesting the new rule. These surely rank among the most extraordinary walkouts in history—these activists were fighting for the right to stab themselves to death.

Minor junshi incidents continued. Delaying suicide until the anniversary of the lord's death proved a successful way of circumventing

---

14. Quoted in Ōkuma, *Seppuku no rekishi*, 160.

the red tape. Some men waited as long as three years. The first test case in Edo came five years after the shogun's decree, with the death of Okudaira Tadamasa in 1668. Tadamasa, who was lord of Utsunomiya and a great-grandson of Ieyasu, passed away at his residence in Edo on March 31. When news of his death reached Utsunomiya, one samurai, a veteran named Sugiura Uemon, announced his intention to kill himself. Colleagues tried to dissuade him, but nothing could prevent Uemon from cutting his stomach. As his colleagues had feared, the punishment handed down by the bakufu was severe. Uemon's sons were forced to cut their stomachs, his nephews and grandson were banished from Edo, and his family was dispossessed. In addition, the incoming lord's yearly stipend was slashed in half, and large portions of the domain's holdings were confiscated or reallocated to distant regions. Hundreds were made to suffer on account of one suicide.

After this devastating ruling against Utsunomiya, other domains imposed similar penalties and the practice of junshi rapidly faded. Aspiring martyrs still submitted petitions. These were always rejected. As an alternative, bereaved vassals were urged to shave their heads and take Buddhist names.

The Principle of Dual Blame

Here is a selection of seppuku rulings from the first half of the seventeenth century, selected from bakufu and domain records:

> March 1608. By order of Lord Mōri Terumoto. Seppuku of vassal Katsura Toki. Offence: killing a civilian.

> April 25, 1613. By order of the shogun. Seppuku of sons of Ōkubo Nagayasu, government administrator. Offense: recently uncovered crimes of their late father. Inheritance also confiscated.

> May 12, 1623. By order of the bakufu. Seppuku of guardsman Matsudaira Jinzaburō. Offense: insulting a superior.

July 1623. By order of Tokugawa Tadanaga, lord of Kōfu. Seppuku of vassal Yoda. Offense: disobeying ban on dismounting within fourth circle of Edo Castle.

February 8, 1629. By order of Tokugawa Yoshinao, lord of Nagoya. Seppuku of vassal Harada Moritsugu and son. Offense: theft and sale of timber.

February 22, 1634. By order of the bakufu. Seppuku of Takenaka Shigeyoshi, lord of Funai, and son, at Kaizenji Temple, Asakusa. Brother banished to northern territory. Offense: corruption.

June 5, 1636. By order of the bakufu. (1) Decapitation of officer Minobe Gonbei and three guardsmen. Offense: fighting. (2) Seppuku of Shima Gonzaemon. Offense: intervening in said fight.

June 6, 1636. By order of the bakufu. Seppuku of Imada Gentarō and decapitation of his family (three persons). Offense: sheltering Christians.

February 29, 1642. By order of Hoshina Masayuki, lord of Yamagata. Seppuku of Natsume Iori, chief horse-handler. Offense: gross misconduct arising from insatiable womanizing.[15]

The "gross misconduct" mentioned in the last case was embezzlement. Iori was found guilty of various financial scams, such as redirecting a portion of the domain's soybeans to his own stables and overcharging for official trips. Among the other names above, Ōkubo Nagayasu, whose sons were executed in 1613, was Ieyasu's chief representative

15. Selected from *Seirinki* (Mitamura, ed.) and *Edo bakufu nikki* (Fujii, ed.).

on the island of Sado, today part of Niigata Prefecture. Sado was for centuries regarded as remote, a place for monks and exiles. Attitudes changed abruptly when gold was discovered on the island in 1601. Nagayasu supervised a series of gold-mining projects on Sado, earning huge profits for Ieyasu. A fair portion of the cash found its way into Nagayasu's pockets, and he was subject to several investigations during his lifetime. Nagayasu enjoyed the good life, and was not one for keeping a low profile. He named a mineshaft after himself and kept an enormous hoard of gold in his house. His entourage was said to have included more than seventy concubines. In his will he left instructions for an opulent funeral, complete with a solid gold coffin. A month after the funeral, when the extent of Nagayasu's pilfering was discovered, Ieyasu systematically exterminated Nagayasu's family and friends. All seven of his sons, aged fourteen to thirty-six, were ordered to kill themselves, his wife and daughter were sold as slaves, business colleagues were beheaded, and several noblemen known to be close to him were dispossessed or banished. On the day that Nagayasu's sons performed their suicide rituals, Ieyasu's men dug up Nagayasu's gold coffin, decapitated his corpse, and exhibited his head on a spike outside Sunpu Castle.

It was not unknown for samurai of the highest echelons to dispute death sentences. In 1640, Inaba Sakon, a governor of Kaga Province, was ordered to kill himself after failing to submit a proper report of the region's finances. Sakon refused, insisting that his accounts were in order. Just at that time the lord of Kaga, Maeda Toshitsune, retired from public life. The task of straightening out Sakon fell to Maeda's son, who dispatched a rider with this message:

> I know nothing of the charges against you. But it is most regrettable that you have felt compelled to disobey a command from Lord Maeda. My father has recently begun his retirement. Now your new lord commands you: cut your stomach and give your life to me.[16]

16. Yamamoto, *Seppuku*, 206–7.

Sakon offered no further argument, and killed himself without delay. Under normal circumstances, the penalty for refusing to cut one's stomach was automatic extension of the sentence to include other family members. Such mass executions were conducted with rigorous efficiency, being performed simultaneously at different locations. François Caron, a Dutch trader resident in Japan during the 1660s, recorded the fate of the male relatives of an unnamed governor near Edo who was found guilty of overtaxing his subjects. The governor had a brother and an uncle in Kyushu; his sons and other brothers were employed as guards and officers in various castles and towns around Japan. The governor and all his relatives, nearly a dozen men in all, were forced to cut their bellies at the same hour on the same day, each at his respective location.[17]

Needless to say, commoners who committed crimes *against* samurai did so at their own peril. In his *Hagakure*, Jōchō records for us the sequence of highly creative punishments administered to a thief who had robbed the storehouse of the Nabeshima family. A team of samurai executioners ripped out his finger- and toenails, severed his tendons, drilled holes in him, shattered his bones, set fire to his pubic hair, and poured boiling soy sauce over his wounds. They finally put him out of his misery by bending the backs of his heels to his head.[18]

By far the most common reason for seppuku rulings was fighting. Unaccustomed to peaceful living, samurai of the early 1600s were quick and eager with their swords. From remarks in records kept by samurai families, it would appear that these sword fights were a source

17. Caron, *A True Description of the Mighty Kingdoms of Japan and Siam*, 58–59.

18. Despite the risks, samurai estates were favorite targets for thieves, since image-conscious samurai lords were reluctant to report break-ins. In September 1832 a thief was captured in the grounds of the Matsudaira residence in Nihonbashi. He confessed to having burgled ninety-nine samurai estates over the preceding seven years. Fewer than a half of these had reported the robberies; twenty estates had been robbed twice. Although the usual punishments for burglary were incarceration and branding, this thief, who preyed exclusively on samurai wealth, was given the full treatment. He was tortured in various unpleasant ways before being decapitated. His head was put on display and the samurai used his body for sword-testing. There was no burial or cremation; his remains were given to dogs. (Koishikawa, *Autorō no kindaishi*.)

of much entertainment to the samurai themselves. The problem for the government was that even a ten-second tavern brawl could leave bad blood between domains that lasted for years. Authorities needed to devise a way of resolving such conflicts politically, as well as judicially. Their solution was *kenka ryōseihai*, the principle of dual blame in any dispute.

The idea is traditionally said to have originated in a 1547 ruling from Kai Province, recorded in the *Kōyō Military Chronicles* (Kōyō gunkan, 1586). Two middle-aged samurai, Uemon and Sekisaemon, got into a brawl. Uemon pushed Sekisaemon against a wall and knocked him to the floor. Sekisaemon managed to land a kick on his way down, winding Uemon and incapacitating him. That was all. News of the scuffle reached the ears of the lord of Kai, Takeda Shingen. Shingen asked why no one had tried to intervene. He was told that nobody paid them much attention since they had been fighting "like eight-year-olds." Shingen was disgusted by this. To his mind, a fight without swords was no fight at all, and was unworthy of those who call themselves samurai. He had the two men arrested and relieved of their ears, noses, and heads—in that order. Shingen then announced that he was adding a new section to the domain's regulations. From now on, in any fight between samurai, both parties would be punished *irrespective of the reason for their dispute*. His intention was not to stamp out fighting, but to stamp out frivolous fighting. If samurai were not ready to die, he declared, they should not fight at all. His advisors expressed their concern that this would promote cowardice, with no one daring to fight no matter how rudely provoked. The rule was added nevertheless.[19]

The Shingen anecdote remains a popular one. But it is a fact that similar laws were in place in other military households before 1547, and their stipulations suggest different concerns. A 1526 amendment to the code of the Imakawa family, rulers of Suruga (now part of Shizuoka Prefecture), introduced a mandatory seppuku death penalty for both parties involved in any violent altercation. In a spirit entirely contrary to Shingen's, the Imakawa amendment allowed exemption

19. Satō, ed., *Kōyō gunkan*, 379–80.

for a samurai who showed restraint when attacked; if he sustained a wound as a consequence, he would not be ordered to cut his stomach, even if he was initially to blame for the dispute.[20] In 1536, Date Tane-mune, lord of the northern territory of Mutsu, introduced a revenge clause in his rules of conduct for his men. It stated, "When a samurai who commits suicide [*jigai*] leaves a note explaining the reason for his suicide, an enemy he identifies in this note shall also be subject to punishment."[21] The text goes on to clarify that such punishment will not be automatic, but will be determined according to the facts of the case by Lord Tanemune himself. These and other examples indi-cate that the dual blame system developed from a desire to stamp out duels, feuds, vendettas, and other such problems, and not to foster warrior spirit.

Ieyasu's government subsequently adopted the principle of dual blame. It was intended as a rule of thumb, not enshrined in law. This allowed for considerable leeway in its application. With the emphasis on public order and face-saving rather than individual justice, it led to some eccentric rulings.

In 1607 Ieyasu rebuilt Sunpu Castle in what is now Shizuoka as a retreat for himself and his family. His luggage was transported from Edo under the supervision of a young samurai from the Ikeda domain, Suga Kozaemon. While the luggage was being unloaded at Sunpu har-bor, a group of seven samurai from Shimazu were having a drinking party on a nearby boat. When one of the Ikeda crew cracked a joke about them, the Shimazu men angrily boarded the Ikeda boat and a fight broke out. Four crew members were injured. Kozaemon, who was on the harborside at the time, was informed of the incident soon after. Kozaemon was more than just the shogun's luggage handler: he was one of the Ikedas' finest swordsmen. He mounted his horse and gave chase, catching up with the Shimazu boat further down the river. He jumped aboard with both his swords drawn and threw him-self at the Shimazu men. Total body count: six dead, one wounded.

20. Shimizu, *Kenka ryōseihai no tanjō*, 178-80.

21. Ibid., 43.

Kozaemon tied the wounded samurai to the boat, and rode off shouting his own name.

The incident provoked a disagreement between heads of the two domains. The Shimazus wanted Kozaemon dead. But the Ikedas resisted, pointing out that he had not started the fight. The Shimazu lord appealed to the bakufu for a ruling. In the meantime he ordered the samurai who had been tied up to cut his stomach, on the grounds that it was shameful to have been so roundly defeated; a true samurai would die before allowing himself to be bound with rope. A government messenger then arrived with the ruling on Kozaemon: since both parties in any dispute were culpable, Kozaemon must also kill himself. In a way this was a concession, since he was not to be beheaded as a murderer. For his fine swordsmanship he was granted the right to cut his belly. His seppuku was an honor; the other's, a punishment. In addition, a stipend of four hundred *koku* was awarded to Kozaemon's three-year-old son.

A somewhat similar incident occurred in the grounds of Edo Castle. On March 22, 1633, a government scribe named Yamanaka Sanemon ambushed a co-worker, Hattori Hanzaburō, for reasons that are not clear. Hanzaburō proved the stronger swordsman, killing both Sanemon and his valet. Hanzaburō was cheered all round for his splendid display, and the next day the shogun ordered him to cut his stomach.

An example of a violent dispute that was deemed exempt from the principle of dual blame is found in the records of Aizu for April 1666. Iida Hachirōhei presented himself at the home of a fellow samurai, Aizawa Heizaemon, and announced that he was there to avenge an insult. Hachirōhei attacked, but Heizaemon managed to wrest the sword from his grip, and struck him in return. The two men were restrained and inspectors were summoned. Hachirōhei, the attacker, claimed that Heizaemon had been making fun of him. Heizaemon denied any wrongdoing; others confirmed this. Hachirōhei was sentenced to death, while Heizaemon went unpunished. The authorities ruled that there was no evidence that he had insulted Hachirōhei. Furthermore, by handling the attack so admirably he had demonstrated that he was worthy of continuing in service. Had he not defended himself so well, it was suggested, he would have been ordered to cut his stomach.

One phenomenon unique to this chaotic period of seppuku history should be noted. Since it was natural to assume that any samurai found dead with his stomach slashed had committed suicide, murderers realized that they could confuse investigators by cutting the bellies of their victims. A manual of 1633 offers tips for determining whether or not a gutted samurai had died by his own hand.[22] A government document of 1656 records a specific case of "seppuku murder." On July 9, the shogun's chief of security, Inaba Masayoshi, was found dead in his bedroom. The coroner's verdict was suicide, but the Inaba family disputed this and launched their own investigation. Within days, two of Masayoshi's guards confessed to murdering him. The two guards were lovers whose affair Masayoshi had discovered. Fearing the consequences of exposure, they had killed him, stabbing him across the stomach in an attempt to disguise the murder as suicide. To kill one's own master (*aruji-goroshi*) was regarded as an especially heinous crime. Punishment was correspondingly severe. A bureaucrat recorded the manner of the pair's execution: "A large hole was dug in the ground and filled with charcoal. This was covered with bamboo poles. The criminals were coated in oil, tied to the poles, and grilled like fish."[23]

In the spring of 1637, the three phenomena of dual blame, martyrdom, and male-male love united in an incident in the Edo district of Asakusa, which was predictably resolved in a bloody eruption of stomachs and necks. Two teenage samurai, Hosono Shuzen and Funagawa Uneme, had been competing for the affections of another, Itami Ukyō. It appears that Shuzen discovered that Ukyō was favoring Uneme and flew into a rage. With his sword drawn he ambushed Ukyō in the street. Ukyō defended himself, killing Shuzen. By the rule of dual blame, Ukyō was sentenced to death by seppuku.

---

22. Sobue, *Seppuku kaishaku den.* The advice given is dubious: "The voluminous loss of blood from a stomach wound so completely drains the blood from the head, as to turn it pure white. If any color remains in the cheeks, suspect foul play."

23. Yoshimoto, ed., *Dankai, gyokuteki inken*, 25:406.

The execution is recorded as having taken place at Keiyōji Temple in Asakusa on April 17. Before a crowd of spectators, Ukyō recited a death poem and made a slight cut in his stomach. When the swordsman acting as kaishaku struck, Uneme broke from the crowd and threw his arms around his headless friend. Weeping, Uneme begged the kaishaku to make him a martyr. The kaishaku obliged, and displayed the two heads side by side.[24]

The incident became famous after the success of a prose adaptation by Ihara Saikaku in 1687. Saikaku gives the ages of Uneme and Ukyō as seventeen and fifteen respectively. For dramatic effect, Saikaku also has a number of older vassals stab each other on the spot, and a third stomach-cutting teenager who leaves a poetic suicide note: "What reason is there to linger in this transient world?"[25]

The Akō Incident (1701–1703)

No swordplay of any kind was tolerated at the shogun's palace in Edo. From the time of Ieyasu, seppuku had been mandatory for any samurai who so much as drew his sword within the palace grounds. To disobey this rule was to insult the shogun himself. Not surprisingly, transgressions were extremely rare. In the first hundred years of Tokugawa rule there were only four such incidents. In 1628, Toshima Nobumitsu, a samurai in the direct service of the shogun, fatally struck down a senior councilor named Inoue Masanari. Nobumitsu also killed one of the guards who attempted to restrain him, and disemboweled himself on the spot. As Masanari was one of the shogun's top aides there were calls for the entire Toshima family to be exterminated, but the final ruling was that Nobumitsu's suicide had concluded the matter. The case of Hattori Hanzaburō, who was condemned to cut his belly after *being* attacked (and killing two of his attackers) in the grounds of the palace in 1633, was mentioned earlier. In 1684, a junior councilor named Inaba Masayasu murdered

24. Nakayasu, *Seppuku: Hisōbi no sekai*, 77–92.
25. Saikaku, *Nanshoku ōkagami*, 244.

the Grand Councilor, Hotta Masatoshi, before being cut to pieces by palace guards.[26] Since Masayasu's son was already dead, that was the end of the Inaba line and no further action was deemed necessary.

The fourth incident proved more problematic. The sequence of events that began with the assault by Asano Naganori, lord of Akō, on Lord Kira Yoshihisa, Master of Ceremonies, in the corridor leading from the White Chamber, and ended with a bloody vendetta against Kira by forty-seven of Asano's men, constitutes the most celebrated samurai story of all. The Akō Incident, as it is known, derives its enduring fascination from the conflict between samurai honor and secular law. At a basic level the story seems to offer everything: handsome young prince, wicked villain, bull-headed king, plucky band of brothers, family crises, spies and sword fights, a resounding victory for justice—and forty-seven ritual suicides. This is the stuff that Kabuki plots are made of, and indeed the Kabuki play based on the incident, *The Treasury of Loyal Retainers* (Chūshingura), is still the most often performed. The Akō Incident is widely believed to embody moral conundrums that are quintessentially Japanese. It is perhaps more accurate to say that the whole affair now comprises the sum of three centuries of scholarly commentary and fictional embellishment, having absorbed a plethora of nuances and complexities that were tagged on post factum.

Asano Naganori was the third lord of Akō in Hyōgo Prefecture. Thirty-five at the time of the incident, he was a popular figure, if little more than a pleasure-seeking playboy who left administrative matters firmly in the hands of his advisors. In April 1701, during a term of service at the shogun's palace, Asano learned that he was to be entrusted with the important task of entertaining a party of imperial ambassadors. As a provincial, unfamiliar with court protocols, Asano was told to seek advice from an expert, sixty-year-old Kira Yoshihisa. Tension of some sort quickly developed between the two. According to an early account, Kira demanded a bribe for his services, and when

26. Hotta Masatoshi was the son of Hotta Masamori, who had committed junshi upon the death of the shogun, Iemitsu, in 1651.

Asano refused to pay, Kira began taunting him by belittling his country ways.[27] The fact is that no concrete evidence exists. All we know is
that on April 21, the day the imperial envoys were due to arrive, Asano
snapped. Rushing Kira from behind, and shouting, "You know what
this is for!" he lashed out with his short sword, hitting Kira on the
shoulder. As Kira turned, Asano cut him again, this time hitting his
eboshi (courtier's headwear). Asano's third strike sank into the wall as
Kira fled shrieking down the corridor. Asano was restrained by a third
man before he could give chase.[28]

As attempted murders go, it was a lame effort. Attacking a man
twice his age, from the rear, and with the advantage of total surprise,
Asano inflicted nothing more than two minor flesh wounds: a cut in
Kira's shoulder and a long scratch across his forehead. Striking with
his short sword, Asano had made the rudimentary error of slashing
rather than stabbing. The outcome: Kira's head healed in two weeks,
while Asano's would be off within hours.

A hundred guards escorted Asano out of Edo Castle, via an
"impure" exit reserved for corpses and criminals, and marched him
to the house of Lord Tamura Dateaki, where he was to be confined
pending an investigation.[29] However, the shogun, Tsunayoshi, was so
outraged by this violation of palace rules that he issued a seppuku
death sentence for Asano without even waiting for the investigators'
report. At just after five o'clock in the afternoon a team of government
representatives arrived at the Tamura residence to supervise Asano's
execution. They included Tsuchiya Yasutochi, the chief inspector, and
Okado Denpachirō, an inspector and official witness. Okado and
Tamura later wrote down the proceedings of that afternoon. Their
notes are the only firsthand accounts we have.

Tsuchiya told Tamura that his prisoner was to die as soon as possible. This was highly irregular, as Tamura knew; he explained that it

27. In fact it was customary to offer gifts to courtiers in exchange for etiquette lessons.
Asano ought to have known this.

28. Watanabe, ed., *Akō gishi shiryō*, 1:34.

29. In Shinbashi 4-chome. Since 1912 the premises have been occupied by Shinshōdō,
a family of confectioners whose best-seller is the "disemboweled bun" (*seppuku monaka*).

would take time to prepare a room. According to Tamura, Tsuchiya replied that the execution could excusably take place outdoors. This was another breach of etiquette. A lord would expect to perform his death ritual in grand chambers. Nevertheless, since Tsuchiya represented the shogun's will, no argument was offered. Two mats were laid out in the garden and covered with white linen. White screens were arranged around three sides.

The sentence was formally read to Asano at six o'clock. "The punishment for attacking Lord Kira, irrationally and with complete disregard for your surroundings, is seppuku, to be performed immediately." Asano expressed no remorse. Asked if he had anything to say, he inquired whether "my enemy Kira" was dead. Tamura told him what he wanted to hear, that Kira was gravely wounded and in terrible pain. Asano was pleased to hear this. The witnesses and assistants took their places in the garden, and Asano was led outside. A junior inspector named Isoda Budaiyū took the role of kaishaku. Since a junior inspector's sword was not sufficiently distinguished for the neck of a lord, Tamura lent Budaiyū a sword from his own collection.

The assistants brought out a small wooden stand with a dagger resting on it. Asano removed his arms from the sleeves of his kimono. Budaiyū stood ready behind him, sword poised. Asano picked up the dagger and seemed to examine it. The moment he pressed the tip to his stomach, Budaiyū's sword came down. Execution accomplished, Tamura sent a servant to the house of Asano's brother to deliver this terse message:

> Sir,
>
> This is to inform you that your brother, Lord Asano Naganori, has just this moment disemboweled himself at my residence, in the presence of Chief Inspector Tsuchiya and two other officials. As next of kin, you are respectfully requested to come and collect the body at your earliest convenience.[30]

30. Watanabe, ed., *Akō gishi shiryō*, 2:383.

One of the many Akō legends has it that Budaiyū's strike was unsuccessful, and that Asano's head dangled from his neck, attached by a flap of skin; Budaiyū is said to have held Asano's topknot as he sliced the head free. Some versions have Asano testing the dagger by making a cut in his left thigh before pointing it to his stomach and slashing his belly with a single horizontal cut. These details are additions not found in the original reports.[31]

There was considerable public distress at the news of Asano's death, and his funeral, at the temple of Sengakuji in Takanawa, was mobbed. But there were more punishments on the way. Asano's stipend of fifty thousand koku, his castle in Akō, and his Edo residence, were all confiscated. His brother was placed under two-year house arrest, and his three hundred samurai were set adrift as *rōnin*, "lordless" samurai.

But that was not the end of the matter. Many people saw the ruling against Asano as a travesty of justice. Edo was soon buzzing with talk of revenge. When would the samurai make their move against Kira? A general antipathy toward courtiers no doubt played its part here. In the public perception, Asano had stood up to government corruption, and paid for it with his life. If his men were anything like him, surely they would seek vengeance? Kira knew the threat was real, and although he had been subject to no official punishment his life had changed forever. He resigned his position at court to take early retirement, and was forced to move to a house in a less coveted area. He hired extra guards, and paid spies to monitor the Akō men's movements. His wife left him.

The leader of the Akō samurai was Ōishi Yoshio, known as Kuranosuke, Asano's chief councilor. Today an untouchable hero, he was not always known for brilliance. As a young administrator he was nicknamed "daytime lantern" (*hiru-andon*); in other words, he was useless. He was not good with money, and needed assistance from senior retainers when handling anything financial. His first talent seems to have been for heavy drinking. All the same he was well educated,

---

31. In some Kabuki versions, Asano's men arrive at the moment of his seppuku; he implores them to avenge him, with the dagger still stuck in his gut.

having studied Daoism and military science under the great samurai sage Yamaga Sokō, and could boast a first-class lineage. The Ōishis had been warriors in Ōmi since the fifteenth century, and Kuranosuke's great-grandfather had been a retainer of Toyotomi Hidetsugu.

Even before their castle was handed over to bailiffs, the Akō samurai were considering suicide. At a series of emergency meetings held in the days following Asano's death, some two hundred samurai debated their options. The sticking point was that the principle of dual blame had been ignored: Kira was still alive. All other concerns were secondary. Some argued that they should not hand over the castle without a fight. Others suggested ripping their bellies in protest, in the hope that their deaths would prompt the bakufu to punish Kira. Against this, it was pointed out that Asano's brother might be executed if the handover was delayed. Older retainers were willing to hand over the castle without resistance, but wanted Kira dead before they killed themselves. A group of hardliners led by Horibe Yasubyōe[32] were for heading to Edo and murdering Kira immediately. This was ruled out due to the increased guard on Kira's residence. If they were going to attack, they would have to bide their time.

The castle was officially handed over on April 26, and three hundred Akō retainers moved their headquarters to nearby Enrinji Temple. Yasubyōe and his gang traveled to Edo while Kuranosuke remained in Akō, pursuing bureaucratic channels. He made repeated petitions for reinstatement, but the bakufu would not budge. This was hardly surprising. To do so would have been tantamount to admitting that the shogun was in error, and shoguns do not make mistakes. Yasubyōe, a stormy fellow who had participated in a vendetta attack earlier in his career, soon grew impatient. He was concerned that Kira might leave Edo altogether and move to his country villa in Komezawa. At one point Kuranosuke even floated the idea of abandoning their plan to murder Kira, and murdering his son instead. The private struggles of the other samurai are evident from their letters. They could not remain unemployed indefinitely. Many found positions elsewhere and moved

32. Not *Yasubei*, as it is often given.

to different parts of Japan. At least two, Hashimoto Heizaemon and Kayano Sanpei, are known to have committed suicide. Heizaemon, who was eighteen, stabbed himself to death in a suicide pact with an Osaka prostitute. Sanpei, who had delivered the news of Lord Asano's execution to Akō, committed suicide. He explained himself in a letter to Kuranosuke. He was being pressured by his father to take a position in Settsu. Sworn to secrecy about plans for a vendetta, he could not give his father a reason for refusing the new position. Stuck between a rock and a hard place, Sanpei eviscerated himself. As months passed, many of the rōnin went their separate ways, and their passion for vengeance waned. After twelve months, fewer than sixty remained committed to an attack on Kira.

Kuranosuke made it clear to them that such an action could mean death, one way or another. Ideally, they would storm Kira's residence, kill him, and deliver his head to Lord Asano's grave at Sengakuji; then they would disembowel themselves. Their actions would be recognized as faithful to the samurai ethos, they would receive posthumous pardons, and their families would not be persecuted. There was no reason to be confident that this would be the outcome. Kira had nearly a hundred samurai in his employ, two for every rōnin. The likelihood was that many of the Akō men would die in the attack. The prospects were not much better for any who might survive. The shogun was sure to be angered by their disobedience, and Tsunayoshi was not known for leniency. They could well imagine the worst-case scenario: the attack is a disaster, they are captured and beheaded without honor, their brothers and sons are executed, their wives and daughters are sold as slaves, and Kira lives happily ever after.

Initially, fifty-seven rōnin agreed to risk it. On the first anniversary of Asano's death, they sealed a vendetta pact with their blood. Unlike the junshi martyrs of the previous century, the Akō men were not driven by personal devotion. Some of them had never spoken a word to Lord Asano. An aphorism of Confucius, quoted frequently in their letters, defines the sentiment that inspired them: "One should not live under the same heaven as the murderer of one's father." Only death—theirs or Kira's—could make things right. At stake was their honor as samurai. Their loyalty was not to Asano personally, but to the warrior code. In this they were out of tune with the times. By this time, revenge, death, and disembowelment were concepts confined largely to the Kabuki stage. The level of public interest in the Akō Incident underlined its rarity. If the incident reveals anything timelessly Japanese, it is this heavy emphasis on the need to save face, a need defined by the status of the men as samurai, rather than on their moral obligations as individuals. Civilians, when wronged, file complaints, find new work, and get on with life. Samurai are supposed to die.

Whatever his previous faults, there is no denying that Kuranosuke planned the attack masterfully. Disguised as merchants and workmen, some of the Akō men gained entry to Kira's house and noted the layout. Kuranosuke and Yasubyōe made sure their men were well equipped. Their final shopping list included sixty heavy mallets, four ladders, two large saws, two axes, twelve spears, forty-seven whistles, forty-seven suits of body armor, and a lantern for illuminating Kira's face. When not plotting murderous revenge, Kuranosuke would head for the pleasure quarters and drown himself in drink. His behavior has been explained as a ruse to throw Kira's spies off the scent. But Kuranosuke had a reputation as a drinker long before the Akō Incident, and there seems no good reason to doubt that he was simply making the most of his last few months on earth. If he was pretending, he certainly fooled his wife: she left him and took the children to her parents' house. Kuranosuke promptly divorced her. Again, this has been interpreted as a calculated ploy to save her from punishment after his death, although it must be noted that none of the other married men divorced their wives.

During these months of preparation, ten more rōnin were forced to drop out, most under pressure from their families. The forty-seven who remained were a mixture of ages and ranks. Most were in their twenties and thirties; five were in their sixties; the oldest was seventy-six. The youngest, Kuranosuke's son Chikara, was just fifteen. One of them, Terasaka Kichiemon, had no business being there at all, since he was almost certainly not of samurai stock. Kichiemon had been a servant in the household of Chūzaemon, the captain of Asano's tiny infantry unit. Chūzaemon had invited Kichiemon to join at the rank of foot soldier after he received his promotion to captain. Another black sheep was Fuwa Kazuemon, the only member of the group who had been "lordless" before the incident began. Asano had banished him from Akō for fighting. Kazuemon drifted to Edo, where he was rumored to have honed his fighting skills by practicing *tsuji-giri*, random nighttime attacks on pedestrians. Tsuji-giri was something of a trend at the time, especially among a certain segment of the samurai class known as *Kabuki-mono* ("Kabuki boys") for their gaudy kimonos and wild antics. Kazuemon was of this type. He turned up at Asano's memorial service and requested permission to participate in the vendetta. He had no special affection for Asano and was basically just looking for a fight. After some initial doubts Kuranosuke welcomed Kazuemon into the group. It was a decision he would not regret.

The attack was set for February 1, 1703.[33] Yasubyōe and Kuranosuke had learned that Kira was holding a party that evening. They decided to attack after the party, in the early hours when house security would be at its weakest. Kuranosuke had devised a two-pronged assault plan. He would head the main attack against the front gate, while his son simultaneously led a second group through the rear entrance.

Letters from the rōnin to their families in the days leading up to the attack show their rising sense of excitement. Writing to a relative, Yokokawa Kanpei compared himself to Minamoto no Tametomo, the hero of the Hōgen Rebellion, and to Hankai, the great Chinese general. Kamisaki Norisuke wrote to his wife: "It would not befit a samurai wife to shed sorrowful tears, so please be strong. Of course I will miss you, but this is what a warrior must do."[34] Neither Kanpei nor Norisuke had ever been in a sword fight before; they were rising to the occasion. Others made gestures of death-acceptance in their own way. Chūzaemon slipped a death poem under his helmet. Following another old tradition, Kuranosuke carried a bamboo stick, to the tip

33. The fourteenth day of the twelfth month, by the old Japanese calendar. For this reason, the Akō Incident is traditionally commemorated in December.

34. Watanabe, ed., *Akō gishi shiryō*, 3:237.

of which he had attached a slip of paper bearing the words: "Ōishi Kuranosuke, retainer of Lord Asano, killed in combat on February 1."

On the night of the attack, the rōnin gathered at three safe houses in Kira's neighborhood. From there it was a twenty-minute walk to his residence. They arrived at just after four in the morning. There was heavy snow that winter, and the rōnin later told how this helped muffle their footsteps as they approached the house. The ladders took some of them over the walls and onto the roofs. Others used mallets to smash through the gates. Guards at the front and rear gates were easily overpowered. The rest of Kira's staff was fast asleep in the dormitories. The older rōnin had been given the task of locking these men inside by jamming the doors. This tactic made all the difference, since only about forty of Kira's men managed to leave their rooms and fight. The younger rōnin cut down anyone who crossed their paths. As they crossed the courtyard, they shouted, "This is a vendetta attack! You are samurai too, and you know why we're here, so don't interfere! Anyone who tries to stop us will die tonight!" Their voices were heard in neighboring houses, and the rōnin were surprised to see lanterns appearing from windows all around them: the neighbors were trying to assist them by illuminating the grounds of Kira's residence.

The rōnin found their way to Kira's bedchamber. He was not there. They searched the house for nearly an hour, running along passageways, in and out of dark rooms, back and forth across the courtyards. To the rear of the kitchen area, they found the door to a small cellar. A group of rōnin surrounded this door. When they opened it, two of Kira's samurai came rushing out. Both were cut down and skewered with spears.[35] There was a moment's pause; then came a third man. The rōnin knocked him down with an axe and stabbed him to death. They peered into the cellar and saw one more face: an old man in a white silk kimono. It was Kira.

The rōnin would later tell investigators that they had dispatched Kira with a single spear-strike. However, lines in a private letter written by Fuwa Kazuemon indicate that all the rōnin present had stabbed

35. One of the two was Shimizu Ichigaku, reputedly the strongest of Kira's swordsmen.

and hacked at Kira until he was dead. They sawed off his head and held it up high. All cheered, and blew their whistles. The job was done.

Sixteen of Kira's men were dead. Another twenty-one had been wounded, four seriously, and twelve had run away. Among the rōnin, only two were seriously wounded, one from a fall, and there was not a single fatality. Their armor had served them well. To investigators the rōnin would speak highly of Kira's samurai, saying they had nothing to be ashamed of. Kira's son was singled out for praise. The eighteen-year-old had fought bravely, and had been badly wounded as a result. On the rōnin side, "Kabuki boy" Kazuemon had an excellent night, with five kills attributed to him. He emerged unscathed, although his sleeves were said to have been shredded to ribbons.

At five o'clock in the morning, an extraordinary procession set out from Kira's residence. Carrying Kira's head, which they had wrapped in cloth and hung from an axe pole, the rōnin made their way across town to Sengakuji Temple. Daylight broke, and some shopkeepers and residents came out to cheer them on. Incorporating a detour that took them past Lord Asano's former residence, now demolished, it took them three hours to reach Sengakuji. There they placed Kira's head before Asano's tombstone, and announced to the spirit of their dead lord that they had killed his enemy. Many of them broke down and wept.

Kuranosuke informed the priests at Sengakuji that he and his men intended to kill themselves in front of the temple. The priests did not like this idea at all. Fearing trouble from the bakufu they stalled Kuranosuke, telling him that they needed proper authorization first. Kuranosuke did not argue with them. This is where the tale of the heroic Forty-Seven starts to falter. Why did the rōnin not kill themselves at Sengakuji? One would not think that a few priests could prevent a large band of swordsmen from doing whatever they wanted to do. Admittedly, the rōnin were probably exhausted. They had been up all night, and had walked three hours since the attack. But Kuranosuke had already sent two of his men to report their attack to the local authorities, suggesting that his intention from the start had been to wait for an official nod before committing suicide. Their vendetta had

violated the original bakufu judgment, yet now they sought bakufu
approval for their suicide. Rather craftily, the priests offered the rōnin
a few kegs of saké. Kuranosuke accepted, and that soon quashed any
ideas of spontaneous disembowelment. More embarrassing still, the
Forty-Seven discovered that they were now the Forty-Six: Kichiemon,
the new recruit, had gone missing. Various theories have been offered
for his disappearance, none of them satisfactory. It seems he had simply run away. Asked about Kichiemon later on, his superior Chūzaemon replied, "I never want to hear that rascal's name again."[36]

From the temple the rōnin first moved to the house of Chief
Inspector Tsuchiya, where bakufu guards came to arrest them. They
were divided into four groups and taken into detention at four separate households: the Hosokawa, the Mōri, the Matsudaira, and the
Mizuno. There were fears of a rescue attempt, and the authorities were
taking no chances. Nine hundred guards marched Kuranosuke and
sixteen of his men to the Hosokawa residence, with ten going to each
of the other three households. (Since Kichiemon was now officially
missing, only nine rōnin went to the Mizuno house.) Chikara, Kuranosuke's son, was among those led to the Mōri household. Father and
son were thus separated, and never saw each other again.

For six weeks, legal experts and Confucian scholars debated the
incident. An extraordinary meeting of high-ranking bakufu officials
was convened to advise the shogun in the matter. First reactions were
enthusiastically supportive of the rōnin, while hostile to the Kira
house. A panel of police constables and inspectors recommended that
Kira's son be ordered to kill himself, along with those of Kira's guards
who had not put up a fight. Ogyū Sorai, a notable Confucian philosopher, summed up the view that ultimately prevailed: "If the rōnin are
condemned to disembowelment in keeping with samurai tradition,
the claim of Kira's family will be satisfied, and the loyalty of the forty-
six will not have been disparaged."

The verdict was announced on March 20, 1703. The oddly worded
ruling declared that the rōnin were guilty of forming a "league" to

36. Quoted in Yamamoto, *Chūshingura*, 216.

perpetrate a "grave and unpardonable act." This demonstrated a lack of respect toward the state, for which their punishment was seppuku. When Kuranosuke heard the sentence he replied, "It must have been a difficult decision. We consider ourselves fortunate to have been sentenced to die by performing seppuku. For this, we are most grateful."[37]

The executions were carried out on the day of the verdict, starting at four o'clock in the afternoon, at each of the respective households. In a large room facing the garden, straw mats were laid out and covered with thin mattresses or cushions. One kaishaku was allocated for each man, the exception being at the Matsudaira house, where there were five kaishaku to decapitate ten men. In a closed room in another part of the house, the rōnin waited for their names to be called. At the Hosokawa house, Kuranosuke was the first to be summoned. He was escorted from the waiting area to the execution place by his kaishaku, who waited for him to be seated before moving to his rear-left. Another assistant appeared with a table carrying the dagger, and placed it before Kuranosuke, who bowed and opened his kimono in readiness. The moment Kuranosuke reached for the dagger, the kaishaku struck off his head. Picking the head up by the root of the topknot, the kaishaku displayed it to the official witnesses, who called out: "Kuranosuke's head, fully severed." Assistants hid the execution area from view with tall screens while they cleared away the body and head, and brought out clean mats and cushions. The same procedure was repeated for each of the other sixteen men.[38]

Ōishi Kuranosuke did not cut his stomach, nor did any of the men who followed him. The official report of the executions compiled by the Hosokawa house is unambiguous here: the men were beheaded as they reached for the dagger. It was the same at the other three households. This is the corresponding passage from the report of the Mizuno house:

> When the stomach-cutter [seppuku-jin] was seated, foot soldiers positioned a table before him, and placed the dagger

37. Watanabe, ed., Akō gishi shiryō, 2:32.
38. Ibid., 33.

thereupon, the blade of this dagger having been wrapped with cloth beforehand. Each stomach-cutter was permitted to offer a polite greeting to the officials observing the ceremony. He loosened his upper robes and bowed to his assistant [*kaishaku*]. The assistant approached, waited at the rear left, and cut off the stomach-cutter's head when he reached for the dagger. The assistant then picked up the head and held it up for the inspection of the officials.[39]

Here the terms *seppuku* and *kaishaku* have wholly forgone their traditional meanings, and now denote nothing more than "condemned" and "executioner." That all four households followed the same format cannot have been coincidental. With forty-six suicide rituals to be performed consecutively, there was ample opportunity for error. The slightest mistake would have sullied the reputations of the rōnin and weakened the validity of the verdict, which depended on their honorable standing as warriors. Notes taken by supervisors at the four households indicate considerable anxiety over this point. Acting on the advice of government officials, the supervisors decided to take no chances, and saw to it that the men were beheaded at the earliest possible moment. It is unlikely that the rōnin would not have been informed of this intention, since it was important that they facilitated proceedings by offering the kaishaku a clear target. Staff at the Mōri house had originally planned to dispense with daggers altogether. They had prepared ten paper fans to be used as a symbolic alternative; using these fans, the samurai would pretend to cut their stomachs before being beheaded. Daggers were provided only after a complaint from government representatives.

Contrary to legend, then, the Akō rōnin did not commit ritual suicide. They were beheaded one after another during a symbolic seppuku ceremony.

There was one outstanding exception. At the Mōri house, twenty-three-year-old Hazama Roku was determined to cut his stomach. The

39. Ibid., 120–21.

official report explains what happened: "Young Hazama Roku surprised his executioner by suddenly reaching forward without bothering to disrobe. Quick as a flash he snatched up the dagger, and by the time his head was off he had already stabbed himself in the stomach. It really was most impressive." There were other impressive moments. The kaishaku for Takebayashi Tadashichi made a very poor strike that cut deep into the shoulder. Tadashichi, knocked off balance by the blow, sat up straight and, with complete composure, told the swordsman to calm himself. The kaishaku did not miss twice. According to the reports, none of the Akō men showed any sign of fear, and nothing occurred that tarnished their names in any way. But there were no bloodletting heroics. Other than Hazama Roku's, no bellies were ripped during the making of this melodrama.

Intellectuals continued to debate the case in print. Not everyone cheered the rōnin as heroes. Satō Naokata, a leading Confucian scholar, saw the attack on Kira as an attack on the bakufu itself. Naokata also wondered why the rōnin had not ripped their bellies at Sengakuji. "To give themselves up and wait for the shogun's ruling," he wrote, "was nothing but a scheme to escape death and bask for a while in their own glory, before finding themselves new employment."[40] His opinion was shared by Dazai Shundai, another Confucian, who was not convinced that their actions were those of men committed to dying: "They should have attacked their enemy at once, without waiting, and ripped their bellies whether they won or lost. The unifying element should have been death. Only through death could they have fully discharged their responsibilities."[41] Jōchō, in his *Hagakure*, repeated these criticisms, and added more. Why, he asked, had the rōnin not killed themselves as soon as they heard of Lord Asano's execution? They could have attacked Kira's residence immediately, and died fighting, or ripped their bellies in defeat. Furthermore, as Jōchō pointed out, Kira was an old man. What if he had died while they were planning their attack? All would have been lost, including any hope

---

40. Satō, *Shijūrokunin no hikki*, in Ishii, ed., *Kinsei buke shisō*, 380.
41. Dazai, *Akō shijūrokushi ron*, in Ishii, ed., *Kinsei buke shisō*, 406.

of redeeming their honor. "Whether you win or lose depends on the circumstances at the time," he proclaimed, "but saving face is different. All you need is the will to die."[42]

The 1700s: Urban Dandies and Paper Fans

The Akō Incident prompted a fresh wave of chivalric nostalgia. A mere twelve days after the rōnin were executed, one Edo theater was offering a Kabuki drama entitled *The Nighttime Vendetta Attack of the Soga Brothers* (Akebono Soga no yo-uchi). Anxious to nip a potential vendetta craze in the bud, the government banned the play after two performances. In 1706 the puppet drama *The Great Peace on a Go Board* (Goban taiheiki), featuring characters that were obviously based on the Akō protagonists, played to a full house in Osaka. But it was the success of *The Treasury of Loyal Retainers* (Chūshingura, 1748) that secured a place for the tale of the forty-seven rōnin in Japan's theatrical canon, where it has remained ever since. These stage versions milked the death scenes for every last drop of bravura, and the facts about the ritual executions blurred into fiction.

Prose writers fared better with the censors. Essayists such as Muro Kyūsō exalted the idea of loyalty-unto-death, as epitomized by the junshi martyrs. Saikaku's parables of a squandered samurai utopia continued to be solid bestsellers. Jōchō wrote *Hagakure*, his paean to sacrificial servitude, during these years, and belly-ripping stories were all the rage in popular fiction. As an example, here is "The Bloodied Daruma" (Chi daruma) from *A Hodgepodge of Juicy Tales* (Kingyoku nejibukusa), an anthology printed in 1704. "Daruma" is the Japanese name for Bodhidharma, the fifth-century Buddhist mystic who was said to have meditated for so long that his arms and legs withered. The author of the story is identified only by a pseudonym, Shōkadō.

---

42. Jōchō, *Hagakure*, 1:45. Interestingly, the murder rate inside the palace actually increased after the Akō Incident. There were four more stabbings over the next four decades.

In the days when Yūsai[43] was head of the Hosokawa family, two brothers, both wandering samurai, came seeking
positions. As they sounded like capable fellows, Yūsai
granted them an audience.

"And what skills do you possess?" he asked them.

"When needs must," they replied, "we can do what no
other samurai can."

Won over by their confident manner, Yūsai offered
the elder brother a stipend of four hundred koku, with
another three hundred koku for the younger.

Then came the Great Fire of Meireki.[44] When the flames
reached the roof of His Lordship's residence, fierce winds
fanned a whirl of smoke and fire that raged beyond anyone's control. Valuables from the house were carried outside to safety, but there was one oversight: the treasured
painting of the Daruma was left hanging in His Lordship's
chamber. Yūsai was first distraught, then furious. His
attendants ran about like headless chickens until someone
suggested calling the two newcomers, who had boasted
of being able to do "what no other samurai can." Yūsai
agreed, and the brothers were quickly sent for.

"Go back into the house," he commanded them, "and
if the flames have not yet reached my quarters, fetch the
scroll of the Daruma that hangs there. But don't take too
many risks—come back if the fire is too strong."

The brothers held their breaths and rushed into the
blazing inferno, just as the fire surged toward their master's quarters. Entering via the rear gate, they ducked
under clouds of smoke and found their way to His Lordship's room. Flames were billowing across the ceiling, but
had not yet reached the floor. Yes, there was the priceless
painting, hanging in the alcove.

43. Hosokawa Fujitaka (1534–1610), whose posthumous Buddhist name was Yūsai.
44. In 1657. Shōkadō has got his dates muddled.

Quick as a flash, the brothers took it down and rolled it up, using their robes to cover it. But as they tried to leave, flames blazed up on all sides. Their escape was cut off. Alas, both were burned alive!

After the fire was extinguished, their charred corpses were discovered among the ash. And what an incredible sight it was.

To begin with, the older brother had chopped off the younger brother's head. Then, reaching in through the neck, he had scooped out the guts and internal organs, and had stuffed the scroll—still wrapped inside the coat—inside his brother's hollowed corpse. He had cut his own stomach wide open in a huge cross shape and pushed his brother's headless torso *inside his own belly*. He died with his arms around his beloved brother, and with the priceless scroll buried deep inside the pair of them. When it was examined, the painting was found to be miraculously undamaged, with just a few bloodstains around the outer edges of the scroll.

As His Lordship declared, the devotion of these two men is a shining example for all true samurai.[45]

The Akō Incident also galvanized the judiciary. Consider this 1709 ruling by magistrates in the case of Lord Maeda Toshimasa, who, in a calculated act of vengeance, had stabbed a rival in the stomach so violently that the man's blood was said to have gushed from his mouth:

The undisputed facts of the case are that Maeda Toshimasa brutally stabbed and killed Oda Kenmotsu at Tōeizan in Ueno on March 26. While the attack seems to have been an act of pure insanity, the fact that Kenmotsu died as a result leaves the sentence in no doubt. Toshimasa is hereby commanded to die by seppuku. Kenmotsu's stipend of

45. Kigoshi, ed., *Ukiyo zōshi kaidanshū*, 290–92.

ten thousand koku shall pass to his son. Toshimasa's stipend, also ten thousand, shall pass to Toshimasa's older brother.[46]

The clear intention here is to tie up loose ends, so as to leave no grounds for a vendetta. The two samurai are dead—one murdered, one disemboweled—and their families keep their respective stipends. The argument for insanity was employed with much greater frequency after Akō, since it rendered further analysis superfluous. Mad lords are not deserving of vendettas.

This strategic use of seppuku rulings was not limited to high-profile cases. In the winter of 1731, Mōri Tahē, a samurai of the Kaga domain, fatally stabbed his younger brother at their home. The brother, Sukeuemon, had been shouting at his wife over some domestic matter. Tahē pulled him away with the words, "You raise your voice to your wife, but you wouldn't have the guts to shout at a man like that!" Sukeuemon flew into a temper and reached for his short sword. He was dead before it was out of its scabbard. The official punishment for murdering a sibling was decapitation. But the magistrates agreed that a straight beheading for Tahē would have exonerated his brother.

> Even if we allow for the fact that Sukeuemon may have been about to attack him, Tahē ought to have attempted to restrain his brother, rather than rashly resorting to a sword strike. To cut down one's own brother in this manner is inexcusable, and demands the strictest punishment [i.e. execution by decapitation]. However, since Sukeuemon's actions also appear to have fallen below an acceptable standard, Tahē's sentence shall be the lesser one of seppuku.[47]

---

46. Yamamoto, *Seppuku*, 52.
47. Ibid., 102.

A very similar incident occurred in Edo some seventy years later. Yuge Kazuya, a captain in the *shoinban*, the shogun's elite bodyguard unit, killed his brother in a fight over money. Magistrates ruled that Kazuya had acted in self-defense, and sentenced him to seppuku. In each of these cases the ruling reflected the actions of both men involved: honorable death for one implied dishonor for the other.

With the emphasis now firmly on ruling rather than ritual, on form rather than content, stomach-cutting faced redundancy. From the 1730s onward, seppuku ceremonies were mostly performed without a cut to the stomach, the condemned man being beheaded before or while reaching for the dagger. Samurai handbooks of the time are explicit in this regard; a swordsman who acts as kaishaku is encouraged not to hesitate, but to remove the head as quickly as possible. Some ceremonies dispensed with the dagger altogether by using a paper fan in its place, as had been suggested in the Akō case. The first documented references to this practice date from the 1680s. For many, no doubt, the paper fan came as welcome relief. Originally however, "pretend" seppuku using a paper fan was not, as might be supposed, a soft option for those too cowardly to cut their stomachs. On the contrary, it was first devised for men who were not at all cowardly. The last quarter of the seventeenth century had seen a number of violent provincial uprisings, during which scores of insurgents and samurai mercenaries were rounded up and brought to Edo for execution. These men did not go quietly. Their executions were marred by angry scenes, shouts of anti-bakufu slogans, and fierce exchanges with the witnesses. In some cases, scuffles broke out after the condemned man picked up the dagger. At the execution of rebel leader Oguri Mimasaka in 1681, assistants had to hold Mimasaka down and pull his head by its topknot, while the kaishaku hacked through the neck. After that, executioners thought twice before offering a dagger to a condemned samurai. Cautionary exhortations in kaishaku handbooks suggest similar problems. The symbolic fan was one solution.

Paper fans also came in handy when executing children. *Notes on Decapitation and Stomach-cutting* (Kaishaku narabini seppuku dōtsuki no shidai), a manual from the 1720s, offers this advice: "As for seppuku performed by little ones, tell the boy that you are going to practice first. Offer him a fan instead of a dagger. When his head is in the right place, decapitate him without a word." A note in the records of the Owari domain for 1708 describes the executions of Satō Kanesaemon and his thirteen-year-old son, the latter being "successfully beheaded after much trickery and deception."[48] Retainers who were well liked, and had given long years of service, might also be granted permission to use a paper fan. In 1760, Kanda Hakuryōshi, a veteran retainer of Ōu, was sentenced to death for a costly financial oversight. Hakuryōshi, an octogenarian, performed the full ritual using a paper fan as if it were a dagger. He removed his upper garments, turned the fan to his stomach, slowly "cut" across, and bowed as he returned the fan to the table. The kaishaku severed his head with one chop.

In his *Thoughts on Belly-ripping* of 1772, Yamaoka Shunmei has this to say on the use of the paper fan:

> In the old days, suicide by stomach-cutting was a spectacular technique, one that warriors considered and studied carefully to familiarize themselves with its nuances. The names of those who performed it well were remembered and repeated in later generations. Today there are so many rules for cutting the stomach. An assistant is always present, and sometimes the dagger plays no part whatsoever, a paper fan being placed upon the tray in its stead; as soon as the man picks up this fan, off comes his head from behind. Since the stomach is not cut, how on earth can we call this "seppuku"? It is no different from an ordinary beheading.[49]

Understandably, in an era when the tradition of seppuku was fading, Edo folk were awed by any samurai who managed a proper stomach-cut. The ritual suicide of Sugimoto Kujurō, the fifteen-year-old sentenced to death after killing another boy over a game of Go,

48. Ujiie, *Ō-edo zankoku monogatari*, 47.
49. Yamaoka, *Hara-kiri kō*, 161.

quickly passed into legend. Kujurō seems to have impressed everyone who met him during his final hours. It was said that he did not complain about the verdict, and refused to say anything disparaging about the boy who had attacked him. He spent his last night writing letters to family benefactors, and visiting the houses of friends and relatives to bid them farewell. He showed no signs of nervousness or fear during the ritual. He bowed politely to the officials, and cut himself cleanly with a single stroke. Those who witnessed his death told the tale for the rest of their lives. Kujurō's name crops up in various samurai essays, some of them, such as Muro Kyūsō's *Sundai's Miscellany* (Sundai zatsuwa), written decades after his death. For the name of the boy he murdered, one must search the small print.[50]

Muro Kyūsō and Yuasa Jōzan, whose tales of suicidal heroics secured a large readership, were doing more than pandering to popular taste. During the long years of peace, martial values were on the wane. More bellies were being ripped on the Kabuki stage than in reality. Samurai strutted about with their trademark long and short swords, but many lacked the skills to use them. Archery and equestrianism were in similar decline. It was a sign of the times when, in April 1779, the shogun's sixteen-year-old son died by falling from his horse.

The extent to which urban effeteness had eroded warrior machismo can be gauged from Ise Sadatake's *The Deadly Ritual* (Kyōrei-shiki), a brief list of seppuku protocols written around 1770:

The Deadly Ritual

Bathing. When the condemned washes himself, whether at a temple or at the house of a local official, he should fill the tub first with cold water, and then add hot water. Hot water may be used first on the hair.

Hair. The hair should be wound with string four times to

50. The boy was Ogawa Tarō, aged twelve. The case is documented in *Kaga-han shiryō* (Heki, ed.), 5:787–93.

the left, lifted higher than usual, and wound again in the reverse direction.

Clothing. White robes are mandatory. The left side should be crossed over the right, as when dressing a corpse. A beige jacket is best, preferably with a white sash.

The tatami. Use two brown mats with white edges and a length of six *shaku* [six feet].

Ceremonial materials. Four sheets of white cloth, also six shaku in length, should first be spread over the mats. When the condemned sits on the cloth, a low table is brought out and placed before him. Two cups are placed upon this table; customarily, one of the cups is plain earthenware and the other is glazed; he may drink from either. Offer him some morsels (suggestion: three slices of scented radish with a pinch of salt). Cups are also provided on tables for the official witnesses. In rare cases, the witnesses may also partake of some morsels. It is sufficient to prepare one small serving for each witness.

The saké. Bring out a bottle of saké. Reaching across the table before the condemned, pour twice into the earthenware cup. Then pour a cup for each of the witnesses. After they have emptied their cups, they should formally greet the condemned. The condemned may be permitted a few more sips, though this is unusual. Do not allow him to drink more than four cupfuls, even if he requests more. Now is the time to bring out the belly-ripping blade.

After the saké. Place the blade on the table before the condemned. The kaishaku now takes his place at the rear, and stands with his long sword poised. The condemned indicates that he is ready. It is said that certain special

movements are to be performed when handing a sword
to a condemned man; these secrets are known only to
swordsmen.

The decapitation. Once his head is off, cover any unsightliness with sheets, and draw the screen so that the corpse
cannot be seen. The screen used at this time is ideally
white on both sides.[51]

Sadatake's fastidious table manners are worlds away from the explo-
sive barbarity of the warriors of medieval war tales. This is seppuku etiquette for the Edo dandy, a stomach-cutting ceremony in which every
tiny detail is crucial—except the actual cutting of the stomach.

Elsewhere too, overtly rhetorical death was under attack. A proclamation of 1722 attempted to stamp out love suicides (double suicides
committed by desperate couples), a popular phenomenon in those
times. The following year saw a ban on depictions of such scenes in
theaters. Bloodletting was acceptable only as an expression of governmental power, not of the self-determining power of the individual. We
can safely assume that most samurai welcomed the erasure of stomach-cutting from ritual protocol, as long as there was no consequent
detriment to the honorable symbolism of the act. But this slackening of
severity assumes a greater significance when considered in its broader
social context. For at the same time that samurai were being spared
the ordeal of cutting their stomachs, the severity of punishments for
non-samurai was increasing. According to new laws known as the One
Hundred Articles, introduced in 1742, death was now the penalty for
forging official documents, making counterfeit coins, and stealing
public funds, no matter how small the amount. Adultery by commoners also became a capital offense. Since the institution of marriage
was considered to be an arm of government, adulterers were technically guilty of treason. Furthermore, the cruelty of the punishment
had to match the cruelty of the crime. A man who killed his uncle was

51. Ise, *Kyōrei-shiki*, 208–9.

beheaded in the usual manner, whereas a man who killed his parents or his master was executed by slow decapitation using a saw. Incisions were made on either side of his head and he was exposed in a public place for two days, passersby being encouraged to saw through his neck at their leisure. Legislators did not neglect traditional techniques, such as roasting and boiling in oil. Arsonists, logically enough, were to be burned in public. As ever, humiliation, before and after execution, was integral to the punitive process. Criminals were paraded through the streets on horseback or in carts, alongside banners proclaiming their offenses. Decapitated heads were displayed for three days. Crucifixion remained a common practice. It was not a mode of execution, but of humiliation; victims were strangled or stabbed to death beforehand. The new laws also included stipulations for pickling corpses prior to public display. Salt was injected through the rectum using a bamboo rod; the body was folded, and squeezed inside a large earthenware jar. The salt liquefied the innards, which leaked from the bottom of the jar. As a general rule, pickling was reserved for celebrity villains. The pickled corpses would turn black but could be exhibited for weeks. As a further degradation, pickling and body disposal were performed by members of pariah castes.

Postmortem humiliations for non-samurai did not stop there. In many regions of Japan, corpses of executed criminals became the property of the executioner, to dispose of as he saw fit. This afforded multifarious money-making opportunities. Headless bodies could be sold to well-to-do samurai residences, where the master of the house and his guards used them for sword practice. An old samurai proverb declared that the finest swords can slice through two bodies in a single stroke. Corpses were therefore normally delivered in pairs, bound by rope at the ankles and wrists. In the pleasure quarters there was said to have existed a tradition known as *yubikiri*: sealing a love-promise with a severed finger. A besotted client would cut off his little finger at the upper joint and send it to the girl of his choice as proof of his commitment; supposedly, enterprising executioners with spare body parts to unload spotted an opening, and began supplying fingertips on demand to anyone who would pay. Most lucrative of all was the trade in human organs for their reputed medicinal benefits. Livers, gallbladders, and brains were dried and compressed into edible pellets so that they could later be dissolved in boiling water to make a broth. Thus, with remarkable efficiency, the corpses of common criminals were chopped, sliced, diced, dried, pickled, processed, packaged, and sold for consumption (and indeed digestion) by a paying public. One prominent family of executioners who worked for eight generations under the name of Yamada Asaemon made a fortune from the sale of their "health-boosting pills."[52]

Related to the "sanitization" of ritual suicide, exemplified by documents such as *The Deadly Ritual*, is the appearance in the late eighteenth century of a new seppuku term: *ikon-bara*, meaning "grudge suicide." This strange expression, which appears to have been used pejoratively, was coined to distinguish aggressive stabbing forms, such as jūmonji, from the more dignified cutting (or "pretend" cutting) of the suicide ceremony. By this time, masochistic histrionics after the manner of medieval warriors were deemed unacceptable. Sobue Tsunetsugu makes this point explicitly in his afterword to *Remarks on Stomach-cutting and Decapitation*:

> We hear tales of men from early times who, at their moment of destiny, first tested the sharpness of the blade against their thigh, or gouged their stomachs into the shape of a cross, or wrenched out their innards. But these were wild strongmen who cared not what the world thought of them. Such antics are out of place during a supervised and orderly ritual.[53]

52. In addition to their work at execution grounds, Asaemon and his men offered a freelance kaishaku service for the samurai estates, another indication of the general decline in swordsmanship. Asaemon's name crops up in a popular ditty from the late Tokugawa years: "He turns corpses into money / gets rich from headless robbers. / Here he comes to trim your pinky / it's Asaemon the Chopper." (Ujiie, *Ō-edo shitai-kō*, 147).

The extraordinary world of pharmaceutical cannibalism provides the backdrop for Saikaku's story *Raw Livers make a Most Unusual Medicine* (Namagimo wa myōyaku no yoshi, 1668). It is the tale of a servant who endeavors to cure his ailing master by feeding him the organs of children whom the servant has murdered for that purpose.

53. Sobue, *Seppuku kaishaku den*.

Authorities were not averse to manipulating the seppuku ceremony to score political points. One lamentable case was the execution of Sano Zenzaemon in 1784. In an incident reminiscent of Asano Naganori's assault on Kira Yoshihisa, Zenzaemon, a young guard, had attacked a bakufu official in the grounds of Edo palace. On the evening of March 24, he ambushed Tanuma Okitomo, a junior councilor, as Okitomo was leaving his office. Like Asano, Zenzaemon is said to have shouted "You know what this is for!" as he lashed out with his short sword. A second similarity was that Zenzaemon struck his victim on the shoulder. In this case, however, no one immediately intervened, despite there being at least twenty witnesses. Zenzaemon chased Okitomo across the courtyard, pushed him into a flowerbed, and stabbed him in the groin. Palace guards then pulled Zenzaemon away. The blade had penetrated to Okitomo's thighbone; he was beyond help, and died on April 2. Two days later, Zenzaemon was sentenced to seppuku.

The ceremony, such as it was, broke all rules of protocol. From the day of his arrest Zenzaemon was locked up in the local jail, rather than being confined in the house of a superior, which was his samurai right. Government inspectors read the sentence to him in his cell, and the execution was carried out the same evening on a patch of open ground in the center of the jail. They refused him a dagger, offering him instead a wooden sword, and beheaded him as he picked it up. His death poem, which surfaced much later, was unfinished, suggesting further malpractice on the part of the inspectors. News of Zenzaemon's treatment caused uproar among the public. Okitomo had been a highly unpopular figure whose trading policies had pushed up the price of rice. Edo folk saw Zenzaemon as a political activist; after his execution they dubbed him a martyr. The truth, when it came out, was mundane: the Sano and Tanuma families had been feuding over a private matter for some time. But the public cheered Zenzaemon all the same, dubbing him "the Divine Reformer." In contrast, stones were thrown at Okitomo's funeral procession. Two of the inspectors who supervised Zenzaemon's execution were disciplined for "ignoring

formalities."[54] It is likely, though, that the mistreatment had been officially sanctioned. Anti-bakufu assassins were not to be given opportunities for heroics.

Once again, wrongs were righted in fiction. Within a few years of
the incident, the Edo puppet and Osaka Kabuki theaters were performing their respective versions of a drama in which a samurai
named Sano Genzaemon strikes at the heart of bureaucratic venal-
ity by murdering a councilor in the shogun's palace. Since theaters
were forbidden from portraying current events, the play was set in the
twelfth century.[55]

For real belly-ripping fireworks we must look beyond the stylized
seppuku ceremonies to the passions of individual samurai, for whom
bloody suicide remained the superlative mode of self-expression.

In the autumn of 1730, Asano Yoshinaga, fifth lord of Hiroshima,
was enjoying himself in Yoshiwara, Edo's main pleasure district. He
had taken a particular liking to one young girl, and came to an agreement with the owner of her brothel to buy her contract. Yoshinaga also
bought contracts for a pair of handsome young boys. For a samurai lord
to buy prostitutes openly was to risk severe official reprimand. Riskier
still, when Yoshinaga returned to Hiroshima his three purchases traveled with him. This was too much for his wife, who shut herself up in
her room and killed herself by slitting her stomach with a single stroke.
She left a note for her husband: "It may not be indecent for a lord to
buy his playthings from the pleasure quarters, but that he should bring
them home with him is unforgivable." She was still breathing when
her staff found her. Two maids and her chief female attendant tearfully
requested permission to die with her. Permission for the maids was
granted; the other was told to stay alive for thirty-five days and then
reconsider. Following their mistress, the maids cut their stomachs. They
were then stabbed to death by the attendant, who, thirty-five days later,
put a dagger through her throat at Seishōji Temple.[56]

The death of Yoshinaga's wife, who was known as Lady Setsu,

54. Yamada, *Sanō Masakoto seppuku yowa*, 533–47.
55. The play was *Yūshoku Kamakurayama* by Katsukawa Shundō.
56. Mitamura, *Daimyō no onna hara-kiri*, 312–14.

caused a sensation. Not since the days of the Ashikaga shoguns had samurai women ripped their bellies like this, and for a woman to act as kaishaku was unheard of. Setsu was the daughter of Maeda Tsunanori, lord of the powerful Kaga domain; her samurai credentials were thus impeccable. Her death is both remonstration and punishment. Her aggressive "male" suicide symbolically strips her husband of his maleness. She is more warrior-like than he is. A similar psychological tactic can be perceived in another female suicide, in Yamato (now part of Nara Prefecture) in May 1736. Perhaps with Lady Setsu fresh in her memory, Mizoguchi Yono disemboweled herself the day after killing her husband. He had been having an affair with the wife of his own lord, Oda Nobukata, while Nobukata was away in the capital. Although Nobukata himself never learned of the affair, Yono did. She wrote an explanatory letter to her father, and stabbed her husband to death when he returned home that night. The punishment for murdering one's husband was strangulation followed by crucifixion. Yono requested seppuku. "I may be a woman," she declared, "but I am a samurai woman. I will die by cutting my stomach." Her request was granted. This was unorthodox, though understandable. Considering the scandalous circumstances, her superiors welcomed the opportunity to resolve things behind closed doors. Yono disemboweled herself at her home in the presence of two official witnesses. A maidservant placed the dagger before her, and Yono ripped her belly in jūmonji, with one horizontal cut from left to right, and a second cut from her navel to the pit of her stomach. She had absorbed the shame of her husband's crime by slitting her stomach in his stead.[57]

In addition to these unusual cases, suicidal practices among non-samurai are occasionally mentioned in official documents of these years. Criminals were often ready to die rather than face capture. Coastal security personnel reported self-stabbings by pirates. In August 1781, thieves looted the cargo of a Dutch ship at port in Deshima. Although several witnesses identified the culprits, the men refused to confess. This vexed the Dutch captain, who wrote in his diary, "The

57. Nakayasu, *Seppuku: Hisōbi no sekai*, 191–93.

watermen are still being tortured daily, but they persist in their denial. The interpreters explain that it is the nature of the Japanese, unless they are caught red-handed, to prefer to die in pain rather than confess, for then their death will not bring disgrace to their families, who will suffer the greatest ignominy if they are executed."[58] It could be more than ignominy. Another Dutchman noted in his diary entry for July 5, 1763: "They told me that the murder in Osaka of one of the senior attendants of the Korean ambassador has been committed by an interpreter. He has been executed, and all the nails and teeth of his brother have been extracted."[59]

The Kiso Anti-flood Project (1753–55)

The greatest display of stomach-cutting in the eighteenth century comes courtesy of the Satsuma domain in Kyushu.

During the summer of 1753, prolonged flooding devastated large areas of the Nōbi Plain (in what is now southern Gifu Prefecture). It was not the first time the region had been struck by floods. Local farmers had often petitioned the central government for help in building anti-flood dams, but officials had balked at the estimated cost. After that disastrous summer, the bakufu authorized the construction of a series of dams and embankments along three major rivers: the Kiso, the Nagara, and the Ibi. The "Kiso Project," as the whole enterprise became known, was conceived on a grand scale: at least ten thousand workmen were needed; more ambitiously still, it was set for completion within the year, in readiness for the following summer. There was a twist: the lord of Satsuma in Kyushu was ordered to foot the bill.

For decades the Satsuma had been at loggerheads with the government over various reforms and centralization policies. The order to fund the Kiso Project was interpreted, no doubt correctly, as an attempt to bankrupt the Satsuma, whose finances were already fragile. To refuse would mean war with the bakufu, a war the Satsuma could

58. Blusse and Remmelink, eds., trans., *Deshima Diaries*, 461.
59. Ibid., 288.

not win. In spite of this, many of the Satsuma samurai wanted to fight. They were pacified by their senior councilor, Hirata Yukie, who presented the venture as a matter of honor. Yes, Satsuma would accept this impossible challenge. Satsuma men would build the dams, they would divide the three great rivers, and in doing so, they would show the government and the nation what Satsuma samurai were made of.

On January 29, 1754, one thousand samurai said goodbye to their families and journeyed from Satsuma to Nōbi. Yukie headed for Osaka to raise funds. At Nōbi the samurai were joined by nearly ten thousand workmen from villages around Gifu. Work officially began on February 27. It did not go well. Heavy rains made conditions difficult from the start. Worse still, the floods of the previous year had left the locals with few provisions to spare for their visitors. The samurai were overworked and undernourished. Nevertheless, with honor on the line they insisted on tackling the most dangerous and difficult tasks for themselves. Bakufu officials, who had traveled from Edo to supervise the project, bullied them at every turn. These officials also kept an eye on the locals, forbidding them from selling discounted clothing to the samurai, and ordering them to report any anti-government talk. More floods in April led to more setbacks. Costs soared, tempers flared. The situation was defused somewhat after Yukie arrived from Osaka, where he had secured massive loans from local merchants. Yukie was a man of high moral character, as well as a skillful diplomatist. But as the project dragged on, he found himself trapped between his men, who resented their ill-treatment, and the bakufu supervisors, who complained of Satsuma truculence.

The first suicides came in the spring, just two months into the project. On April 14, two samurai, Nagayoshi Sōbe and Otogata Sadabuchi, were found dead in their lodgings. They had stabbed each other to death. They left no suicide note, and had divulged their intentions to no one. Since their section of the embankment had collapsed three times during the previous weeks, it was assumed that they had killed themselves out of shame, or in protest at bakufu mismanagement. Yukie did not report their deaths as suicides. Instead, he told officials that the two had succumbed to sickness.

As it turned out, sickness was the next problem. During the summer, hundreds of Satsuma men were afflicted with dysentery. Many died. Things became chaotic. More bellies were ripped, and Yukie could no longer conceal matters from his supervisors. This was the list of suicides in August:

August 3	Matsuzaki Nakazaemon
August 5	Tsuneyoshi Guntarō
August 8	Hachi Rōzaemon
August 9	Setoyama Ishisuke
August 14	Nomura Hachirōuemon
August 15	Hirayama Bokuuemon
August 19	Maeda Hyōemon
August 20	Tokuda Sukeuemon
August 21	Ōyama Ichibei
August 22	Hagiwara Kansuke; Sonoda Shinbei
August 23	(one death, name unknown)
August 24	Ishizuka Jinsuke
August 27	Hamajima Kiuemon
August 29	Nagayama Magoichi; Takigiku Heihachi[60]

The men's ages and ranks are unknown. In their reports to Edo, the supervisors recorded every one of these deaths as *kappuku* (suicide by tearing the stomach), rather than *seppuku*. This confirms that the term *seppuku* was reserved for officially sanctioned execution ceremonies, now normally performed without disembowelment. To indicate that the men had actually cut their stomachs, and that they had done so without official approval, the supervisors reached for a different word.

Yukie struggled to maintain morale as, one after another, his men eviscerated themselves. Although documentary evidence is scant—there were no suicide notes or valedictory speeches—these deaths appear to have been exceptionally gruesome. The samurai expressed their frustration and anger by committing bloody *ikon-bara*—grudge

60. Ōkuma, *Seppuku no rekishi*, 203–4.

suicides. None of the men sought kaishaku; each disemboweled himself alone, in his lodgings. This meant removing the sword from his
belly, and either thrusting it into his throat or allowing his chest to fall
onto the blade. That was easier said than done. Naitō Jūrōsaemon,
who stabbed himself in his room during the night, was still breathing
when a servant discovered him the next morning. He was treated by a
local doctor but died that afternoon. To colleagues who rushed round
to see him, Jūrōsaemon explained his reasons. The workmen under
his command had disregarded his instructions, causing a delay; he
was dying from shame at this failure, which he regarded as his own.
The doctor's report precisely states Jūrōsaemon's injuries:

1. Large horizontal incision across the abdomen, approximately 8 *sun* [9 inches] wide and 4 *sun* [5 inches] deep.
   Treatment: wound was sewn up and ointment was
   applied.
2. Two incisions in the right thyroid region, both small.
   Same treatment. Injuries clearly self-inflicted.[61]

In other words, Jūrōsaemon had performed ichimonji before stabbing himself twice in the throat. He survived for fourteen hours.

Subsequent deaths followed the same pattern. There was also one
suicide among the bakufu contingent. On the morning of January 14,
1755, Takenaka Denroku, a twenty-nine-year-old inspector, was found
dead in his room at a local inn. He was crumpled face-down in the
middle of the room, which was bespattered with blood. He had torn
open his stomach, completely removed his intestines, and flung them
about the room. We do not know whether Denroku died in support of
the Satsuma men, or to take the blame for some failure of his own.

The Kiso Anti-flood Project was finally completed on May 22,
1755. In all, eighty-four samurai were dead, nearly one out of every
ten who had left Satsuma. Thirty-two of these men had perished from
dysentery; fifty-two had ripped their bellies. Among the thousands of

61. Itō, *Hōreki chisui to Satsuma hanshi*, 191.

regional workmen, there were only two deaths: one from dysentery, one by drowning. The final bakufu report praised the Satsuma men for their perseverance. At an official ceremony on May 24, supervisors congratulated Yukie for his handling of the project, and presented him with an array of gifts. Yukie accepted their thanks, while declining the gifts. He wrote a letter to the lord of Satsuma, informing him that the project had been successfully completed. The next day he cut his stomach and died. He left no note, but it was accepted by all that he was bearing the blame for the deaths of so many of his men.

All the drama and tribulations notwithstanding, the project was hailed as a triumph. The dams were built, and any lingering problems had been solved by suicide. No one thought badly of men who ripped themselves up like this. Once the government contingent had returned to Edo, the locals built a shrine and prayed for the souls of the dead Satsuma samurai.

The 1800s: "Revere the Emperor, Expel the Barbarians!"

In the 1630s, under the third Tokugawa shogun, Iemitsu, the government had embarked on a program of semi-seclusion. Japanese citizens were not permitted to leave the archipelago, the penalty for infractions being death. Foreign visitors were unwelcome. Spanish and Portuguese traders were expelled from the Japanese islands; some Dutch who remained were confined to the Deshima trading station in Nagasaki. Japan was otherwise almost completely closed to Europe. Two centuries of isolation followed.

Conditions began to change around 1800. Russians, who were exploring Sakhalin and the Kuriles to the north of Japan, attempted to request supplies at Japanese ports. British expeditions to Japan did likewise. Their requests were generally denied. Some port authorities responded by opening fire. As foreign ships continued to stray into Japanese waters, the prevailing view was that the government was not dealing with the problem effectively. On July 8, 1853, four American warships sailed straight into Edo Bay, announcing themselves with cannon fire. The Americans demanded establishment of trade relations, hitherto restricted to the Dutch at Nagasaki. A month later, a Russian contingent arrived with similar demands. Almost overnight, the Japanese made the painful discovery that centuries of samurai tradition were no match for Western military science. Japan had no navy, few modern weapons, and her fighting men were under the scattered control of regional domains. The Americans and the Russians won their trading rights, and Japan began moving toward centralization. Within barely twenty-five years, Western rifles replaced swords and spears, and feudal militias were abolished in favor of a national army based on European models. The samurai accepted these and other momentous changes, though not without a predictable show of intractability.

Foreign encroachment was only one among numerous problems confronting the government. Decades of maladministration and failed economic reforms had badly undermined public confidence. Civil uprisings plagued Japan during the 1830s. Some of these disturbances were on an alarming scale, and government forces had difficulty repressing them. One consequence of this was that samurai in the employ of the government acquired a reputation for being weaker fighters than samurai in provincial domains.

Political sympathies began to shift toward the imperial household, which for centuries had occupied a symbolic position outside the realm of national affairs. But a new awareness of the outside world prompted Japanese scholars and intellectuals to look to their cultural roots. Some advocated a religious nativism based on literal readings of ancient texts. For instance, it was argued that while men everywhere saw the sun rise and set, only the Japanese were directly blessed by (and descended from) the sun goddess. The greatness and uniqueness of Japan stemmed from this divine lineage, embodied in the emperor, a living god. A refrain of nationalist tracts was "Our Japan is a sacred land." This rise in what might be termed cultural fundamentalism spawned a host of anti-government protestors, many of whom ripped their stomachs.

One of the first to do so was an imperialist named Takayama Hikokurō (1747–93). The son of a wealthy samurai family from Gunma, Hikokurō's sympathy for the imperial court derived from an early fascination with the *Taiheiki*, the medieval chronicle that tells how

Emperor Go-Daigo attempted to smash the hegemony of the Ashikaga
shoguns. After studies in Kyoto Hikokurō went out into the world to
promote imperial devotion. He traveled ceaselessly, involving himself
in various academic disputes relating to the Kyoto court. His most
notorious act of subversion was to decapitate three statues of the Ashikaga shoguns and display the heads on Sanjō Bridge, a customary
exhibition spot for executed criminals. Bakufu agents began tracking
him down. Hikokurō spent the first half of 1793 in hiding at a friend's
house in Kurume, and it was there, on August 4, that he committed
suicide. He was still alive when he was discovered, crumpled forward
with his sword in his hand. The wound went halfway across his stomach and his innards had spilled out. Eyewitnesses noted that he had
not bothered to free his shoulders from his kimono, and wondered
if this might have hindered him from completing the full motion.
Although Hikokurō had stabbed himself at noon, and successfully
severed both his long and short intestines, he did not expire until nine
o'clock the next morning. His last testament, entitled "Suicide Note
for my Descendants," is characteristically combative:

> I wandered the land, observing the condition of our
> nation, to ascertain the true state of things. But few would
> join me. Meanwhile the loathsome bureaucrats grew ever
> more powerful, and the Imperial Way faded each day.
> Angered by this, I secretly wished to restore the imperial
> court to power, and scoured the land for virtuous and
> upstanding men who would join me in that endeavor.
> Alas, it was not to be, and now the craving for justice that
> fills my belly feels ready to burst forth. Since I take no
> pleasure in a docile existence in this world, I have decided
> to slash my stomach. I have no regrets, since I act in the
> firm conviction that you will continue these efforts on my
> behalf and one day make them a reality, thereby bringing
> peace to my departed spirit.[62]

62. Takayama, *Takayama Hikokurō zenshū*, 4:356. Hikokurō had three daughters but no

Hikokurō uses the graphic term *tofuku* ("stomach-slash") for effect here; *seppuku*, so familiar from court judgments, smacked too much of officialdom. Hikokurō's suicide took his friends by surprise, and appears to have been intended as a spontaneous expression of the depth of his convictions rather than as a specific protest. His death had more impact than anything he had accomplished while alive, as he surely knew it would. Hikokurō was one of the first samurai thinkers to make imperial devotion synonymous with morality, and to seal that belief with death. He was to have many imitators.

The sense of moral crisis so forcefully articulated by Hikokurō is also apparent in Bushido treatises written around this time. Shame is replacing death as the leitmotif. Rikimaru Tōzan's *Martial Enlightenment* (Bugaku keimō) of 1802 makes no mention of self-sacrificing servitude, and is concerned chiefly with combating decadence. Prominent among Tōzan's "Seventeen Shameful Things for the Samurai" is the danger of "suffocating in the pleasures of female company."[63] Yamaoka Shunmei concludes his *Thoughts on Belly-ripping* with these doleful observations:

> People today, with more than a hundred years of peace behind them, have forgotten how to prepare for battle. They are too cautious to confront matters resolutely and with total commitment, as demanded by the ancient tradition of suicide [*jigai*]. Stomach-cutting [*seppuku*] is a spectacular technique; but these days a kaishaku always cuts off the head. Truly, the martial ways are being forgotten.[64]

Elsewhere there is a conspicuous use of the past tense. In *Principles of the Samurai Way* (Shidō yōron) of 1835, Confucian scholar Saitō Setsudō admonishes his readers with nostalgic flashbacks:

> A samurai who knows no shame is no samurai at all. In olden times, shame was the most terrible injury a samurai

sons, which perhaps explains the title of his suicide note.

63. *Bugaku keimō*. In Inoue, ed., *Bushidō shū*, 2:415–16.

64. Yamaoka, *Hara-kiri kō*, 165.

could contemplate, and he would rather die than suffer it. If charged with a crime and sentenced to death, he considered it an honor to be permitted to cut his stomach. He could not countenance the thought of being bound with rope—he was better off being a corpse. A samurai who knowingly commits shameful acts is worthless. He does not know right from wrong. He has no inkling of even the basic concepts of Bushido.[65]

Anger at the "shameful" conduct of lawmakers and bureaucrats soon resulted in violence. During the 1850s, assassinations were a regular feature of Japanese political life. That decade ended with the assassination of Ii Naosuke, a powerful bakufu official who bore the title of *tairō*, "Great Elder." In 1858, Naosuke signed a commercial agreement with America without obtaining authorization from the emperor, who was known to oppose the treaty. Naosuke was also responsible for a draconian purge of over one hundred anti-treaty agitators. A band of samurai from Mito, whose lord had been vociferously hostile to the treaty, vowed to kill Naosuke. To avoid implicating their lord, they left his service and became rōnin. They then said goodbye to their families and gathered in Edo to plan their attack. On March 24, 1860, they ambushed Naosuke's entourage as it approached the Sakurada gate of Edo Castle. Unusually for that time of year there was a thick snowfall; for that reason, Naosuke's bodyguards were carrying their swords in protective covers. This delayed the speed of their reaction and cost eight of them their lives; thirteen other guards were wounded. In the confusion, one of the rōnin was able to drag Naosuke from his palanquin by his topknot and chop off his head.

The aftermath of the killing furnishes us with a good example of the awkward coexistence of the two modes of seppuku, judicial and voluntary. Four of the rōnin, including ringleaders Takahashi Taichirō and Arima Jizaemon, delivered Naosuke's head to the house of another government official—a gesture of contempt. All four then

65. *Shidō yōron*. In Inoue, ed., *Bushidō shū*, 2: 473–74.

cut their bellies in front of the house gate and bled to death in the snow. The rest of the rōnin band fled and went into hiding, but were eventually captured; some died while resisting arrest, those taken alive were tortured to death in captivity. On the opposing side, the guards who had sustained severe wounds were exiled or demoted; the lightly wounded were ordered to cut their stomachs; those who had emerged completely unscathed were charged with cowardice, and consequently forfeited the right to die by their own hand. These men, thirteen in all, were decapitated without honor—as were their fathers, uncles, brothers, and sons. Confucian scholars noted that the ruling adhered to vintage samurai logic: only the brave were permitted to cut their stomachs. But in that case, were the assassins who voluntarily gutted themselves in the snow not the bravest of all? Either way, for many commentators, the dismal performance by the bodyguards confirmed the decline of martial standards in general, and among bakufu retainers in particular.

Another factor in the rise of anti-government activism was the philosophy of the Chinese scholar Wang Yangming (1472–1529), which had secured a following in Japan during the second half of the seventeenth century. Wang had advocated a subjective idealism grounded in the conviction that knowledge and action are one. Knowledge consists not of external facts but of knowing how to act, and man exists only insofar as he realizes himself through pure action. Only passionate sincerity, carried forward into action *whatever the outcome*, endows him with value. While these ideas translated easily to the Tokugawa samurai virtues of purity and righteousness, Wang's refusal to tolerate any disjunction between emotion and action (between words and deeds), and his consequent insistence that man's conscience must be expressed in action, were radical. In Wang's system, as interpreted by Tokugawa thinkers, there is no courage other than displays of courage, no passion other than that expressed in passionate deeds, no heroism other than that manifested in heroes. A man who does not experience passion, or perform courageous and heroic acts, cannot claim to carry within himself unfulfilled potentialities or untapped heroic qualities; he is nothing more than the sum of his actions.

Japanese educators quickly perceived the subversive dangers of Wang's thought, and for a time his name was taboo in Edo schools. But by the 1800s he had many followers. Although Wang bears no direct relation to the suicide tradition, his doctrine, interpreted by many Japanese as one of active nihilism, inspired more than a few suicidal revolutionaries. Among them were Ōshio Heihachirō (1793–1837), Yoshida Shōin (1830–59), and Saigō Takamori (1828–1877). Each of these three men made a close study of Wang's writings.[66] None committed seppuku, though two came very close. Shōin, an imperialist and inveterate troublemaker in the mold of Takayama Hikokurō, was executed at the age of twenty-nine. Government officials refused to let him perform the seppuku ritual, and instead ordered him beheaded in jail. Heihachirō, a retired Osaka policeman, led an uprising in protest at economic hardships inflicted on the townsfolk by government maladministration. Authorities crushed the revolt in a single day. After three months on the run, Heihachirō killed himself when government soldiers surrounded his hideout. He set fire to the house, and no doubt would have cut his stomach if time had allowed it. But with soldiers at the door, he apparently perished by stabbing himself in the throat. His charred corpse was retrieved from the ashes and preserved in salt. After an inquiry that lasted many months, whatever remained of Ōshio Heihachirō was dragged through the streets behind a donkey cart and strung up at the Osaka execution ground. Many of his fellow rebels were crucified. Saigō Takamori rose from lowly origins in Satsuma to become one of the most powerful members of the government in the 1860s. A fiery, uncontrollable figure, he won early fame as a military commander; in a subsequent career as a statesman, his repeated political turnabouts made him many enemies. The vicissitudes of Saigō's career were correspondingly hectic: he was banished twice, pardoned twice, went from national hero to traitor and, after a third pardon, back to hero again. After leading a violent anti-government insurrection, the so-called Satsuma Rebellion of 1877, he died

66. A poem by Shōin perhaps best encapsulates the extremist interpretation of Wang's thought: "To know full well what will happen / and to do it all the same / —that is the samurai spirit." (Seki, *Yoshida Shōin: Hito to kotoba*, 134).

on a Kagoshima hillside in a hail of bullets. An admiring populace had dubbed him the Great Saigō, and all his supporters were eager to hear of his glorious seppuku suicide. Some could not wait. Several weeks before his death, Saigō's spirit was spotted ascending to heaven from the coast of southern Kyushu. (It was a small comet.) Full-color woodblock prints of him driving the sword into his belly were on sale within hours of the final battlefield bulletins. The truth—that Saigō had been felled by a single bullet, and, having no strength left to cut his stomach, was decapitated on the spot by a tearful comrade—took years to seep into the public consciousness.

Samurai terrorists did not always rip themselves up after an attack as Ii Naosuke's killers had done. As hostility toward government reforms increased, so did rebel boldness. In the spring of 1861 a group of samurai from the Tosa domain in Shikoku swore a blood-oath of loyalty to each other and to the emperor, and formed a society they called Tosa Kinnō, the Tosa Imperial Loyalists. Basing themselves in Kyoto, they began a concerted anti-bakufu campaign. This principally involved the assassination of bakufu supporters. One noteworthy success was the murder of Yoshida Tōyō, a pro-bakufu Tosa leader, in May 1862. The Loyalists did not commit suicide after their attacks, and when the ringleaders were ambushed by police agents in the winter of 1863, all allowed themselves to be captured alive.

The head of the group was Takechi Hanpeita (1829–65), a tall, handsome man of noble birth, and one of Tosa's strongest swordsmen. Hanpeita was well educated and rigidly moral. Despite his comparative wealth he favored an austere lifestyle, shunning luxuries and frivolous pleasures. Hanpeita was a man of extraordinary charisma, and the substantial public support enjoyed by the Loyalists was mostly to his credit. But the death-drive was strong in Hanpeita. He often talked of the glorious seppuku that he believed would be his destiny, and boasted to his men that, when the time came, he would slit his belly no fewer than three times.

With many of his men still on the run, Hanpeita initially denied involvement in the Tōyō assassination. Out of respect for Hanpeita's high birth, his interrogators did not torture him. Instead they tortured his men, often in the adjacent cell. Letters written by Hanpeita's wife during these months reveal that she attempted to smuggle poison into the jail several times, in the hope that he could pass it to his men.

By the summer of 1865, after twenty months of interrogation and torture, officials had the information they required to secure a death sentence for Hanpeita. But there was uncertainty about the mode of execution. Hanpeita and his supporters naturally hoped for a seppuku ruling. Officials delivered the verdict to him in his cell on the morning of July 3. For his "contempt for authority" and his "flagrant mockery of national law" he was condemned to death. As for the method: "On the evening of this same day, you will be taken to the north corner of the Minami Kaijō garden, where you will execute yourself by cutting your stomach, on a flooring of boards or straw mats laid down for the aforementioned purpose."[67]

Authorities could not risk the debacle of a shoddy execution. Accordingly, the ceremony was conducted with impeccable attention to protocol, and with noticeably more pomp than was usual. At precisely eight o'clock, guards led Hanpeita from his cell to the execution ground. Thirty witnesses and inspectors sat in a semicircle around the stage, which was covered with fresh tatami mats and illuminated with tall candlesticks. On a small cedar table, the finest dagger from the Tosa collection awaited him. Hanpeita, dressed in white death robes tied with a silk sash, looked sickly and emaciated. Two kaishaku, one a close friend, the other Hanpeita's nephew, followed him to the center of the mats. All three knelt and bowed as an official read out the sentence. Hanpeita picked up the dagger, examined it carefully, and returned it to the tray. He removed his arms from the sleeves of his kimono and adjusted the position of his sash. Taking the dagger in his hands a second time, he tightened the cord that was wrapped around the hilt. Without a pause, he plunged the blade into the top left side of his abdomen. He cut across to the right, removed the blade, and began another cut. He succeeded in making three full cuts across his stomach. After the third he appeared to lose strength, and collapsed forward, dropping the dagger. His shoulders crumpled until he was supporting himself on his forearms; in this position, it was impossible for his kaishaku to strike at his neck. Still on their knees, the two men ran him through with their swords from each side. Witnesses counted six deep stabs. The entire performance was accomplished with great deliberation and in complete silence: at no time did Hanpeita cry out or utter a sound. The only words he had spoken were those he offered to his kaishaku seconds before stabbing himself: *go-kurō*— "Thank you [for your trouble]."[68]

Takechi Hanpeita's corpse was carried in a litter to his home, where his wife and family members were waiting. The train of mourners at his funeral the next day was ten miles long.

The terrorist tactics of groups such as the Tosa Loyalists were politically ineffectual. Reforms followed one after another, and the influx of foreigners accelerated. Many samurai could not tolerate their presence: armed white men were walking the streets of Edo with impunity. The situation became more precarious when the young emperor Kōmei, who was known to oppose the policy of making trade treaties with foreigners, broke with centuries of protocol by expressing his opinion publicly. In March 1863 he issued an order to "expel all barbarians." The government ignored him, but by the time of Kōmei's sudden death from smallpox in January 1867, the damage was done. Samurai who were already fuming at the presence of foreigners felt that they could commit acts of violence against them with a clear conscience, knowing that they were acting in accordance with the emperor's wishes. Pompe van Meerdevoort, a Dutch naval physician who resided in Japan from 1857 to 1862, noted the xenophobia in his journal:

> In those districts where there are many soldiers (so-called military servants, or *samurai*), in Edo, Kyoto, Kagoshima, etc., every morning several dead bodies are found in the streets, victims of duels or because drunken military men tested their swords on them for bets. Many military men,

68. Ibid., 332–35.

especially when they are drunk, show more resemblance
to wild animals running loose than to defenders of the
law; the majority of them can lay no claim to education
and erudition. When coming across one of them who is
drunk, it is often evident from the brutal expression in his
eyes when he looks at Europeans that he would gladly like
to test his sword on them too. At such meetings it would
be wise to avoid misunderstanding.[69]

It was only a matter of time. On September 14, 1862, Shimazu
Hisamitsu, the retired lord of Satsuma, was returning to Kyoto from
Edo with a guard of seven hundred samurai. Four British visitors on
horseback met them at a crossing on the Tōkaidō road outside Yoko-
hama. Rather than wait for the Satsuma procession to pass by—the
polite and obvious thing to do—one of the four Britons, a business-
man named Charles Richardson, decided to push his way through the
samurai line. It was the last decision he ever made.

The killing of Charles Richardson—he was slashed and stabbed so
many times that the coroner could not determine which wound was the
fatal one—caused outrage.[70] The British Foreign Secretary demanded
the execution of the murderers and a financial indemnity from the
bakufu; when neither was forthcoming, British warships bombarded
the city of Kagoshima, the main port of the Satsuma domain. There
were more assaults on foreigners in the following months. While some
were genuine misunderstandings, others were premeditated attacks. In
October 1863 three samurai ambushed a French diplomat at Idogaya
and killed one of his bodyguards. Two British army officers were
murdered in Kamakura a year later. In February 1868 shots were fired

69. Wittermans and Bowers, trans., *Doctor on Desima*, 54.

70. A report into the incident identified the first samurai to strike as Narahara Kizaemon.
Despite the furor that followed the killing, neither Kizaemon nor any of the other guards
implicated were ordered to cut their stomachs. Kizaemon seems to have been quite a fire-
brand. When the British struck at Kagoshima to persuade the Satsuma leadership to pay
compensation, Kizaemon, posing as a watermelon vendor, attempted to board one of the
British ships; his plan—to sabotage the vessel and commit suicide aboard it—failed. A year
later, he was killed in a fight with pro-bakufu supporters outside the imperial palace in
Kyoto.

during an altercation in Kobe between samurai of the Bizen domain and a group of French sailors. Sir Harry Parkes, the British consul general, survived three assassination attempts.

In those cases where the attackers were captured and executed, foreigners were sometimes present at the executions. Journalistic reports of Japanese executions appeared in the European press. The following account by Charles Wirgman of the execution of Shimizu Seiji, one of three rōnin condemned for the Kamakura murders, was printed in the *Illustrated London News* on March 18, 1865:

> The criminal was mounted on a pack-horse and promenaded through the town. His sentence was written on a large flag carried before him, and also on a board. A guard of twelve Japanese soldiers, with fixed bayonets, marched in front; and the rear was brought up by two mounted officers and a crowd of Europeans on horseback. The streets were crowded with Japanese and Europeans. The murderer, who was an athletic man, with a fine head and a determined expression, sang all the time and looked about him with an air of indifference. At the end of a street he smoked a pipe and had something to eat; then he was taken to the execution-ground, where bonfires and torches lighted up the scene; but the execution was put off till next day, because it was too late for the garrison to attend. The man was then conducted back to prison; and next morning, at nine o'clock, the whole garrison—Royal marines and light infantry of the 20th Regiment, under the command of Colonel Penrose; and half a battery of artillery, under the command of Lieutenant Wood—marched out to the execution ground, where they formed a square. The Japanese troops were drawn up on the road. After waiting some time, the prisoner, escorted as before, but carried in a *norimon* or litter, made his appearance. He had some wine and food and then walked to the straw, on which he knelt, with the hole for his head to fall into in front of

him. He had made a request that he should not be blind-
folded, which was granted, and also that his body might
be buried and sent to the place he named, and that a tab-
let should be placed over his tomb. After speaking to the
executioner, he sang or yelled out a long recitation, which
no one seems to have understood, and turned to the executioner, who had his sword ready to strike. Saying, "Wait
a little," he settled himself with his head over the hole,
and said, "Now!" The sword came down, but only severed
a part of his neck; so that the executioner had to make
three cuts before the head was off. A gun was then fired,
and the head was taken, in a mat bag, to be exposed at the
entrance of the town.[71]

Seiji had offered no explanation for the murders other than
his anger at the admittance of foreigners to Japan, and showed no
remorse. He did not turn himself in, but was captured after a three-day
pursuit. For these reasons he was not permitted to perform seppuku.
His rōnin status may also have been a factor. Since no collective honor
was at stake, the authorities were at liberty to make an example of
him. Their sole concession to his samurai rank was a glass of saké.
Nonetheless, foreign observers discerned something exceptional in
Seiji's bearing, and were unanimously won over by it. A German man
in the crowd, Rudolph Lindau, wrote of him: "His intention to die
without weakness in the face of his enemies could be read clearly on
all his features." Even the official report of the British Legation noted
that the samurai "tendered his neck to the executioner with the greatest imaginable indifference." Lindau concluded, "If his intention had
been to show the foreigners that a Japanese could go to meet death
calmly, he had attained his end. He had compelled the admiration of
everyone who saw him."[72]

71. Williams, *The Kamakura Murders*, 96–98.
72. Ibid., 98–99.

The confrontation at Kobe was much more contentious. Two French sailors had cut through a procession of hundreds of Bizen samurai. A Bizen commander drew his sword, and in the ensuing commotion his men fired shots in the direction of the foreign settlements. Three days of turmoil ensued. Order was restored when a sentence of seppuku, endorsed by the emperor himself, was handed down upon the commander, whose name was Taki Zenzaburō.

Representatives from the legations of Britain, Holland, Italy, and Germany attended the seppuku ceremony, held on February 9, 1868. Two young British diplomats, Ernest Satow and Algernon Mitford, subsequently published reports of what they had witnessed. These are the most detailed eyewitness descriptions of seppuku in existence, and are often quoted by Japanese historians. Here is Satow's version:

> We were guided to the Buddhist temple of Eifukuji at Hyogo, arriving there at a quarter to ten. Strong guards were posted in the courtyard and in the ante-chambers. We were shown into a room, where we had to squat on the matted floor for about three-quarters of an hour; during this interval we were asked whether we had any questions to put to the condemned man, and also for a list of our names. At half-past ten we were conducted into the principal hall of the temple, and asked to sit down on the right hand side of the dais in front of the altar. Then the seven Japanese witnesses took their places. After we had sat quietly thus for about ten minutes footsteps were heard approaching along the veranda. The condemned man, a tall Japanese of gentleman-like bearing and aspect, entered on the left side, accompanied by his *kaishaku* or best man, and followed by two others, apparently holding the same office. Taki [Zenzaburō] was dressed in blue *kami-shimo* of hempen cloth; the *kaishaku* wore war surcoats (*jimbaori*). Coming before the Japanese witnesses they prostrated themselves, the bow being returned, and then the same ceremony was exchanged with us. Then

the condemned man was led to a red sheet of felt-cloth
laid on the dais before the altar; on this he squatted, after
performing two bows, one at a distance, the other close
to the altar. With the calmest deliberation he took his
seat on the red felt, choosing the position which would
afford him the greatest convenience for falling forward.
A man dressed in black with a light grey hempen mantle
then brought in the dirk wrapped in paper on a small
unpainted wooden stand, and with a bow placed it in
front of him. He took it up in both hands, raised it to his
forehead and laid it down again with a bow. This is the
ordinary Japanese gesture of thankful reception of a gift.
Then in a distinct voice, very much broken, not by fear
or emotion, but as it seemed reluctance to acknowledge
an act of which he was ashamed—declared that he alone
was the person who on the fourth of February had outrageously at Kobe ordered fire to be opened on foreigners as
they were trying to escape, that for having committed this
offence he was going to rip up his bowels, and requested
all present to be witnesses. He next divested himself of his
upper garments by withdrawing his arms from the sleeves,
the long ends of which he tucked under his legs to prevent
his body from falling backward. The body was thus quite
naked to below the navel. He then took the dirk in his
right hand, grasping it just close to the point, and after
stroking down the front of his chest and belly inserted
the point as far down as possible and drew it across to the
right side, the position of his clothes still fastened by the
girth preventing our seeing the wound. Having done this
he with great deliberation bent his body forward, throwing the head back so as to render the neck a fair object
for the sword. The one *kaishaku* who had accompanied
him round the two rows of witnesses to make his bows to
them, had been crouching on his left hand a little behind
him with drawn sword poised in the air from the moment

the operation commenced. He now sprang suddenly and delivered a blow the sound of which was like thunder. The head dropped down on to the matted floor, blood from the arteries pouring out and forming a pool. When the blood vessels had spent themselves all was over.[73]

There are indications of Bizen umbrage here. It was highly unusual, if not altogether discourteous, to keep an official witness waiting for forty-five minutes. Satow himself notes Zenzaburō's somewhat disobliging manner. Needless to say, the usual ornamental niceties, such as refreshments, were not proffered. Zenzaburō was no urban dandy or docile bureaucrat. He was an officer in the Bizen guard corps, and his self-execution was in every respect a martial ceremony.

Mitford's account appeared in London's *Cornhill Magazine* in November 1869 under the title "The Execution by Hara-Kiri":

A further delay then ensued, after which we were invited to follow the Japanese witnesses into the *hondo* or main hall of the temple, where the ceremony was to be performed. It was an imposing scene. A large hall with a high roof supported by dark pillars of wood. From the ceiling hung a profusion of those huge gilt lamps and ornaments peculiar to Buddhist temples. In front of the high altar, where the floor, covered with beautiful white mats, is raised some three or four inches from the ground, was laid a rug of scarlet felt. Tall candles placed at regular intervals gave out a dim mysterious light, just sufficient to let all the proceedings be seen. The seven Japanese took their place on the left of the raised floor, the seven foreigners on the right. No other person was present.

After an interval of a few minutes of anxious suspense, Taki Zenzaburō, a stalwart man, thirty-two years of age, with a noble air, walked into the hall attired in his dress of

73. Satow, *A Diplomat in Japan*, 344–45.

ceremony . . . the *kaishaku* was a pupil of Taki Zenzaburō,
and was selected by the friends of the latter from among
their own number for his skill in swordsmanship.

With the *kaishaku* on his left hand, Taki Zenzaburō
advanced slowly toward the Japanese witnesses, and the
two bowed before them, then drawing near to the foreigners they saluted us in the same way, perhaps even with
more deference: in each case the salutation was ceremoni-
ously returned. Slowly, and with great dignity, the condemned man mounted on to the raised floor, prostrated
himself before the high altar twice, and seated himself on
the felt carpet with his back to the high altar, the *kaishaku*
crouching on his left-hand side. One of the three attendant officers then came forward, bearing a stand of the
kind used in temples for offerings, on which, wrapped in
paper, lay the *wakizashi*, the short sword or dirk of the Japanese, nine inches and a half in length, with a point and
an edge as sharp as a razor's. This he handed, prostrating
himself, to the condemned man, who received it reverently, raising it to his head with both hands, and placed it
in front of himself.

After another profound obeisance, Taki Zenzaburō, in
a voice which betrayed just so much emotion and hesitation as might be expected from a man who is making a
painful confession, but with no sign of either in his face or
manner, spoke as follows:

"I, and I alone, unwarrantably gave the order to fire on
the foreigners at Kobe, and again as they tried to escape.
For this crime I disembowel myself, and I beg you who are
present to do me the honor of witnessing the act."

Bowing once more, the speaker allowed his upper garments to skip down to his girdle, and remained naked
to the waist. Carefully, according to custom, he tucked
his sleeves under his knees to prevent himself from falling backwards; for a noble Japanese gentleman should

die falling forwards. Deliberately, with a steady hand, he took the dirk that lay before him; he looked at it wistfully, almost affectionately; for a moment he seemed to collect his thoughts for the last time, and then stabbing himself deeply below the waist on the left-hand side, he drew the dirk slowly across to the right side, and, turning it in the wound, gave a slight cut upwards. During this sickeningly painful operation he never moved a muscle of his face. When he drew out the dirk, he leaned forward and stretched out his neck; an expression of pain for the first time crossed his face, but he uttered no sound. At that moment the *kaishaku*, who, still crouching by his side, had been keenly watching his every movement, sprang to his feet, poised the sword for a second in the air; there was a flash, a heavy, ugly, thud, a crashing fall; with one blow the head had been severed from the body.

A dead silence followed, broken only by the hideous noise of the blood throbbing out of the inert heap before us, which but a moment before had been a brave and chivalrous man. It was horrible.

The *kaishaku* made a low bow, wiped his sword with a piece of paper which he had made ready for the purpose, and retired from the raised floor; the stained dirk was solemnly borne away, a bloody proof of the execution.[74]

Mitford included this article, along with some "hara-kiri" anecdotes and an abridged translation of Kudō Yukihiro's *Records of Suicide by Sword*, in his collection *Tales of Old Japan*, published in London in 1871. The book was a popular success, and familiarized Europeans with the concept of "hara-kiri." Mitford appears to have been ignorant of the term *seppuku*. Even Satow, whose Japanese was excellent, elected to stick with *harakiri* in his memoir. It is pertinent to note that both men formed the opinion that the ritual suicide was a noble and

74. Mitford, *Tales of Old Japan*, 356–59.

dignified death. Against the charge, voiced in some English newspapers, that Christians should not have attended such a barbaric spectacle, Satow offered this retort: "I was proud to feel that I had not shrunk from witnessing a punishment which I did my best to bring about. It was no disgusting exhibition, but a most decent and decorous ceremony, and far more respectable than what our own countrymen were in the habit of producing for the entertainment of the public in the front of Newgate Prison." Mitford especially was won over. In public lectures after his return to England he hailed "harakiri" as "the sublimation of all those ideas of honor which constitute the very essence of chivalry."[75]

To others, however, it was becoming clear that the emphasis on chivalry-in-death rather than chivalry-in-deed fostered a reckless belligerence and made nationalist zealots impossible to control. There would be no improvement in security as long as the penalty for attacking foreigners was glorious death. The incident that convinced Western diplomats on this point occurred one month after the Kobe confrontation, at the port of Sakai, about three miles from Osaka. The events of March 8, 1868, which the Japanese delicately refer to as the "Incident at Sakai," constituted in fact a small-scale massacre: eleven French sailors shot dead in cold blood by samurai from the domain of Tosa.

At around noon on that day, a group of Tosa guardsmen, who were armed with both swords and rifles, intercepted the party of the French vice-consul as he was walking from Osaka to Sakai, where a steam launch was due to meet him. Despite having obtained official authorization for their visit, the vice-consul and his group feared for their safety, and temporarily sought refuge in a local house. The steam-launch arrived on time, and waited. During the wait, thirteen French sailors from the steam-launch boarded a skiff and rowed ashore. Since Sakai was officially closed to foreigners, the arrival of the Frenchmen caused some commotion. The Tosa side later claimed that the sailors had been misbehaving and "out of control." It was alleged that they had broken into a private residence, where they "intimidated

75. Mitford, *A Tragedy in Stone*, 131.

and insulted a number of young ladies."[76] But townsfolk testified that the sailors had done nothing more than purchase some fruit, which appears to have been the purpose of their brief expedition. There was no question, however, that by landing without a permit the French sailors were in breach of the law. News of the "foreign invasion" quickly reached Tosa command, and two teams of guards sprinted to the scene. Within minutes of the guards' arrival, eleven Frenchmen were dead. Although the Japanese and French accounts differ in regard to many points, there was no disagreement over how the sailors died. They were shot as they scrambled into the skiff and attempted to row back to their ship. The Tosa samurai, some firing from a bridge, others from the shoreline, had no difficulty picking off their targets. The youngest Frenchman killed was nineteen, the others were all in their twenties. None was armed.

The French consul general in Japan, Léon Roches, bayed for blood. To the bakufu he presented a list of demands that included the execution of the culprits and sizeable financial compensation for the bereaved families. The bakufu conceded. Due to the large number of Tosa guards involved, however, the apportioning of individual blame was problematic. It was decreed that twenty men must cut their stomachs. The captains of the two units volunteered immediately. Eighteen guardsmen, nine from each unit, were then selected by drawing lots. The executions were set for March 19 at Myōkokuji, Sakai's oldest temple. Roches declined to attend in person, and sent one of his captains, Bergasse du Petit-Thouars, as his representative.[77]

Du Petit-Thouars and twenty of his men arrived at Myōkokuji at two o'clock, anticipating a brisk round of beheadings. However, with twenty seppuku suicides to be performed consecutively, and with swords, shroud, and mats being replaced each time, the entire ceremony was scheduled to last several hours. Du Petit-Thouars described the ceremony in his journal, published posthumously fifty years later:

76. Sasaki Kaizō, *Senshū Sakai-to hanshi rekkyo jikki*, 36.

77. Japanese historians invariably place Roches at the execution ground. This is erroneous. In his journal Du Petit-Thouars makes it clear that he, and not Roches, was in attendance.

A bell rang to announce the time for redressal. The court-yard was surrounded by a fence and partitioned into a small room by columns covered with a large white curtain (the color of mourning) bearing the coat of arms of the clan whose vassals were on guard. On one side, two wide podiums were provided, one of which was for the Japa-nese officials whose duty it was to supervise the execution. To the front was a square space laid with tatami mats, over which was arranged a large white shroud, and above that, strips of red cloth. This space was protected from sun and rain. The military contingent sat on the right, with the tower holding the condemned on the left.

An official appeared immediately before each execution, slowly carrying a small wooden stand on which lay the dag-ger that the condemned man was to use to commit hara-kiri. He placed it on the shroud, and withdrew, at which point the condemned man appeared. The official confirmed the man's identity, read to him some sort of document announcing his sentence, and made a deep bow. The offi-cial who had positioned the stand then came forward again, greeted the man, and directed him to the exact spot where he would be executed. The two approached slowly with the executioner following behind them. When they reached the edge of the tatami, the official bowed once more to the con-demned, showed him the dagger, and told him where to kneel. When the man made a gesture of agreement, the offi-cial restraightened his back and proceeded slowly forward. The condemned kneeled roughly in the center. If he himself was an official, he planted his lord's flag in front of him. He moved the stand closer to him, then slowly and quietly removed all his garments one by one, picked up the dagger, and cut horizontally across his stomach. His entrails spew out, he collapses.

When the condemned man took up the dagger, the exe-cutioner standing directly behind him gripped his sword with both hands and delivered a single blow. The head and torso were usually severed. The executioner then looked at the body, and squatted over him. If the head was not completely severed and the body was still moving, he delivered a second strike. Once the body had completely stopped moving, the executioner slowly rose, wiped his sword, and returned it to its scabbard. He then bowed deeply to the corpse, and returned to his position among the others. Eight men cleared away the corpse and the tools used in the execution, wrapping them up in straw matting and a large shroud. Preparations then began for the next execution.[78]

The official Japanese account of the executions naturally depicts things from the Tosa viewpoint, and includes many details that are absent from Du Petit-Thouars's curt outline. Informed that foreigners would be attending the ceremony, the Tosa supervisors gave their men a pep talk, urging them to do their best "to startle and impress the Frenchmen with our valiant Tosa spirit."[79] Upon arriving at Myōkokuji, the twenty samurai strolled around the temple grounds. This gave them an opportunity to examine the twenty graves that had been dug for them. Meanwhile, guards posted at the temple gate were busy holding back a crowd of excited onlookers. A sudden rain shower then delayed commencement until four o'clock.

The first samurai to take the stage, a captain named Minoura Inokichi, set the tone. Holding the dagger to his belly, he glared at Du Petit-Thouars's group and shouted, "Oi, you despicable Frenchmen! We're not dying for your sake. We die for our emperor and for Japan. Now watch how a Japanese man cuts his belly. You won't want to eat meat after this, Frenchmen!"[80] Clearly this was going to be a seppuku ceremony like none before it.

Such impertinence would never have been tolerated under normal circumstances; the kaishaku would instantly have lopped off the

78. Du Petit-Thouars, *Furansu kanchō no mita Sakai jiken*, 30–31.
79. Sasaki, *Senshū Sakai-to hanshi rekkyo jikki*, 44.
80. Ibid., 47.

offending head. But here, before an audience of foreigners, normal
rules did not apply. At the execution of Shimizu Seiji mentioned earlier, a member of the crowd jotted down these words from Seiji's final
outburst: "These are indeed bad times for Japan when a samurai must
die merely because he cut down a foreigner."[81] No doubt the Tosa
samurai shared this sentiment. Their resentment and frustration were
manifest before and during the ceremony. The only achievable solution was to aim for "aggressive" suicides akin to those of the Sengoku
period, where a vanquished warrior defied his enemies by contemptuously self-destructing before their eyes.

Such, at least, was the hope of the Tosa samurai. However, as
hinted at in Du Petit-Thouars' account, the ceremony was marred by
incompetence on the part of the kaishaku. There were twenty of them,
one for each of the condemned; fewer than half successfully decapitated their man with a single chop. The Japanese report makes no
attempt to conceal this fact. This was the messy end of Inokichi, whose
kaishaku required three strikes to finish him off:

> Inokichi bravely ripped himself open with two crossed
> cuts. Then, thrusting his hand inside the wound, he pulled
> out a lump of his entrails and glared again at the French
> observers as if about to fling his guts at them. Flustered by
> this, his kaishaku, a man named Mabuchi Momotarō, hur-
> riedly stepped forward and struck; but his aim was clumsy,
> and the blade only achieved a shallow wound to the top
> the head. Inokichi roared at him, "Steady yourself, Mabu-
> chi!" The second strike cut deep into his neck, and with a
> sharp ripping sound the head toppled forward—but only
> partially, for it was not completely severed. Inokichi, now
> drenched in his own blood, was able to scream: "I'm not
> dead! Cut again, cut again!" His voice echoed far beyond
> the execution area to the streets outside. Everyone watch-
> ing was mortified, particularly the French, who were very

81. Williams, *The Kamakura Murders*, 97.

obviously scared out of their wits. When Inokichi reached again into his belly in an attempt to put an end to his torments, the Frenchmen turned sickly pale and made the most peculiar noises, such as *Oooo* and *Arrrr*. They were squirming in their seats as Mabuchi landed his third strike, which was successful. Thus Minoura Inokichi was dead. He was twenty-four years of age.[82]

The farce continued when the kaishaku for the next man, Nishimura Saheiji, also struck too soon, before Saheiji had time to lean forward and steady himself; the head flew six yards to the front. Ōishi Jinkichi, a sergeant who was fourth to die, gutted himself magnificently, but his kaishaku ruined the moment by failing to sever the head after seven attempts. This inept display culminated with the kaishaku kneeling beside Jinkichi and carving through his neck with a short sword.

The ceremony proceeded in this manner, frenzied belly-rip followed by clumsy decapitation, until, as the eleventh corpse was being cleared away, Du Petit-Thouars decided that enough was enough. He had been sitting for over two hours, yet the ceremony had barely passed the halfway point. Through his interpreter he told the Japanese supervisors that he was leaving, and that he would not be demanding the deaths of the remaining nine men. Du Petit-Thouars intended this as a gesture of goodwill. He deemed justice to have been served, at least numerically: for their complicity in the murder of eleven French sailors, eleven Tosa samurai had now forfeited their lives. Ignoring the protestations of the Japanese organizers, Du Petit-Thouars and his entourage walked out.

Du Petit-Thouars' premature withdrawal was a publicity disaster. Apart from the breach of etiquette—it was unheard of for an official witness to march out of a seppuku ceremony—the stunt did nothing for the image of foreign warriors. Sasaki Kaizō, the scholar who prepared the official Japanese report, duly entitled the relevant section "The Flight of the Frenchmen." According to Sasaki, Du Petit-Thouars

---

82. Sasaki, *Senshū Sakai-to hanshi rekkyo jikki*, 47–48.

was looking "decidedly pale and queasy"; he was "sweating profusely" and was "unsteady on his feet." Given the strong anti-French bias of Sasaki's report, we can assume a fair degree of exaggeration here. Considering that Du Petit-Thouars had patiently observed eleven disembowelments, it seems unlikely that he should have been afflicted with a sudden bout of queasiness just before number twelve. Satow and Mitford, who were not military men, had suffered no such discomfort at Eifukuji. Sensitive to accusations of squeamishness, in his own account Du Petit-Thouars offers as many excuses as he can think of:

> When the number of executions reached eleven, one for each of the men we had lost, I decided to end proceedings at that point. There was no doubt that we had done more than enough to demonstrate our power to the Japanese. I judged that leniency would be the most efficacious course of action. Furthermore, it was already evening. A wind had come up and was disturbing the curtains around the stage. For security reasons also, it seemed prudent to return to the ship before darkness fell. That was why, after the execution of the eleventh man, I called the Japanese supervisor and conveyed my intentions to him.[83]

Leniency, in the sense meant here by Du Petit-Thouars, is a concept wholly alien to Bushido. Conciliatory tactics that lack a face-saving component are perceived only as weakness. Du Petit-Thouars admits that Roches was displeased with his walkout. Satow bemoaned the decision in print:

> These Japanese massacred a boat's crew of inoffensive and unarmed men, who were never alleged to have given the slightest provocation. Twenty were sentenced to death, and one could only regret that Captain du Petit-Thouars judged it necessary to stop the execution when eleven had

83. Du Petit-Thouars, *Furansu kanchō no mita Sakai jiken*, 32.

> suffered, for the twenty were all equally guilty, and requir-
> ing a life for life of the eleven Frenchman looked more
> like revenge than justice.[84]

Understandably, the Japanese claimed a psychological victory. Sasaki had no doubts about the outcome when he came to compile his report, and the novelist Mori Ōgai set the seal on the matter in a celebrated short story, "The Sakai Incident," published in 1914. Due largely to the success of Ōgai's fictionalized account, which was based on Sasaki's report, the incident—or rather, the suicide ceremony that ended it—is today remembered as a classic example of fragile Western sensibilities wilting in the face of fearless samurai machismo.[85]

Parkes, the British consul general, was careful to learn from the mistakes of the French at Sakai. On March 23, three samurai ambushed a party of British representatives, including Mitford, who distinguished himself by chasing down and capturing one of his attackers after the man was wounded by a guard. The next day Parkes wrote to his wife:

> Out of this affair I expect to get a law rendering attacks on
> foreigners by two-sworded men—hitherto looked upon
> as heroism—punishable by an infamous death. The *hara-
> kiri* which Roches mistakenly accepted in the Sakai affair
> makes heroes or martyrs of the men who undergo it, and
> rather encourages than deters from crime.[86]

Parkes got his new law. On April 8, an imperial decree was posted on public signboards around Kyoto. A translator at the British legation prepared this English version:

---

84. Satow, *A Diplomat in Japan*, 345.

85. During the French premiere of Mishima Yukio's short film *The Rite of Love and Death* in 1966, some members of the audience apparently fainted during the seppuku scene. Mishima was jubilant, and wrote to a friend, "I am proud to be the first Japanese to have made a Frenchman faint since the Incident at Sakai." (Mishima, *Zenshū*, 38:742.)

86. Dickens, *The Life of Sir Harry Parkes*, 88.

> Henceforth those persons who, by violently slaying for-
> eigners, or otherwise insulting them, would rebel against
> the imperial commands, and brew trouble in the country,
> and all other persons whatsoever, are hereby ordered to
> behave in a friendly manner. Those who do not uphold
> the Majesty and Good Faith of their country in the eyes
> of the world, being guilty of the most audacious crime,
> in accordance with the heinousness of their offence, will,
> even should they belong to the samurai class, be stripped
> of their rank, and will meet with a suitable punishment.[87]

The key phrase here is "even should they belong to the samurai class." The fact was that samurai were the exclusive perpetrators of attacks on foreigners. But a samurai stripped of his rank was a commoner, for whom the "suitable punishment" was most likely to be a common beheading. Other factors had already stalled samurai enthusiasm for attacking foreigners. The lords of Satsuma and Tosa had been forced to pay astronomical sums in compensation for the murders committed by their men, and British warships had bombarded Kagoshima. From these consequences other samurai leaders learned their lesson. But fines and cannonballs would not deter rogue vigilantes. The new law was the decisive factor here: there would be no more seppuku sentences for xenophobes. Attacks on foreigners ceased immediately. Degradation succeeded where disembowelment had failed. With no prospect of a glorious death, samurai lost the desire to kill.

A minor incident from 1870 also warrants our attention. Summer of that year saw a clash between rival factions in Tokushima. Eight hundred samurai loyal to the Hachikusa family attacked the residence of the family's chief councilor, Inada Kunitane, who had been attempting to establish a breakaway group of his own. Kunitane was away in Tokyo on the day of the attack, and his men were caught off guard. Twenty were killed and scores were injured; two later killed themselves in shame. Authorities stepped in, handing out an assortment

---

87. Mitford, *A Tragedy in Stone*, 283–84.

of punishments from incarceration to banishment, and sentencing ten ringleaders to death by decapitation. The Hachikusa family petitioned for seppuku. In the hope of diffusing tensions on both sides, the government acquiesced. The ceremony was held in Tokyo on September 15. There were no paper fans in sight: all ten samurai cut their stomachs before being beheaded.

This, as things turned out, was the last judicial seppuku in Japanese history. From the late 1860s the trend was firmly toward modernization and Westernization, and the practice of seppuku was doomed to extinction. Politicians had debated the matter one year earlier, when a motion to abolish judicial seppuku was brought before parliament. This was the motion as proposed to parliament by reformist lawmaker Ono Seigorō in March 1869:

> In our nation, seppuku is the punishment reserved for samurai. What crime, if any, the accused has committed remains obscure, and many for whom no punishment has yet been determined have cut their stomachs to atone for their alleged wrongdoings. Our military men speak highly of stomach-cutting. But it is a fact that the practice does not exist in any of the Western nations.
>
> Traditionally it is deemed reasonable for a man to throw away his life by cutting his stomach. Could it not be argued, however, that a man who cuts his stomach without regard for his life acts immorally? If he has done no wrong, he should plead his innocence. On the other hand, if he is guilty, the nation has laws to judge him; he should admit his crime and face his punishment. In either case there is no good reason for him to cut his stomach. To do so is, moreover, an additional crime, since it signifies his contempt for the law, and his refusal to face the consequences of his actions.
>
> Many samurai who cut their stomachs in the past were endowed with vigorous spirit and a deep sense of honor. With proper persuasion they might have endeavored to

continue living, and would undoubtedly have served
their nation well. Condemning men to death for the first
and only crime they commit allows them no chance to
improve their character, and is a waste of national talent.
At this time of widespread reforms, I hereby propose that
the institution of seppuku be abolished.[88]

On its first reading, the motion was defeated. Lawmakers argued
that seppuku enshrined the national spirit and encouraged the pursuit
of honor. But these were no more than nostalgic farewells to a waning
tradition. After a second reading the motion was roundly approved
and passed into law in 1871.

But the history of samurai suicide does not end with its excision
from the legal system. On the contrary, these turbulent years gave rise
to the bloodiest mass suicides seen in Japan since the wars of the Muromachi period nearly four centuries earlier. To understand this spectac-
ular reversion, we must recall seppuku in its original manifestations,
before it was swallowed up by officialdom and the judiciary, before it
was controlled, regulated, monitored, and choreographed. In the dying
moments of Japanese feudalism, suicide reassumed its ancient function as a fearless flash of defiance by warriors so proud they would
rather die than admit defeat. The rawness returned, and the polished
formality of *seppuku* gave way to the convulsive anarchy of *hara-kiri*.

Belly-ripping was now an atavism.

The Aizu White Tigers (Died October 7, 1868)

On January 3, 1868, radicals from Satsuma and Chōshū occupied the
imperial palace in Kyoto and announced a return to imperial rule
under the young emperor Meiji. The bakufu government was abolished, and the shogun, Yoshinobu, demoted to lord status.

The Meiji Restoration, as it became known, triggered a brief and
hectic civil war. Samurai loyal to the bakufu attempted to recapture

88. *Parliamentiary Minutes* (Gianroku), March 1869.

the palace and reinstate Yoshinobu. Prince Arisugawa, the emperor's cousin, led an army against Edo, where Yoshinobu eventually offered his formal surrender. Diehard bakufu loyalists, including most of the navy, retreated north. They were pursued by the forces of Satsuma and Chōshū, and samurai of other anti-bakufu groups, collectively known as the army of the "new government" (*shinsei*). The British, with an eye on the future, involved themselves in the war by equipping and training the Shinsei army, which numbered over a hundred thousand men. The Shinsei also managed to acquire three thousand US-made Spencer rifles, which were capable of firing off twenty rounds per minute. (Considerable training was needed to familiarize the Japanese troops, who knew nothing more modern than flintlock muskets, with these new weapons.) Several pro-bakufu domains in the north, such as Sendai and Yonezawa, made a lackluster show of resistance and were swiftly subdued. In September 1868, Shinsei forces converged on the last pocket of resistance: the stronghold of Aizu in the mountainous region of what is today western Fukushima.

Aizu was ruled by the Matsudaira family, whose bond to the shogun was unbreakable. Samurai from this region had supported Tokugawa Ieyasu in his struggle to establish the first centralized government. Ieyasu himself was of Matsudaira stock. Aizu's military code stipulated loyalty to the shogun, "whatever the consequences." In 1868 the Aizu leader was Lord Matsudaira Katamori, then in his early thirties. Imperialists had special reason to want Katamori dead. In April 1863 vandals decapitated three statues of the Ashikaga shoguns at Kyoto's Tōjiin Temple. It was a copycat stunt obviously inspired by the legacy of Takayama Hikokurō (see p. 158). Katamori, who had spent his student years in Kyoto, retaliated by creating a death squad of two dozen swordsmen to hunt down and exterminate anti-shogun activists in the capital.[89] The Satsuma and Chōshū men who were now marching north remembered this, and had vengeance in mind.

89. This group evolved into the Shinsengumi, the shogun's elite security unit. Of the initial twenty-four members, only ten survived. Eight were killed in action, one was assassinated, one was executed, and four were forced to cut their bellies—by their fellow members, for breaking the unit's own rules of conduct.

Buried under snow for nearly six months each year, Aizu was not an easy place to wage war. Yet there had been a fortress at Wakamatsu, Aizu's main town, since the 1300s, and generations of northern warlords had based their operations there, most notably Ashina Moriuji (1521–80) and Date Masamune (1567–1636). Aizu samurai had earned themselves the sort of reputation that typically adheres to men from such places: strong, rugged, fearless, and merciless as wolves. The women were no softer. While some regions of Japan are renowned for the beauty of their women, Aizu females were known for their athleticism and physical strength. In a popular event at one annual festival, the fair maidens of Aizu competed against each other in lifting 120-pound bales of straw over their heads.

Militarily the Aizu were well organized. A fighting force of six thousand men was on standby at any time. These troops had recently received some welcome assistance with weapons and ammunition from the French, who were betting on a bakufu victory. Even so, the Aizu could not hope to match the Shinsei's firepower. To supplement the army and existing militias, Aizu leaders set up some forty reserve units. The four main reserve units took their names from mythological creatures: the Black Tortoises, the Green Dragons, the Red Phoenixes, and the White Tigers. Reservists were grouped by age. Tortoises were over fifty years of age, Dragons were thirty-six and above, Phoenixes were aged eighteen to thirty-five. Tigers officially consisted of boys aged sixteen and seventeen; in fact, many younger boys managed to win places by lying about their age. Each reserve unit was further divided into five subunits according to the men's rank, or, in the case of the Tigers, the ranks of their fathers. Other reserve units included a "barefist unit" comprised of martial artists, a "temple unit" of monks armed with wooden staffs, a "sumo unit" of wrestlers and assorted heavyweights, and various semicombat or support units for women. Nakano Takeko, Aizu's eighteen-year-old female *naginata* (glaive) champion, started teaching an intensive course in self-defense techniques for girls. Two hundred local farmers formed an unofficial unit of their own, calling themselves the *kanshitai*, "the Deathwishers." In this manner, the entire population mobilized for war.

Aizu's military commanders anticipated multiple attacks from all sides. Accordingly, they divided their army and dispatched small-scale defensive units to various locations around the region. This proved a tactical disaster when the Shinsei struck at a single point, the Bonari Pass on Aizu's eastern border, decimating the force of eight hundred defenders entrenched there. There was now no line of defense between Wakamatsu Castle and the invaders. More Aizu divisions hurried out from Wakamatsu to stall the enemy advance. Fighting was fierce, and battle reports describe feats of outstanding bravery on both sides. Meanwhile the remaining divisions of the Aizu army raced across country to join the battle. But they were out of time. On October 5, the bells at Wakamatsu rang out the warning: the enemy was within sight of the castle walls.

The realization that Wakamatsu might fall sent the people into an apocalyptic frenzy. They armed themselves with whatever weapons they could find. Women who had lost husbands at Bonari joined the rear-guard lines dressed in their husbands' kimonos. Old folk with their grandchildren took positions along the barricades. Japan had seen nothing like this since the sieges of the sixteenth century. Two dozen female reservists requested permission to fight on the front line. The commander refused. He relented when the women drew their daggers and unanimously threatened to commit suicide on the spot.[90] Among the male reserve units, the Tortoises were sent to merge with the main defense brigade in the town center, as were the two junior units of the White Tigers. The upper three Tiger units marched three miles northeast of the castle to the area of Takizawa, where one branch of the Shinsei vanguard was focusing its attack. The boys whose fate interests us here belonged to one of these three units, which comprised sons of Aizu's most noble families. Before following their progress further, let us take a closer look at the teenage samurai of White Tiger Unit 2, Team 1.

---

90. These women, who were led by Nakano Takeko, later fought alongside the men— and died with them.

All the boys in this team were pupils at the Nisshinkan, Aizu's fin-est school. Education here was grounded on the primary Bushido vir-tues of loyalty, purity, and fortitude. Each morning the boys recited a "Code of Conduct":

> We will obey our elders.
> We will bow to our elders.
> We will not tell lies.
> We will not behave badly in any way.
> We will not bully those weaker than us.
> We will not eat anywhere other than in our own homes.
> We will not talk to women outside our own families.[91]

Nisshinkan boys learned mathematics, astronomy, medical science, and Confucianism. Martial skills featured prominently in the curricu-lum; kendo, judo, shooting, swimming, and horsemanship were com-pulsory for all pupils. The people of Aizu were immensely proud of the Nisshinkan, which was regarded as one of the best schools of its kind in Japan. It was even known abroad. In 1864, a young teacher at the Nisshinkan, Sawara Morizumi, along with three of his senior pupils, visited France at the special invitation of the French Education Ministry. They returned with tales of bustling Parisian streets, of mysterious for-eign foods, and of a blue-eyed emperor who rode in a golden carriage.[92]

Historians have done their best to unearth evidence of latent heroic potential in the twenty boys whose names are remembered today, but they sound like boys everywhere. Nishikawa was a strong sportsman. So was Nomura, his best friend. Nagase and Hayashi, both sixteen, were next-door neighbors; they had played together since they were toddlers. Shinoda, seventeen, was the oldest. Then there was Yanase, captain of the school swimming club, Ibuka, who was teased for being a mother's boy, and Mase, who everyone agreed was the most hand-some. The youngest of the group was Iinuma. He had lied about his

91. Hiraishi, *Aizu Boshin sensō*, 2–3.
92. Napoleon III.

age in order to join. Nearly sixteen on his application form, he was in fact just a few weeks past his fourteenth birthday.

The Tigers assembled in the third circle of Wakamatsu Castle on the morning of October 6. There was concern about the availability of workable weapons. In training, the boys had used antique German-made flintlock muskets, which they found to be dangerously unreliable; their requests for something better had been declined. Today, to everyone's great relief, they were given French cavalry rifles. Short, light, and easy to carry, these were ideal for the boy soldiers. In addition to his rifle, every Tiger carried a sword or dagger of some kind.

The Tigers reached Takizawa in the early afternoon. They joined the fight, reinforcing the Deathwishers and other volunteer troops in an impetuous charge. Forty Aizu men were killed in this clash, including all the officers. A few hours of respite followed. As night was falling, a Shinsei artillery unit arrived with Gatling guns. The Aizu men retreated into the forest, intending to regroup in more secluded positions on the opposite side. In the poor light, a band of around twenty Tigers lost contact with their unit leader. They rallied around the oldest boy they could find, Shinoda, who attempted to lead them back to Wakamatsu and rejoin the main division. But the Shinsei surged forward, chasing the Tigers out of the woodland to the base of a tall hill known locally as Iimoriyama. Having no choice, the boys started up the hillside.

They climbed through the night. From midnight an unrelenting gale brought harsh squalls of heavy rain. The boys heard occasional gunfire from below, and assumed that the battle was continuing. In fact the Shinsei army had unexpectedly pulled back, allowing scores of Aizu stragglers to slip quietly back into the castle.

By first light the boys had successfully crossed the peak of Iimoriyama. They descended to a point midway down, where they found a small shrine. Thankfully, it was one they recognized. Further along was a waterfall where they sometimes played. From there they knew they could find their way back to Wakamatsu without using any of the existing paths. But as they approached the water they were fired on by Shinsei snipers. The Tigers scattered for cover. During this ambush, Nagase was shot in the leg. The others bandaged him up, and supported him on their shoulders as they proceeded carefully through the trees.

They stopped before reaching a stone bridge that led across to the waterfall. To one side was a tunnel, remnant of some long-abandoned construction scheme. With Shinsei soldiers close by, the boys knew it was too risky to pass in front of the waterfall. Instead they headed into the tunnel. The followed the long and twisting route in pitch darkness, knee-deep in mud, with bats swooping over their heads. When they emerged, they realized that they were on the side of the hill that faced Wakamatsu. They climbed higher to a grassy plateau from where they knew they could see the castle.

But when they came out onto the plateau they saw a picture of hell. Wakamatsu was on fire. Thick clouds of black smoke rose high enough to blot out the castle's turrets and towers. Shrieks and shouts could be heard, and explosions, as Shinsei canons pounded the walls from very close range.

The boys sank to their knees in the tall grass. One shouted out, "The castle has fallen! His Lordship must be dead!" Some boys started to cry.

Nishikawa, after Shinoda the most senior member of the group, called them to order. "We've done all we could," he said, "but the castle is on fire and the enemy is all around us. It is time for us to die. Everyone, prepare yourselves."[93]

Nobody argued. Iinuma produced the poem his grandmother had written for him, and read it aloud. The older boys, conscious of the need to set an example, knew they must act first. Ishida, one of the wounded, was too weak to move his arms. A boy named Shibata drove his sword into Ishida's throat. Shibata pressed the blade against his own throat and fell forward, dying instantly. Next were Hayashi and Nagase. Hayashi put his sword to Nagase's chest, Nagase put his to Hayashi's throat, and they stabbed simultaneously. Nagase's wound was fatal, Hayashi's was not. Nomura stepped forward and cut off Hayashi's head; Nomura then slit his own stomach with the same

93. Hiraishi, *Aizu Boshin sensō*, 260–62.

sword. Iinuma secured the base of his sword against a rock and drove the blade into his throat. The others followed suit, stabbing each other and cutting their own throats or stomachs. The last to die was Nishi-kawa. He waited until all the boys had stabbed themselves before shooting himself in the head with his revolver.

The bodies were soon discovered. Ide Hatsu, a woman from a nearby village, was searching the area for her two teenage sons; both non-Tigers, they had gone missing that morning, taking their grand-father's rifle with them. Hatsu feared the worse. Coming out onto the plateau she caught sight of the bodies in the grass. All were cov-ered in blood; several bore shrapnel and bullet wounds; a few had been decapitated. Hatsu moved closer, and noticed that one boy was still alive and conscious. We have a reliable record of the words they exchanged, as gunshots rang out on the hillside just below them:

> "Young man, what is your name?"
>
> "Iinuma Sadakichi, White Tiger Unit."
>
> "You and your friends acted too soon! The castle has not fallen. Your mother and father are safe. There was no reason to kill yourselves."
>
> "You're lying. The castle is on fire . . . we didn't know whether His Lordship was still alive . . . so we turned our swords on ourselves."
>
> "No, His Lordship is safe, and so is Wakamatsu. If you don't believe me, I'll take you to your parents right now."[94]

Hatsu lifted the boy onto her back and carried him to the nearest house. A doctor was sent for, while some village girls took turns nurs-ing the brave young hero.

The truth was that Hatsu had no way of knowing whether Iinuma's parents were still alive or not. But she was right about Wakamatsu. The absent divisions of Aizu's army had returned just in time to repulse

94. Ibid., 278–79.

the latest Shinsei attack. The castle was not ablaze. The smoke obscuring it was the product of cannon and rifle fire. The teenagers, experiencing combat for the first time, had indeed acted too hastily.

The following day, locals buried the bodies in shallow graves on the hillside.

At Wakamatsu the Aizu samurai battled on, refusing all appeals to surrender. It took three more weeks of daylong heavy bombardment to wear them down. Katamori offered his formal surrender on November 6. More than three thousand Aizu samurai were dead. Hundreds of women and children had also perished. There were many suicides. Twenty-one wives of Aizu leaders killed themselves at the home of the chief councilor; for fear of being discovered in an immodest posture, the women tied their knees together before cutting their own throats; moments earlier they had stabbed their infant children to death. Takeko, the naginata instructor, had sustained a terrible head wound; she requested kaishaku and was decapitated by her mother. The exact number of seppuku suicides among the Aizu men is not known, and only a few stories have survived. Tanaka Harukiyo, the chief councilor, fought on the front line with his men. After sustaining a severe wound, he cut his stomach in an impromptu ceremony along with another councilor. On the penultimate day of the battle, an elderly retainer named Doi Nobukata saw his master fatally struck down before him. Nobukata pleaded to be allowed to join the fight at the castle's main gate, where he was shot dead; he was ninety-two years old. In addition to the boys who committed suicide on Iimoriyama, at least another thirty boys from the White Tiger units lost their lives in the fighting. Then there were boys who, for one reason or another, had not been permitted to join the Tigers. Over sixty non-enlisted teenagers were killed in action or took their own lives. The youngest recorded suicide was an eight-year-old boy who cut his stomach in panic when an ammunition storehouse exploded behind him. The teenage sons for whom Hatsu was searching on the hillside had gone to fight on the barricades in the town center. Both were killed.

Following Aizu's surrender, Katamori and his new chief councilor, Kayano Gonbē, were taken to Tokyo, where ministers of the new government pressed for their trial and execution as traitors. To save his lord's life, Gonbē volunteered to enter a guilty plea and commit suicide. He cut his stomach in a ceremony on June 27, 1869. Katamori took the tonsure and lived out the rest of his life as a Shinto priest.

In the aftermath of the battle, the deaths of the Tigers on Iimori-yama did not receive special recognition. After all, many thousands were dead. What was special about those twenty? Once Aizu folk began to reflect on the meaning of their defeat, however, they craved heroes. The tragedy of the teenage martyrs now struck a chord. At first it was a local story. Then, on April 28, 1869, the Tokyo *Terigu-rafu* newspaper featured a report about the Aizu boys who had "faced death without flinching." Idolization had begun. In the years that followed, Aizu painters and sculptors produced countless representations of the boys' seppuku scene. Magazines around Japan serialized fictional versions of the story. Poets hailed the boys in verse. These included Sawara Morizumi, the boys' tutor at the Nisshinkan. His rousing poem "Aizu's White Tigers," written nearly twenty years after the battle, became especially popular and appeared in many anthologies. Here is a translation of the closing verses:

> They looked south to the castle, lost in smoke,
> Holding back their tears until one boy spoke:
> "Our cause is lost! Remember your pride!"
> The young warriors slit their bellies and died.
>
> Cold blow the winds on Iimori Hill,
> But the glory of their deed blazes still,
> Aizu's brave White Tigers!
> Aizu's brave White Tigers![95]

Later still, amid the frenzied nationalism of the 1930s, the Tigers were obvious targets for glorification. Their fame spread even beyond Japan. A Japanese diplomat related the Tigers' story to Mussolini, who

---

95. Ibid., 324. Sawara avoids the word *seppuku* here, and opts instead for *tofuku*.

sent the people of Aizu a bronze eagle in tribute. Via an insidious
process of mythmaking, twenty tragically confused schoolboys were
resurrected and reconstructed as nationalist mascots.

An objection could surely be made that the White Tigers' deaths
were no more or less significant than any of the other thousands who
lost their lives at Wakamatsu. The extraordinary performance by Aizu's
female population during the battle, for example, is woefully under-
represented in historical literature. Perhaps the only valid response
to this objection is an appeal to samurai aesthetics: death must be as
beautiful as it can be. The deaths of the White Tigers are thought to
come as close as possible to achieving to this aesthetic ideal. Every
aspect of their story seems to lend itself to dramatization: the showdown between rival samurai armies; the chase from the battlefield; the
night in the mountain woods, the waterfall, the flight through the tunnel; the hillside plateau, the distant castle half-hidden by smoke; the
tears, the poems, the dying embraces; so much blood needlessly shed,
so many beautiful boys . . .

As for Iinuma, the fourteen-year-old whom Hatsu found alive and
carried to safety, he was treated for his injuries and in time made a full
recovery. It is of course to him that we owe the details of the story.
Iinuma's honor was intact. Yet he struggled under a heavy sense of
shame at having failed to die with his friends. He declined to discuss
the incident until his final years, and even then would speak only
with professional historians. After his recovery, Iinuma completed his
education and joined the new imperial army. He rose to the rank of
captain, but always refused to carry a revolver, insisting that only a
sword would do. When anyone questioned him about this, he replied:
"I am a dead White Tiger."[96]

Iinuma Sadakichi died in 1931 at the age of seventy-eight. He was
buried on Iimoriyama, today a popular stop on Aizu's tourist trail.
Visitors will find that his gravestone is set at a distance from those of
the other boys.

96. Nakamura, *Byakkotai*, 225.

Revolt of the League of the Divine Wind (October 24, 1876)

A minority of reactionaries remained vociferously hostile to Westernization well into the 1870s. Meanwhile the Meiji government promulgated one new law after another, each delivering a fresh insult to traditionalist pride. With the abolition of hereditary class distinctions in 1869, commoners were no longer obliged to bow their heads to samurai on the street. In 1871, the year of the prohibition of judicial seppuku, the samurai domains were converted into governmental prefectures. The following year Prince Iwakura led an official delegation of diplomats to America and Europe—a prince of the imperial blood was negotiating with foreigners. For many samurai, however, the point of no return was reached on March 18, 1876. After that date, it was decreed, only commissioned army officers and designated security officials were permitted to carry swords. There were howls of protest. Disgruntled samurai across the country formed anti-reformist groups. An old saying, "The sword is the soul of the samurai," was on everyone's lips. Stalwarts predicted the end of the Japanese state, activists distributed angry manifestos—all to no avail.

Kaya Harukata (1836–76), head priest of the Nishikiyama Shrine at Kumamoto Castle, resigned his position in protest at the proscription on swords. He was already outraged at religious reforms that granted Christianity equal rights with Shinto. In his youth Harukata had studied at a private school run by Hayashi Ōen, an influential nationalist and Shinto fundamentalist—Ōen's school was named Gendōkan, "The School of the Fundamental Way." Inspired by Ōen's teachings, and galvanized by the sword ban, Harukata and a former classmate, Ōtagurō Tomō (1835–76), established a Shinto faction of their own. They called it the *Keishin-tō*, the Party of Divine Reverence. The group is better known today by its popular cognomen, *Kumamoto Shinpūren*: the Kumamoto League of the Divine Wind.[97]

Harukata and Tomō had no difficulty attracting members, and

97. *Shinpū* is an alternative reading of the characters for *kamikaze*. This Shinto term originates in the ancient *Chronicles of Japan*, but more popularly denotes the serendipitous typhoon of 1281 that sank Kublai Khan's invasion fleet off the coast of northern Kyushu. The samurai of the Divine Wind were thus self-styled saviors of Japan.

within a month the League was nearly two hundred strong. Many of the recruits were still in their teens, hotheaded sons of samurai families and students from the Shinto schools. Tomō himself was formerly a priest. Both he and Harukata had spent time in jail. In 1872 they had been rounded up and interrogated, along with scores of other activists, after the assassination of Hirosawa Saneomi, a luminary in the new progressive government. Other members of the League had similar histories. They were dangerous, fanatical men, united by their disgust at what they considered the systematic erosion of Japan's religious and cultural traditions.

Harukata and Tomō devised a plan worthy of the group's name. The samurai of the Divine Wind would split into three groups and launch three separate attacks—against the residence of Major-General Taneda, who headed the Kumamoto garrisons; against the residence of the Kumamoto governor; and against the main infantry barracks. They would kill everyone in charge—Taneda, the governor, the army commanders, and the head of the Kumamoto assembly. They would then occupy all the major governmental and military compounds in Kumamoto. Moreover, faithful to their professed opposition to Westernization, they would accomplish all this using only their swords. Firearms were for foreigners and conscripts.

Pitting fewer than two hundred swordsmen against an estimated two thousand armed troops, this was a plan that would have delighted the suicide eulogist Jōchō, a plan imbued with what he had called *shinigurui*—a "mania for death."[98] Nonetheless, some degree of success was not beyond the realm of possibility, at least in the preliminary stages. A large section of the army's Kumamoto force was away in Saga Prefecture in anticipation of further uprisings there. The battalions that remained were scattered across several encampments. The castle itself was defended by only two hundred guards. Since these government soldiers were mostly commoners drafted under new laws,

98. Jōchō attributes this neologism to a saying of his lord, Nabeshima Naoshige: "Bushido is a mania for death. Ten men cannot overcome one who is mad enough to die." Jōchō comments: "Great deeds are not accomplished by playing it safe. You must go insane, you must have this mania for death." *Hagakure*, 1:65.

it was a fair assumption that they would be no match for the samurai in close-quarter fighting. Outwardly at least, Harukata and his men pinned their hopes on these factors. What they dreaded above all was capture. Since the abolition of ritual suicide as an institutionalized samurai privilege, capture now necessarily meant unthinkable humiliations, irrespective of crime or rank. Etō Shinpei, the leader of a short-lived uprising in Saga two years previously, traced his genealogy as far back as the Chibas of Kamakura, renowned warrior-administrators in the thirteenth century. It made no difference. Shinpei was decapitated in public and his head was exhibited alongside those of thieves and pickpockets. The head was also photographed by the press—a new degradation courtesy of the modern age.

While it would be an exaggeration to categorize the League of the Divine Wind as a suicide squad from its inception, that is undoubtedly what it became. Certainly the samurai had no political objectives to speak of. Their chief aspiration, in its psychological essence, was to realize the perennial samurai fantasy of inviolable rectitude and fearless self-sacrifice culminating in sanguinary apotheosis. But above that, a solid conviction in the historical magnitude of their act elevated their zeal to the edge of intoxication. Harukata and his men believed themselves to be the last samurai. Their deaths would be the death of all samurai. That being so, what manner of death would they choose if not the glorious death of seppuku, the crowning symbol of samurai tradition?

Late in the evening of October 24, the samurai gathered at the Fujisaki Shrine, five miles east of Kumamoto Castle. They prayed together, and performed rites of purification. Each wore a headband with a victory slogan of his own composition. In addition to the customary long and short swords, each man carried a third sword behind him, tucked under his belt. Although rifles and pistols were banned, gunpowder, which had a long history in Japan, was not; accordingly, a small number of the samurai also carried homemade grenades. It was agreed that, if their initial assault was repelled, they would fall back to the shrine and regroup. Their passwords, in case they were separated from one another, were *ten* and *chi*—Heaven and Earth.

The attacks started well. In the middle of the night, the first team successfully scaled the outer walls of the castle and slit the sentries' throats.
A second team arrived at the infantry barracks and smashed through
the gates with sledgehammers. Guards at Taneda's residence were easily
overpowered; some took one look at the intruders and fled. The samurai made their way to Taneda's bedroom. Harukata had instructed them
not to kill anyone unnecessarily, but in the heat of the fight they seem
to have cut down whoever got in their way. At least one maid was killed,
and various grooms and servants were wounded. Five samurai burst
into the bedroom and stabbed Taneda to death, inadvertently slashing his wife at the same time. While she cowered under the blankets,
they cut off her husband's head and wrapped it in cloth, exactly as the
Akō rōnin had done with the head of Lord Kira. In the morning, Mrs.
Taneda, who was herself of samurai stock, hurried out to Kumamoto's
newly opened telegram office to wire a message to her parents. The
message, which subsequently appeared in all the major newspapers and
did much to popularize the telegram service in Japan, was a marvel of
samurai sangfroid. In its entirety it read: "Husband dead me just cut."[99]

The fighting was much fiercer at the artillery barracks, where the
troops were most numerous. Anticipating this, Harukata and Tomō
headed a squad that included the older and more experienced swordsmen. But once the Kumamoto guards had armed themselves with
rifles and taken up firing positions, the samurai could make no head-
way against them. Harukata and Tomō rallied their men by shouting
the name of Hachiman, the god of war. All joined in a desperate final
charge against the rifles. Eighteen of the samurai were killed, including Harukata, who was fatally shot in the head. Tomō took a bullet in
the chest, but was still breathing as his men dragged him beyond the
range of the rifles. He asked to be turned toward the east, so as to face
the imperial palace; one of his men then struck off his head. Seeing
that their leaders were dead, the samurai pulled back and headed for
the Fujisaki Shrine. Those who were too severely wounded to move
stabbed themselves to death on the spot.

99. Ōkuma, *Shinpūren kekki*, 35.

Army reinforcements arrived at three o'clock in the morning and pursued the samurai through the streets of Kumamoto. More samurai were killed; a few were captured alive; around sixty made it back to the shrine. There was an argument over what to do next. The younger men wanted to turn back and die fighting, but the likelihood of capture seemed too great. It was agreed that the group would disband at this point, return to their homes, and "follow the will of the gods." The meaning of this was clear to all.

The suicides began later that day and continued well into November. With army and police search parties combing the area around Fujisaki, some two dozen samurai were forced to seek refuge in the hills. One group killed themselves at a village there. Those who made it home explained matters to their families before disemboweling themselves. Wherever possible, the samurai endeavored to maintain a degree of ritualistic solemnity, though with police on their heels some stabbed themselves in great haste. Others, unable to reach their homes, went instead to the houses of friends and relatives in other towns, or to temples, where they died at the graves of their forefathers.

Fifteen-year-old Ota Saburōhiko came down from the hillside at noon on October 26, and made his way home without being apprehended. After a long sleep, he announced to his parents that he was going to kill himself. His relatives gathered for the occasion. Leaving him alone with his dagger, they waited in the next room. After a minute's pause, they heard the boy's voice: "Father, I can't do it. Come and help me push [the blade in]." His father entered the room and found that the boy had missed the carotid artery. He stood behind his son and helped him cut his throat.[100]

Later the same day, Nishikawa Masanori, twenty-four, led three teenage samurai back to his house, where all four committed suicide together. On a fresh headband, each wrote his name followed by the words: "Dead by his own hand."

Four young sons of the Koshino family had participated in the attack. All survived with only cuts and scratches. After two days on the run, the four boys made their way to Sakurayama Temple, and slit their stomachs at the family grave.[101]

Another teenage member of the League, seventeen-year-old Shimada Kitarō, was uncertain how to perform seppuku, and sought advice from his old jujitsu instructor. Police later took a statement from the instructor:

> "I told the boy how to do it. He had his last drink with his family, said his goodbyes, and went into the next room. His father and I followed him, and we stood watch. He did as I instructed him, slipped his kimono from his shoulders, and cut across his belly in one flat line. Then he put the tip of his sword to his throat, and asked me, 'Is this right?' I said, 'Yes—do it!' He gave us a smile, and drove it in deep."[102]

On the afternoon of October 30, senior members Ishihara Unshirō and Abe Kageki, along with Kageki's young wife Ikiko, slit their bellies and throats minutes before police raided their house. Ikiko left a brief note for her mother:

> I can leave you only a few words. Kageki joined with Harukata and Tomō in the incident and suffered heavy losses— one hundred and sixty-nine are already dead, slain in the fight or by cutting their stomachs. Though I am a woman, I intend to follow my husband into death.[103]

Another senior member, Tsuruda Goichirō, evaded the search parties for three days, and quietly slipped into his house on the evening

---

101. The loss seems to have been altogether too much for the family dog, Tora ("Tiger"), who passed away a few days later. The Koshinos solemnly announced that Tora had committed suicide (by swallowing his own tongue), and buried him beside their sons at Sakurayama Temple. The little grave of "the martyred hound" can still be seen there today.

102. Ōkuma, *Seppuku no rekishi*, 245–46.

103. Ibid., 249.

of October 27. He and his wife put their two daughters to bed and drank a few cups of saké. Goichirō then retired to a separate room where he cut his stomach and put the sword through his neck. The next day his wife learned that their teenage son, who also took part in the attack, had killed himself at the home of an uncle.

A group of six samurai avoided capture by rowing out of the harbor on a fishing boat. They included Morishita Teruyoshi, whose sword had severed the head of Major-General Taneda. All six headed into the hills, where they ritually killed themselves on October 29. According to the police report, the strongest swordsman among them, indentified only as Tajima, acted as kaishaku for the first four. Then, he and the last man, Teruyoshi, cut their stomachs together.

Of the 173 samurai who participated in the Kumamoto attacks, 28 died fighting and 87 committed suicide. The rest, many of whom had been wounded, were captured and imprisoned or executed. Only five escaped.[104] The overall fatality rate was therefore roughly seven men out of every ten.

The beautiful madness of the Divine Wind rebels was one of the last furious paroxysms of the seppuku tradition. They had issued no manifesto; other than victory headbands, death poems, and a few letters, they left no written explanations of their conduct. None was needed. Their deaths carried the meaning.

Nogi Maresuke (Died September 13, 1912)

Three decades separate the League of the Divine Wind from the celebrated suicide of General Nogi Maresuke (1849–1912), former Commander of the Imperial Third Army. Japan's metamorphosis from feudal dictatorship to modern nation-state was accomplished. The rapidity of change had been remarkable. Japan's administrative and judicial systems, financial institutions, and armed forces had all been remodeled in line with those of Western nations, with whom Japan

104. These numbers vary slightly from account to account. I follow Watanabe Kyōji, *Shinpūren to sono jidai*, 224.

now dealt on equal terms. Intellectual trends, as well as fashions in music and literature, enthusiastically followed Western standards.

In terms of seppuku history, those three decades are largely a blank. There was no place for stomach-cutting in the new Japan. Words such as *kaishaku* and *junshi* now belonged to a vanished past. Basil Hall Chamberlain, a British scholar resident in Japan during the Meiji years, wrote in 1904: "The dear old Samurai who first initiated the present writer into the mysteries of the Japanese language, wore a queue and two swords. This relic of feudalism now sleeps in Nirvana."[105] In 1900 Nitobe Inazō, a professor at the imperial university in Tokyo, had published a book in English entitled *Bushido: The Soul of Japan.* Nitobe's tone is unmistakably one of nostalgia for yesteryear, and his chapter on suicide and vendettas is firmly rooted in the past. Chamberlain, perhaps with a nod to Nitobe, admitted the existence of some Japanese who "still secretly cherish the swords bequeathed to them by their knightly forefathers," but dismissed this as "merely a backwater." Speaking generally, he declared, "the educated Japanese have done with their past."[106] No wonder then, that when Count Nogi Maresuke, a general of the imperial army, was found dead at his home, with his stomach ripped open in two crossed cuts and his neck impaled on the finest antique sword in his collection, and with his wife Shizuko collapsed beside him, dead from multiple stab wounds, the nation was stunned. On the day of Emperor Meiji's funeral the Nogis had committed ritual suicide.

No one close to Nogi seems to have anticipated his decision to die. Yet even a cursory examination of his life suggests an archetypal samurai self-immolator in the mold of Nishina Morinobu, Shibata Katsuie, Takechi Hanpeita, and many others whom we have examined, one of those men for whom, to borrow a phrase from Nitobe, "death was lighter than a feather."

For many generations, Nogi's ancestors had been samurai retainers of the Mōri family. Biographers have traced the Nogi lineage to

105. Chamberlain, *Things Japanese,* 1.
106. Ibid., 2–3.

the tenth-century emperor Uda (867–931). Nogi was born in 1849 at his father's house on the Mōri estate in Tokyo, one of the four estates where the Akō rōnin had performed their seppuku ceremonies a century and a half earlier.[107]

In his student days Nogi demonstrated a literary talent, and for a time he seems to have contemplated an academic career. But his father wanted him to be a soldier, and, after some bohemian years, Nogi obliged by enrolling in the new imperial army. It was an early example of the committal to duty that defined his character.

As an officer during the 1870s, Nogi commanded the 14th Infantry Regiment and assisted in suppressing a spate of samurai uprisings similar to that of the League of the Divine Wind. An especially notable success came in October 1876 when Nogi's men swiftly overwhelmed four hundred rebel fighters from Akizuki in Fukuoka, killing dozens and capturing more than a hundred. Seven rebel leaders cut their stomachs.

The insurgent army led by Saigō Takamori during the Satsuma Rebellion of 1877 presented a more formidable challenge. In fierce fighting against Satsuma samurai on the Kumamoto hills in February 1877, Nogi's men were repeatedly surrounded and forced to withdraw. During one such retreat, the soldier carrying the regimental flag was shot dead. In the confusion of the moment, the flag vanished, and was presumed to have fallen into enemy hands. Nogi was mortified. He attempted to charge back, alone, to retrieve it, but was restrained by junior officers.[108]

Emperor Meiji had personally presented the flag to the regiment in a ceremony at the imperial palace. Nogi could not forgive himself for losing it. Over the following weeks he fought with near-suicidal recklessness. On February 27 he was shot through the leg and taken to a military hospital in Kurume. After a few days he left the hospital without permission. Unable to walk properly, he ordered two privates

---

107. The former Mōri estate is today the site of the Roppongi Hills complex.

108. Testimony from the rebels later revealed that they did not seize the flag immediately, but picked it from the field the following day. The flag found its way to one of the samurai generals, whose widow handed it in to police after hostilities ceased.

to carry him back to the front line on a handheld vegetable cart. He was shot again, this time in his left arm. By April, imperial troops had broken into Kumamoto Castle, and Takamori's rebels were on the run. The flag, however, was still missing. According to a memoir by a fellow officer, Nogi attempted to kill himself at least twice during this period. The officer, Kodama Gentarō, discovered Nogi as he was preparing to disembowel himself outside Kumamoto Castle. Kodama stopped him just in time and confiscated his sword. Nogi then went missing. A search party found him three days later. He had headed into a remote area of hills, taking no food. Kodama persuaded Nogi to seek punishment via official channels. On April 27, Nogi wrote a letter of self-admonishment to General Yamagata Aritomo at military headquarters:

> On the night of February 22, second lieutenant Kawara-bayashi, bearer of our regimental flag, was killed during a skirmish at Ueki. I could not locate his body, and it was unclear whether the flag had been captured by the enemy or destroyed. Despite countless searches I have been unable to retrieve it. I can offer no explanation for my carelessness in this matter. My failure is inexcusable.[109]

This, in effect, was a veiled request for permission to kill himself. But Nogi had done more than enough to redeem himself through his extraordinary efforts since the loss of the flag; and in any case, the rebel forces were now in retreat. This was the reply he received from General Yamagata on May 9:

> The loss of your regimental colors is certainly a matter of grave importance. However, considering the extreme circumstances at the time of the incident, the death of your flag bearer cannot be regarded as arising from incompetence on your part. It has therefore been decided that no action will be taken against you.[110]

109. Kuroki, *Nogi Maresuke*, 100.
110. Ibid., 102.

The letter bore the seal of Prince Arisugawa, supreme chief of the armed forces and cousin to the emperor. Nogi kept it with him for the rest of his life. It should be emphasized that regimental colors were a very recent introduction. The emperor had presented the first ones in 1874. Each flag, a red sunspot with radiating stripes, was treated as a sacred object, part of the emperor's own person. Nogi's despair over the loss entered military lore, and inspired a tradition of suicidal flag-defending.[111]

As the eldest son of a conservative samurai family, Nogi found himself in an awkward position during the rebellions. Many of his relatives and friends were sympathetic to the rebels. When a group of reactionaries began laying plans for an insurrection in Hagi, Nogi's younger brother joined them. He tried to persuade Nogi to do the same, but Nogi refused. The pair shared a bottle of saké and said their farewells. They never spoke to each other again. When Nogi's troops later crushed a rebel army at Hagi, his brother was among those killed.[112]

Following the double trauma of his brother's death and the loss of the regimental colors, Nogi entered a long period of dissipation and excess. This pattern was repeated throughout his life. Anecdotes about Nogi's drinking binges, brothel crawls, and barroom fistfights constitute a sizeable chapter in every biography.

The vicissitudes of Nogi's subsequent career need not detain us too long. Suffice it to say that they were extreme. On four separate occasions he felt obligated to tender his resignation. Each time he later returned. Between these moments of drama, Nogi spent long periods

111. The most famous incident took place at sea. On June 15, 1904, Russian warships surrounded and torpedoed the Japanese tanker *Hitachimaru*. In addition to the naval crew, an army infantry unit was on board the ship with their regimental colors. The Japanese officers refused to surrender; they ceremonially burned the colors, and almost everyone aboard went down with the ship. Newspapers later reported that nearly a thousand men had perished.

112. Another victim was Nogi's old school tutor, Tamaki Bunnoshin. After the failure of the Hagi uprising, Bunnoshin cut his stomach at the grave of his ancestors. He was beheaded by his forty-year-old wife, Oyoshi, a rare case of a woman acting as kaishaku for a man. Bunnoshin had told colleagues that he wished to be assisted by the person he loved. Oyoshi was the sister of executed nationalist fanatic Yoshida Shōin.

at his country cottage, tending to his vegetable patch. He had married Shizuko, the youngest daughter of an army doctor from Kagoshima, in 1878, and now had two grown sons who were both pursuing military careers of their own.

It was the war against China in 1894–95 that made Nogi a national hero. Port Arthur, strategically positioned on the southern tip of the Liaodong Peninsula, was said to be impenetrable. Yet in an ingeniously executed attack, Nogi, commanding the First Army, captured the port in a single day. Nearly five thousand Chinese soldiers were killed; the Japanese lost fewer than three hundred. It was an astounding victory.

Nogi had less success as governor-general of Taiwan, an appointment he received in 1896. According to one account, his unbending moral righteousness caused friction with his administrators, who were inclined to inflict hardship on the natives. After countless difficulties, Nogi returned to his vegetable patch.

He was recalled to service in February 1904, after war broke out between Japan and Russia. When Russian forces captured Port Arthur, Nogi was given command of the Third Army in the hope that he could repeat his stunning victory of ten years earlier. But the Russians had fortified their positions with great diligence, and the siege was prolonged and bloody. Nogi sent wave after wave of infantry against the fortress. Losses on both sides were terrible, though military historians have been especially critical of Nogi. For the assault on Nanzan, north of Port Arthur, he formed a special unit of three thousand men called the White Sashes (*shirodasukitai*), and ordered them to charge the Russian lines after dark with bayonets drawn; the entire unit was annihilated before midnight. As corpses piled up outside their defenses, the Russian defenders covered their mouths with handkerchiefs soaked in camphor to overcome the stench.

In Tokyo, crowds of outraged protesters gathered outside Nogi's house. They threw stones at the roof and chanted hostile slogans. Nogi's wife, Shizuko, later recalled the words of a young military officer, who stood at the gate and shouted out:

"Nogi, you fool! Why don't you kill yourself? A real samurai wouldn't stand such shame! Why are you still alive? Why don't you apologize to the people and cut your stomach? Must we form a militia and kill you ourselves?"[113]

Nogi's forces prevailed at Port Arthur on January 2, 1905. By then nearly sixty thousand men under his command had lost their lives. After a final ten-day battle at Mukden, where another eighty thousand men were killed on each side, Russia surrendered.

Japan's victory stunned the world. It was the first time that an Asian army had defeated a Western one since the Mongol invasions of the thirteenth century. The Japanese government showered Nogi with awards and put him on parade. But his army's terrible loss of life weighed heavily on Nogi, and these were honors that he felt he did not deserve. The war was also a personal tragedy for him: his two sons, both infantry officers in the Third Army, were among those who had fallen at Port Arthur. Presenting his official report at the palace, Nogi broke down in tears. According to one account, he prostrated himself before the emperor and begged for permission to commit seppuku. The emperor is said to have replied: "I understand very well the feelings that make you want to apologize by cutting your stomach, but this is not the time for you to die. If you insist on killing yourself, let it be after I have departed from this world."[114]

As we know, Nogi obeyed this command to the letter. In the years after the war he lived a life of formal engagements. He traveled to London to attend the coronation of King George V. He was appointed headmaster of the Gakushūin, Japan's most exclusive school, and entrusted with the education of the young crown prince Hirohito. All the while, Nogi paid secret visits to the families of men who had died under his command, and anonymously donated a large part of his personal fortune to fund military hospitals and memorials. Newspapers later uncovered these activities and hailed Nogi all the more. He became a figure of worship.

113. Sasaki, *Nogi Maresuke*, 64.
114. Translation in Keene, *Emperor of Japan*, 712–13.

On July 19, 1912, it was publicly announced that Emperor Meiji was gravely ill. Nogi visited the palace twice a day to pray at the emperor's bedside. Deeming it inappropriate to ride in his carriage through palace grounds while the emperor was bedridden, Nogi made a point of arriving and leaving on foot each time. The emperor passed away on July 30, and the state funeral was set for September 13. This gave Nogi six weeks to prepare for death.

He spent August clearing up his papers. He rewrote his will, leaving sums of money to everyone whose service he valued, including his maidservants, his stable boy, and groundsmen at the Gakushūin. During the first week of September he visited former colleagues, and on September 11, he paid a formal visit to the crown prince. They did not know it, but Nogi was saying his farewells.

On the morning of September 13, the day of the emperor's funeral, Nogi and Shizuko had their photographs taken in the garden of their house. Nogi wore his full military regalia, Shizuko wore a white mourning gown. They had already informed the palace that they would not be attending the funeral, pleading a bout of ill health.

From the early evening, the couple retired to their room on the second floor. At around 7:30 Shizuko came downstairs to tell the servants to go outside and join the crowd of mourners who were lining the streets. All did so, excepting two maidservants. Shizuko returned to the second floor, taking a bottle of saké with her.

The imperial hearse set off from palace at 8 p.m. The funeral cortege included palace officials, military generals, and members of the nobility. As the procession passed over the palace bridge at 8:15, an artillery unit fired salutes and temples around Tokyo tolled their bells. The hearse then continued on its way; it would take another two hours to reach the Aoyama parade grounds, where the funeral service was to be held.

At 8:50 the Akasaka police station received an emergency call from the Nogi residence. Officers arrived at the house within minutes, bringing with them a police doctor. The maids directed them to the second floor.

The room, which was actually two rooms divided by a sliding door, was a fairly large one of fourteen tatami mats. White sheets were laid out over a section of the mats. One window of the room faced the imperial palace. Beneath that window Nogi had arranged a low table covered with a white cloth, on which stood a portrait of the emperor. Various items had been set out. These included pieces of ceremonial paper with poems written on them, a dozen or so letters, a file of documents, some military medals, and photographs of Nogi's sons.

Nogi was near the center of the room. According to the police doctor's written report, presented a week later, Nogi was "facing directly toward the emperor's portrait, with the left side of his head against the floor, and his upper torso somewhat crumpled; his right leg was outstretched and fully visible, while his left was bent and tucked under." When the doctor unbuttoned Nogi's tunic, he discovered a large stomach wound consisting of two cuts: a six-and-a-half-inch horizontal cut about two inches above the navel, and a six-inch near-vertical cut that crossed the first from upper left to lower right. The wound was deepest at the intersection between the two cuts, where the blade had penetrated to a depth of three quarters of an inch. Nogi being of thin, gaunt build, this had been deep enough to slice through his abdominal wall. Elsewhere the cut was no deeper than a quarter of an inch. The blade of Nogi's sword was buried in his throat. The sword was later identified as one made in the early fourteenth century by Bizen Kanemitsu, one of the foremost sword smiths of the Kamakura period.

Shizuko was facing her husband, collapsed forward over her knees, with her hands in her lap and her forehead against the floor. The doctor found four wounds in her chest; one of these, which penetrated as far as her heart, he determined to have been the fatal wound. Shizuko's robes were not disheveled, and her legs were aligned with knees touching. In his report the doctor conjectured that the Nogis had acted according to the following sequence: to begin with, Nogi had slashed his stomach twice; he buttoned his tunic over the wound, probably with his wife's assistance. Nogi then rose to his feet and stabbed Shizuko, who was still kneeling, in her chest; however, weakened by loss of blood from his stomach wounds, it was only on the fourth strike that Nogi had succeeded in perforating his wife's heart. He adjusted her kimono and repositioned her legs before returning to his first position, seated on the floor; there he had forced the sword into his throat. From the bloodstain on the blade, the doctor calculated that Nogi had pushed the sword sufficiently deep that eight inches of the blade protruded from the rear of his neck. Finally, Nogi had driven the hilt sharply to one side, while at the same time twisting the angle of blade. This, the doctor concluded, had brought death within a few seconds.[115]

Nogi's letters expressed his shame over losing his regimental colors in the battle against the Satsuma rebels; he had hoped for death ever since. This was his farewell poem:

> The Divine Lord of the World is gone.
> In reverence, I shall follow Him.[116]

Newspapers around the globe carried reports of Nogi's death on their front pages. "Gen. Nogi and Wife Kill Themselves as Gun Booms for Mikado's Funeral" announced the *New York Times* on September 14. "Calmly in his home near Tokio [*sic*] Port Arthur's captor awaits signal for cortege to move—then cuts his throat. His devoted companion at once follows his example and commits hara-kiri . . . . Japanese here approve his act as the highest patriotism and a fitting end for [a] hero." Stanley Washburn, an American journalist who had accompanied Nogi during his campaign at Port Arthur, later wrote: "To us, far off in England or America, the deed seems a dreadful one, but to those who knew Nogi and understood a little of his ideals and of his simple worship of his emperor, the act seems not strange, but almost natural."[117]

In Japan, initial reaction was varied: disbelief, shock, embarrassment, incomprehension, outrage, awe. There was unanimous agreement

115. The full report, entitled "Report on the Examination of the Bodies of General Nogi and His Wife" (Nogi taishō fusai shitaikenjo shimatsusho), can be found in Kuroki, *Nogi Maresuke*, 685–88. One detail from the report did not appear in later newspaper accounts: Nogi had inserted two cork-sized plugs into his rectum to prevent portmortem leakage. This problem is never addressed explicitly in samurai literature, though the sixteenth-century *Kōyō Military Chronicles* does warn against "unsightly messiness after death." Presumably, Nogi needed no warning. He had seen his share of corpses.

116. Nogi, *Nogi Maresuke zenshū*, 3:549.

117. Kuroki, *Nogi Maresuke*, 124.

that junshi was an anachronism, though that was hardly a serious charge. Unsympathetic commentators condemned Nogi for his ego-tism, for sullying Japan's newly modernized image, and for many other reasons. The harshest critics dubbed him a madman and com-pared his suicide to Van Gogh's. There was intense speculation about the Nogis' state of mind, the timing of their decision, and so on. Mori Ōgai probed the psychology of junshi in more fiction. But the essence of Bushido was to push on to one's own logical conclusion without hesitation, rationalization, or introspection. Nogi had studied the writings of Jōchō and the philosophy of Wang Yangming. Shi-zuko, from an old samurai family, was as steeped in tradition as Nogi. We can assume that husband and wife were of one mind. Both knew *Hagakure*'s famous imperative: "In an either-or situation, do not delay: choose death."[118] Rationality is a threat to integrity, since to rationalize is to assess loss and profit. Only by pressing forward to the end can the samurai achieve self-completion. One's single-mindedness must be unflinching—all the way to death.

If there is a tragic element to Nogi Maresuke's fate, it resides not in his death, but in his life. It is articulated below by a character in *Kokoro*, a celebrated novel of 1914 by the great Meiji writer Natsume Sōseki:

> I read in the paper the words that General Nogi had writ-ten before killing himself. I learned that ever since the Sat-suma Rebellion, when he lost his banner to the enemy, he had been wanting to redeem his honor through death. I found myself automatically counting the years that the general had lived, always with death at the back of his mind. The Satsuma Rebellion, as you know, took place in 1877. He must therefore have lived for thirty-five years, waiting for the proper time to die. I asked myself: "When did he suffer greater agony—during those thirty-five years, or the moment when the sword entered his bowels?"[119]

118. *Hagakure*, 1:23.
119. Sōseki, *Kokoro*, 246.

Paradigms

Ikkasai Yoshitoshi. *Seppuku of Obata Sukerokurō* (Obata Sukerokurō Nobuyo), 1868. Copy of woodblock print held by Tokyo Historiographical Institute.

Iga Mitsusue called for Juō, his young son. "The time has come for us to die," he told him. "You must kill yourself."

The boy replied that he did not know how.

"Just cut your belly."

Juō removed the belt from around his waist and tied up his sleeves. He fetched a sword with a redwood hilt; he removed the hilt to leave only the bare blade, and with this he tried several times to cut his stomach. As might be expected for one so young, he could not do it.

"Fire will do just as well," said his father. "Go on, jump into the flames!"

Juō stood and faced the fire. But each time he was about to jump, he felt the blazing heat against his cheeks, and hesitated.

Tears welled in Mitsusue's eyes. "Come here, son." He took the boy on his knee. "I refused to flee," he said, "for fear that people would call me a coward. But now it has come to this! It is because I do not want another man to kill you, my son, that I must do what I now do." So saying, he gave his son one last hug and cut off his head. He cast the boy's head and body into the fire. He faced east and prayed to Hachiman, the god of war, and faced the west, chanting the name of Amida Buddha. Then Mitsusue ripped his belly and followed his son into the flames.

Chronicle of the Jōkyū Disturbance (1240)[1]

1. Matsubayashi, ed., *Jōkyūki*, 67–68.

And so the two young sons of Miura Taneyoshi ripped their bellies. Their last words were a message to be relayed to their dear mother, regretting their defeat in battle and promising to meet her in the next world. The foot of one of them continued to shake after he was dead; Taneyoshi pressed down on it until the shaking stopped. Having watched his sons perform their suicides, Taneyoshi now prepared to perform his own. To his men he gave some instructions concerning the proper disposal of the heads. He faced west toward the Pure Land and called ten times for Buddha's mercy. Then he ripped his belly from side to side, and died.

Chronicle of the Jōkyū Disturbance [2]

The castle at Kanegasaki had been under siege for six months. Yoshiaki and his guards had used up all their arrows and spears, and had eaten all the horses. The captains came to Yoshiaki saying, "My lord, it is hopeless. Let us take the prince to safety by boat and kill ourselves. Until then we will try to keep the enemy at bay." But they had not eaten for days and barely had the strength to stand. They had no choice but to cut some flesh from bodies lying dead near the second gate, and eat it to replenish themselves.

Yoshiaki informed Prince Takayoshi of their decision. "We are warriors," he said. "The time for killing is over, now is the time to die. Your Highness will be safe, for the enemy will not dare to harm a son of the emperor."

But the prince replied, "When my father returned to Kyoto, he appointed me to lead you. If I abandon you now, I am no leader. I will die with you. Please show me how it is done."

Hearing these words, Yoshiaki's eyes moistened with tears. He pointed his sword toward himself, stabbed his left side and tore the blade across to his right, cutting clean through his ribcage. He then extracted the sword and offered it the prince. Prince Takayoshi accepted the bloodied blade and plunged it into his own chest. The warriors who remained chanted sutras as they slit their stomachs, three hundred men in all.

Taiheiki (ca. 1375)[3]

Thirteen of Kusonoki Masashige's generals and sixty of their men sat in two rows among the pillars of the great hall. Ten times they chanted a Buddhist prayer, in preparation for death.

Masashige, sitting at the head, turned to his brother, Masasue. "They say the last thought you have before you die determines whether your next life will be good or bad. Tell me brother, what is your final wish?"

Masasue laughed. "I wish that I could be reborn seven times in the human world, and destroy my enemies!"

Masashige was delighted by this. "Brother, that is a truly wicked thought," he said, "and I feel exactly the same way! Very well then, let's both be reborn and realize our wish."

Having made this vow, the two brothers stabbed each other and died side by side. The eleven other commanders and the sixty retainers then ripped their bellies all at once.

Taiheiki [4]

Lord Tokiharu's men had fled, leaving him with only his wife, his two sons, and some twenty retainers. As Tokiharu watched the enemy troops surging like clouds toward his castle, he knew he could not fight them off. He told his men to do their best to hold the castle gates, and sent a messenger to a nearby temple. A priest arrived shortly and prayed for Lord Tokiharu's children, so that they might have safe passage into Paradise. To his wife Tokiharu explained, "Though our boys

3. Hasegawa, ed., *Taiheiki*, 228.
4. Ibid., 159.

are very young, the enemy will not spare them. I shall take them with me on my journey to Death." [. . .] Tokiharu took the boys outside to the river. He told them to repeat the name of Amida Buddha, and as they did so he drowned them. Tokiharu then cut his belly in a cross and lay down facing west. The priest wept, before burning the bodies until they became a hill of dust. It was from this priest that these stories, and the names of those who died, have survived.

Taiheiki[5]

And so, not knowing whether they would live to return, the shogun and his army boarded a fleet of several hundred ships and rode the waves to Akama, where they landed on February 20, 1336. They were joined six days later by five hundred mounted archers commanded by Yorinao, son of Shōni Sadatsune. Yorinao greeted the shogun and presented him with a silver kimono as a token of unswerving loyalty.

After three days they set sail again, reaching Naikai a day later, and eventually landing at Ashiya in Echizen. But on the evening of February 29 they learned that Sadatsune had killed himself at Uchiyama. Apparently, the sons of Kikuchi Taketoki had joined the imperial side and launched a treacherous attack. Sadatsune fought for two days, but was forced into retreat. Seeing that all his horses and weapons and those of his vassals had been lost in the fire, he declared, "It is very rare for the shogun to pay us a visit. I did my best, hoping to join my son. But I have shamed myself in losing this battle. What use is there in an old man like me continuing to live? I have no other wish than to give my life to the shogun. If I can achieve that, my descendants will never doubt my sincerity." With these words he headed for a temple in the hills near Dazai, and after one final clash with the enemy, Shōni Sadatsune tore open his stomach. Before he killed himself, he sent a priest to deliver this touching letter to his son: "The time has come for me to lay down my life for the shogun. Son, after I am dead, do not bother

5. Ibid., 569–70.

with the usual mourning rites. You and those who survive must unite, stand fast, and give the shogun many more years of loyal service. Consider this your duty to Buddha, and do not waste your years chanting sutras in the name of your dead father, for I shall not hear them."

Baishōron (1349)[6]

As fighting continued into the evening, the warrior Kataoka suddenly found himself surrounded by six enemy riders. He defended himself as best he could, and succeeded in killing three, but his arms were weak from the long battle. Not wanting to die on an enemy's sword, he ended his life by slashing open his belly.

The Tale of Yoshitsune (ca. 1390)[7]

For Lord [Miyoshi] Yukinaga and his two sons, their luck had run out and there was nowhere else to run. On June 4 [1520], they took refuge in Donge-in Temple, but were soon discovered. Lord [Hosokawa] Takakuni surrounded the temple with several lines of troops. It looked certain that Yukinaga and his sons would have to cut their bellies. Wishing to extend their lives, however, they surrendered and apologized to Takakuni. The sons Jirō and Magojirō left the temple first and faced Takakuni, who ordered them to be detained at a house in Kyoto. The next day, Yukinaga and his loyal servant Shinshirō were pardoned, and they too were allowed to leave Donge-in.

But one of Takakuni's generals, Awaji Hikoshirō, was unhappy about this, as Yukinaga had long been his sworn enemy. Hikoshirō requested that Yukinaga and Shinshirō be handed over to him. And so it was that on June 6, Yukinaga was taken to Chionji Temple in Kyoto and forced to cut his belly. He was beheaded by Shinshirō, who

6. Yashiro, ed., *Baishōron*, 99–100.
7. Kajihara, ed., *Gikeiki*, 487.

then killed himself. People remarked how quickly a man's fate can change.

Hikoshirō also wanted the two sons dead. His soldiers headed to the house where the boys were being detained. "Your father has cut his stomach," they said. "Now you must do the same." When they learned of their father's death, the boys wept and declared that they wished they had died by his side. The soldiers waited while the boys composed letters of farewell. Magojirō was first to cut his belly, with Jirō as his kaishaku, then Jirō cut his own belly. His last words were: "This is the fate of a samurai. Please, someone, assist me." They severed his neck with a glaive. People who were watching wept tears of pity.

Records of the Two Hosokawa Families (1550)[8]

At four o'clock in the morning on November 21, 1581, Lord Kikkawa Tsuneie heroically disemboweled himself at Shinkyōji Temple in the grounds of Tottori Castle. His death ritual was attended by Horio Yoshiharu, official representative of Lord Hideyoshi. Lord Kikkawa had awoken early, and, having performed his ablutions, he selected the sword with which he would be decapitated. He appointed Shimazu Genpei to act as his kaishaku, and granted permission for three samurai to join him in death; they were to be beheaded by a different swordsman. For his death robes, Lord Kikkawa selected a light undergarment made of a fabric tailored in Echigo Province; over that, a pea green kimono, and a coat of black silk with a matching pea green lining. He and his men went to the main hall of the temple, where they had their last drink together, using their armor boxes as seats. Lord Kikkawa wrapped some paper around the thick end of the blade of his dagger, leaving the tip exposed. He removed his coat and his robes and recited two short poems, with his eyes fixed on his comrades all the while. That being done, he pointed the dagger to his left side and cut himself cleanly across to his right. His second strike was to the center

8. *Hosokawa ryōkeki*, 590–91.

of his chest; from there, mustering his strength, he drove the dagger all the way down his front. He put his palms to the floor, and, tilting his head forward for Genpei, spoke these, his last words: "Generals will be inspecting this head. Make sure you cut it off well!" Such was the glorious end of Lord Kikkawa, who was thirty-four years of age.

Life of Lord Kikkawa Tsuneie (1585)[9]

Those who opposed Lord Nobunaga were destroyed one after another. In the autumn of 1573, Asakura Yoshikage, lord of Echizen, was cruelly forced to cut his stomach by his cousin, Kageakira, who had betrayed him to Lord Nobunaga. Two of Yoshikage's men, Torii Yoshichi and Takahashi Jinzaburō, assisted him in his final moments, and both cut their stomachs after him; Jinzaburō's death was said to have been particularly impressive. A rider delivered Yoshikage's head to Lord Nobunaga's camp. In addition, Lord Nobunaga ordered his men to hunt down Yoshikage's wife and infant son, and kill them both. Yoshikage's head was then taken to Kyoto, where it was exhibited outside the jailhouse . . .

Three days later, one of Lord Nobunaga's generals, Hashiba Hideyoshi, attacked the Azai clan at Odani Castle. Lord Azai Hisamasa was forced to cut his stomach. One of Hisamasa's favorites, a dancing instructor named Tsurumatsu, assisted him, before slitting his own stomach. It was said that each died a noble death.

The next day, Lord Nobunaga himself led the attack against Azai Nagahisa, son of Hisamasa, and successfully forced him to cut his stomach. The heads of both Azais, father and son, were sent to Kyoto and exhibited at the prison. But Azai Nagahisa also had a grandchild, a boy ten years of age. Lord Nobunaga relentlessly hunted this boy, and crucified him at a place called Sekigahara.

Ōta Gyūichi, *The Life of Oda Nobunaga*, (ca. 1600)[10]

9. Segawa, comp., *Kikkawa Tsuneie-kō jiseki*, 25–27.
10. Ōta, *Shinchō kōki*, 1:236–37.

As countless treacherous rebels swarmed into the grounds of Honnōji Temple, Lord Nobunaga fought valiantly alongside his men. First he used a bow, and fired several arrows that met their target. But in no time the bow had snapped. He then sustained a wound from a spear, and was forced to withdraw from the fight. To his wives and their maidservants he said, "You must flee while you can!" Tearfully, the women made their escape.

By now the building was engulfed in fire. Lord Nobunaga stood amidst flames. Loath to allow his enemies the sight of his corpse, he went further into the depths of the building. He found a storeroom, locked himself inside, and killed himself.

His Lordship's son, young master Nobutada, was on the other side of Kyoto, preparing to head out and join forces with his father. But just as Nobutada and his men were leaving, a messenger arrived with the terrible news that His Lordship had perished during the attack on Honnōji. Knowing that the rebels would come for him next, Nobutada led his men to Nijō Castle, where they intended to fight. Some of his commanders wanted to retreat to the great castle at Azuchi. But Nobutada declared, "Rebels such as these will not allow us to flee. If we are slain by a common foot soldier, our names will be laughed at. Let us cut our stomachs here."

It was not long until the traitor Akechi and his army arrived, and laid siege to Nijō. Nobutada's commanders boldly led their riders out to meet the attackers, and a bloody fight ensued. Sparks flew from the blades of the swords. All fought like heroes. But the enemy scaled the walls and appeared on the roofs. Arrows showered down and musket shots sounded constantly. The enemy penetrated the defenses and lit fires. Nobutada instructed his men: "After I have cut my belly, do your best to conceal my body." He ordered his vassal Kamata Shinsuke to serve as kaishaku. Nobutada's bodyguards threw themselves at their attackers and died fighting. Nobutada looked on with great sorrow as his best men were turned to corpses. Now flames were rising all about. Nobutada cut his stomach, and with a breaking heart Shinsuke chopped off his young master's head.

Ōta Gyūichi, The Life of Oda Nobunaga[11]

When one of these Lords die, ten, twenty, or thirty of his Vassals kill themselves to bear him company: many that do so, oblige themselves to it during their Lords lives; for having received some more than ordinary grace and favor from him, and fancying themselves better beloved than their companions, they think it a shame to survive their Benefactor; and therefore in return of their thanks they usually add, *My Lord, the number of your faithful Slaves is great, but what have I done to merit this honour? This Body, which is indeed yours, I offer you again, and promise it shall not live longer than yours; I will not survive so worthy a Patron.* For confirmation of this they drink a bowl of Wine together, which is solemn; for no covenants thus made are to be broken. Those that thus bind themselves cut their own bellies, and do it as follows. They assemble their nearest kindred, and going to Church, they celebrate the parting feast upon mats and carpets in the midst of the Plain, where having well eat and drink, they cut up their bellies, so that the guts and entrails burst out; and he that cuts himself highest, as some do even to the throat, is counted the bravest fellow, and most esteemed.

François Caron
A True Description of the Mighty Kingdoms of Japan and Siam (1671)[12]

Obata Sukerokurō Nobuyo was born in Ueno. He was the third son of Kōzuke-no-suke Nobushige. At the age of fifteen he went to Osaka, where he served apprenticeships with various samurai families. He became an officer of Ishida Mitsunari, Toyotomi Hideyoshi's most trusted servant, and was awarded a yearly stipend of two thousand koku of rice.

11. Ibid., 2:303–5.
12. Caron, *A True Description of the Mighty Kingdoms of Japan*, 49–50.

When Mitsunari's forces were routed at the battle of Sekigahara [in 1600], Sukerokurō was cut off by enemy troops and lost sight of Mitsunari. He managed to escape, and found his way to a village called Ishiyama. But when he inquired as to his lord's whereabouts, the villagers placed him under arrest. They delivered him to Ieyasu's headquarters at Ōtsu Castle, and received a reward of twenty gold pieces for their trouble.

Sukerokurō was taken before Ieyasu, who demanded to know where Mitsunari was hiding. He received this reply:

"I am Obata Sukerokurō, retainer of Lord Ishida Mitsunari. For sure, I know where my master is. But as one who has been honored by his many kindnesses over the years, I will not betray him to save myself. Torture me if you wish, break my bones—I will tell you nothing."

Ieyasu was impressed by these words. "This is a man who knows the meaning of loyalty," he exclaimed. "But I'll wager he hasn't the faintest notion where Mitsunari is. Why else would he have been captured alone? It would not do to mistreat a samurai of this caliber. On the contrary, we should show respect for men who demonstrate such loyalty. Untie him, and let him go."

Sukerokurō headed straight for the nearest temple. After recounting the details of what had happened to him to the priests, he announced his intention to die.

"I never expected to be set free. How can I go on living? Sooner or later I will be forced to confront the shame of my predicament. I shall die here, at this temple. Please see to it that my body is buried in secret."

And so, at the age of just twenty-three, Obata Sukerokurō cut his belly and died. It is said that when the news reached Ōtsu, Ieyasu was deeply saddened.

Yuasa Jōzan, *Tales of Jōzan* (1739)[13]

13. Yuasa, *Jōzan kidan*, 23–24.

I have found that Bushido is all about dying. In an either-or situation, do not delay: choose death. It is as simple as that. Keep calm, and press forward.

Some say it is pointless to die without achieving your goals. This is a shallow understanding of Bushido. Faced with two extremes, no one can be sure of choosing the right path; naturally we all prefer life to death, and we invent reasons to go on living. But the crucial point is this: the real coward is the man who *continues to live* without attaining his goal. Even if you have failed, no one will think ill of you as long as you choose death. This is the essence of Bushido.

Meditate daily on the inevitability of death. Each morning, when your mind and body are composed, think of being torn to pieces by arrows, bullets, spears, and swords; of being washed away by surging waves, or hurled into raging flames; of being struck by lightning, shaken to pieces by an earthquake, or cast from towering cliffs; of dying from horrible disease, or killing yourself after the passing of your lord. Consider yourself dead, every day of your life.

Jōchō, *Hagakure* (1716)[14]

The most important question for any samurai, whatever his rank, is this: *How will I behave when the time comes for me to die?* No matter how clever his words, no matter how proudly he may have carried himself in life, if he loses his composure during his final moments and dies a pitiful death, all his accomplishments will have been for nothing and he will die disgraced.

Daidōji Yūzan, *Basics of the Martial Way* (1720)[15]

14. Jōchō, *Hagakure*, 1:23; 3:207.
15. Daidōji, *Budō shoshinshū*, 95.

As for when to die, make sure you are one step ahead of everyone else. Never pull back from the brink. But be aware that there are times when you should die, and times when you should not. Die at the right moment, and you will be a hero. Die at the wrong moment, and you will die like a dog.

Izawa Nagahide, *The Warrior's Code* (1725)[16]

A servant in the employ of Lord Inaba Ittetsu was sentenced to death for some crime he had committed. Just before his execution, the man began to cry.

Someone in the crowd shouted out, "Afraid to die, eh?"

"No," said the man, "I'm crying because if I lived, I might have had a chance to use my sword in the service of my lord, but now that'll never happen."

The crowd did not like that one bit.

"Shut him up!"

"Chop his head off!"

Just then Lord Inaba arrived and pushed them back. "Let that man go!" he commanded. The executioners immediately untied the man's hands. "If you want to chop someone," Lord Inaba roared at the crowd, "try your swords on me!"

His subjects cowered before him, while the servant prostrated himself in gratitude.

Many years later [in 1589], Lord Inaba fell seriously ill. As his condition worsened, the servant came to his side. "Sire," he said, with tears streaming down his cheeks, "I have done my best to serve you, but I never had an opportunity to use my sword on your behalf."

After Lord Inaba passed away and the funeral rites were completed, the servant went to his master's grave.

"The only reason I have lived so long is because I said I wanted use my sword in your service. If I carry on living now that you are gone, people

16. In Inoue, ed., *Bushidō shū*, 2:173.

will say, 'You see—that fellow only cried because he was afraid to die'."

There and then, the servant ripped open his bowels.

Yuasa Jōzan, *Tales of Jōzan*[17]

During the siege of Arima Castle [in 1539], Nakano Shigetoshi found Mitsuse Genbei sitting on a path between rice fields near the central keep of the castle. When Shigetoshi asked him why he was not moving forward, Genbei replied, "I have terrible stomach pains, and can go no further. I have sent my men on ahead. Please take command." The incident was reported to the generals, who judged it to be a case of sheer cowardice. Genbei was ordered to remedy his stomach pains immediately—by disemboweling himself.

One of Mori Monbei's sons was involved in a fight, and came home bearing the wounds. When Monbei asked the fate of the opponent, his son replied that he had cut him down.

"And did you kill him?" asked Monbei.

The son nodded.

"Then you have done well," said his father, "Regret nothing. But whatever happens now you will have to kill yourself. Rest a while, then cut your stomach. You need not die by another man's sword. You can die by mine."

Soon after, Monbei performed his final service to his son by striking off the boy's head.

One evening in Edo, a group of samurai gathered for a game of Go. During the game, one of the men excused himself to go to the lavatory. While he was out of the room, a fierce argument erupted between two of the others. He returned to raucous commotion: the lights had been extinguished and one man lay dead.

"All of you, calm down!" he commanded. "Light the lamps again,

17. Yuasa, *Jōzan kidan*, 276–77.

and let me sort this out." Once everyone had calmed down, he struck off the head of the other man involved in the argument. He explained himself as follows: "It was bad luck for me to miss the fight. I am a samurai. People would say that I was a coward for not being involved. If I explained the reason for my absence, they would only laugh at me more, and say I fled to the toilet to save myself. Either way it would be hara-kiri for me. If I must rip my stomach, let it be because I have killed an adversary, rather than on a charge of cowardice."

When the shogun heard of this incident, he praised the samurai most highly.

Jōchō, *Hagakure* [18]

Forty-nine years
of sleep and dreams.
A long and fruitful life?
It was nothing but a cup of saké.
Death poem of Uesugi Kenshin (1578)

Those who kill
and those who are killed
are drops of dew, mere glints of lightning—
thus should we view the world.
Death poem of Ōuchi Yoshitaka (1551)

The best time to die
is when the whole world is against you.
Fall at that moment
and you will blossom like a flower.
Death poem of Shimizu Muneharu (1582) [19]

18. *Hagakure*, 2:106; 3:30; 3:153–54.
19. Fuji, *Sengoku shōgun no jisei*, 57, 25, 65.

As I tighten my stomach
to endure the pain
I hear the cry of a morning crow.
>   Death poem of Yamaoka Tesshū (1888)[20]

Death poems
are a delusion.
You just die.
>   Death poem of Kanzawa Tokō (1795)[21]

On the cultivation of courage:

Courage is born by calming the spirit. Nowadays too many people confuse courage with physical toughness. Courage has nothing to do with your body. It is a thing of the mind. Courage is what enables a samurai to be decisive. Men who hesitate or dillydally like females and little ones, how can they make the life-or-death decision that is a samurai's duty?

How to behave in an argument:

In a verbal dispute, if you notice that the other fellow is becoming too excited, you should keep calm. Either speak less, or stop talking altogether while you wait for him to regain his composure. If all else fails, move in close, stab him, and cut his throat. Depending on the circumstances, you will then have to cut your stomach or leave it to your superiors to decide your fate.

>   Hoshino Tsunetomi, *Miscellany of Military Studies* (1820)[22]

20. Kuzū, *Kōshi Yamaoka Tesshū*, 392.

21. Kanzawa, *Okinagusa*, 358.

22. Hoshino, *Bugaku shūsui*, 251, 265.

Man only makes attempts upon his own life when in a state of delirium; suicides are insane persons.

>   Jean-Etienne Esquirol, *Mental Maladies* (1838)[23]

A true warrior does not think of winning or losing; he just plunges madly toward death.

>   Jōchō, *Hagakure*[24]

We all thought, "These guys are some kind of nutcases."

>   *Jim Verdolini, USS Randolph, describing*
>   *"kamikaze" attack of March 11, 1945*[25]

100 Million Die Together!

>   *Japanese World War II slogan*

The Japanese papers occasionally contain, sandwiched between notes of railway, mining, and tram concessions, announcements like the following: "Dr. —— committed hara-kiri last night at his private residence in such and such a street. Family complications are assigned as the reason of the act." Nor does *hara-kiri* merely mean suicide by any method. *Hara-kiri* is *hara-kiri*, and the private performance is even more ghastly than the official one. It is curious to think that any one of the dapper little men with top-hats and reticules who have a Constitution of their own, may, in time of mental stress, strip to the waist, shake their hair

---

23. Esquirol, *Mental Maladies: A Treatise on Insanity*, 312.

24. Jōchō, *Hagakure*, 1:45.

25. Interviewed in Nicholson, *Day of the Kamikaze*.

over their brows, and, after prayer, rip themselves open. When you come to Japan, look at Farsari's hara-kiri pictures and his photos of the last crucifixion (twenty years ago) in Japan. Then at Deakin's, inquire for the modelled head of a gentleman who was not long ago executed in Tokyo. There is a grim fidelity in the latter work of art that will make you uncomfortable. The Japanese, in common with the rest of the East, have a strain of blood-thirstiness in their compositions. It is very carefully veiled now, but some of Hokusai's pictures show it, and show that not long ago the people revelled in its outward expression. Yet they are tender to all children beyond the tenderness of the West, courteous to each other beyond the courtesy of the English, and polite to the foreigner alike in the big towns and in the rural areas. What they will be after their Constitution has been working for three generations the Providence that made them what they are alone knows!

Rudyard Kipling, *From Sea to Sea* (1899)[26]

In 1892, at the time of the district elections in Nagano Prefecture, a rich voter named Ishijima, after having publicly pledged himself to aid in the election of a certain candidate, transferred his support to the rival candidate. On learning of this breach of promise, the wife of Ishijima robed herself in white, and performed *jigai* after the old samurai manner. The grave of this brave woman is still decorated with flowers by the people of the district, and incense is burned before her tomb.

Lafcadio Hearn, *Japan: An Attempt at Interpretation* (1905)[27]

We in this country are apt to look on *hara-kiri* as a barbarous and even theatrical form of suicide. It is nothing of the kind. It is indeed the sublimation of all those ideas of honour which constitute the very

---

26. Kipling, *From Sea to Sea*, 8.
27. Hearn, *Japan: An Attempt at Interpretation*, 318.

essence of chivalry. The first doctrine which is instilled into the mind of the young Japanese is that death is preferable to dishonour, and that no amount of worldly prosperity and no amount of success are worth having unless the honour of the man be as spotless as the steel of his blade. This spirit is carried into all relations of life, and it is the dominant influence which forms the character of the Japanese.

A. B. Mitford, *A Tragedy in Stone* (1912)[28]

NARRATOR. Hangan takes up the dagger with the point toward him. Plunging it into his left side, he starts to pull it across his abdomen. His wife, too horrified to look, murmurs the invocation to the Buddha, tears in her eyes. The sliding door to the passageway is thrown open and in rushes Ōboshi Yuranosuke. One look at his master and he throws himself down before him in dismay. Other members of the household rush in after him.

HANGAN. Yuranosuke. I waited for you as long as I could.

YURANOSUKE. To be able to look on your face while you're still alive . . .

HANGAN. I am pleased too, very pleased. No doubt you've heard all that has happened. Ah—it's exasperating, humiliating.

YURANOSUKE. I heard everything. Now that the last moments are upon us, words fail me. All I ask is that you die nobly.

HANGAN. Do you think I need to be reminded?

NARRATOR. With both hands on the dagger he pulls it across, piercing deep. He gasps with pain.

HANGAN. Yuranosuke, I leave you this dagger as a memento of me. Avenge me!

NARRATOR. He thrusts the point into his windpipe; then, throwing down the bloodstained weapon, he falls forward and breathes his last. His wife and the assembled retainers stand for a moment, transfixed, their eyes shut, their breaths bated, their teeth clenched; but Yuranosuke crawls up to his lord and, taking the dagger, lifts

28. Mitford, *A Tragedy in Stone*, 131.

it reverently to his forehead. He gazes at the bloodstained point and, clenching his fists, weeps tears of bitter regret. Hangan's last words have penetrated to his vitals. At this moment there takes root within Ōboshi Yuranosuke that noble purpose which will give him a name for loyalty and rectitude to resound through all the ages.

Takeda Izumo
The Treasury of Loyal Retainers (Kabuki play, 1748)[29]

Tenroku removed the dagger from its scabbard and put the tip of the blade to his tongue. Then he tested the blade by making a cut of about an inch into his leg.

Sanai, the young page, was staring at the floor, his knuckles tightly gripping his knees. His face was pale and he was trembling.

"Sanai! Watch now!"

As the boy looked up, Tenroku put the tip of the dagger to his left side, while using his left hand to pull his belly-skin to the right, making it tight and ready for the blade.

"Keep watching."

Sanai's eyes shone with the intensity that comes from extreme nervousness. His head and torso were frozen stiff. The dagger seemed to transmit a force that reached all the way to the backs of his eyeballs.

The tip of the dagger coldly did as it was commanded, and disappeared into Tenroku's flesh.

"Ah . . . ah . . ." It was like the groan of a ghost. Pain now showed itself in Tenroku's face, which changed to a purplish color.

"Sanai . . . are you watching?"

"Yes, sir."

Somehow it felt more painful for the watcher than the cutter. Tenroku's right hand began to shake a little. The wound opened: one inch, two inches . . . . Blobs of white fat came dribbling out, like elongated bubbles. A trickle of blood began. Tenroku kept cutting, three inches,

29. Takeda, *Chūshingura*, 70–72. Translated by Donald Keene.

four inches, wider and wider . . . His intestines were now visible. Sanai noticed that they were gray. Blood poured out. Tenroku stopped cutting and rested the dagger on his right leg. He was breathing heavily, shoulders rising and falling, as he reached out and placed his left hand on the white sheet spread out beneath him.

"Are you . . . are you watching, boy? This is . . . how a . . . a samurai . . ." He struggled to catch his breath. Trying hard not to let his eyes waver, he focused his remaining strength on Sanai's face. Very softly he said, "Did you see?" Then he mumbled something incomprehensible.

It was the sound of a human being wrestling with the agony of death.

Soon Tenroku's right hand, which was still holding the dagger, flopped down to the floor. His intestines had been pushed completely out, and the blood was still gushing. Sanai tried to stand, hoping to assist in some vague way, but his legs failed him.

"Ahh . . ." A strange sound, neither high nor low. Tenroku's face had turned the color of ash. His half-vacant expression appeared to proffer a smile. Now his trembling hands brought the blade to his neck. The tip quivered, as if blown by the wind. Perhaps realizing that he could no longer control the blade, Tenroku leaned further forward, until he was holding the dagger with both arms resting on the floor, and positioned his throat directly above the tip. When his trembling hands drove the blade into his carotid artery, a fountain of blood shot out over the white sheet. Even the silk screen behind was drenched with the blood of the dead hero.

Naoki Sanjūgo
The Bloody History of Yui Kongen (Novel, 1929)[30]

---

30. Naoki, *Yui Kongen daisatsuki*, 266–68.

Picture it. There is a solitary hill. The snow has stopped but the sky is gray under low-hanging clouds. From far off in the distance, as if the snow had sprouted wings and was swooping down upon us, there gallops a single white horse bearing a man who is a god.

The white horse tosses its head and neighs, its breath steaming in the chilly air. As it charges towards us over the snow, we offer a salute with our swords.

Daring to glance up at that divine countenance, we see a look of extraordinary determination and know that our resolve has been communicated. He speaks to us:

"Your loyalty pleases me. From this day forth I shall govern this land in person, as you had hoped. So die peacefully. You must die at once!"

Without a moment's hesitation we unbutton our tunics. As if to tear apart the snowy sky we cry, "Long live His Imperial Majesty!" and plunge our bloodied swords deep into our bellies. Thus the blood of the evil men we have slaughtered mingles with the immaculate purity of our own blood, and is cleansed at the emperor's feet.

We feel no pain. For us this death is bliss itself.

Mishima Yukio
Voices of the Heroic Dead (Short story, 1966)[31]

---

31. Mishima, "Eirei no koe," *Zenshū*, 20:487–88.

GLOSSARY OF FREQUENTLY USED JAPANESE TERMS

bakufu   the military government, controlled by the samurai class.

Bushido   "the way of the warrior," a modern name for the code of conduct to which the samurai once supposedly adhered.

hara-kiri   literally "belly-cutting"; though familiar to English speakers, in Japan this term has hardly ever been used.

ichimonji   seppuku performed with a single horizontal cut.

jūmonji   the classic form of seppuku, performed with two crossed cuts.

junshi   voluntary suicide on the death of one's lord.

kaishaku   the swordsman who decapitates the person performing seppuku.

rōnin   a samurai who has abandoned his service or been dismissed; a "lord-less" samurai.

samurai   originally meaning "servant," as one who serves a lord or master, this became a generic term to denote the military class of premodern Japan; in earlier times the word *bushi* (warrior) was more common.

seppuku   suicide by cutting the stomach, or samurai suicide in general.

shogun   the supreme leader of the military government.

BIBLIOGRAPHY

All Japanese-language publications were published in Tokyo, unless otherwise indicated.

Adachi Shōkei, ed. *Shibata Katsuie-kō shimatsuki* (The Downfall of Lord Shibata Katsuie). Vol. 10 of *Kenkyū kiyō*. Fukui: Fukui City History Museum Bulletin, 2002.

Araki Seishi. *Kanpūren jikki* (The League of the Divine Wind). Shinjinbutsu Ōraisha, 1971.

Aston, W. G. *Nihongi: Chronicles of Japan from the Earliest Times to AD 697.* 2 vols. London: George Allen & Unwin, 1956.

Atsumi Seitarō, ed. *Akō gishi geki shū* (Akō samurai drama anthology). Vol. 15 of *Nihon gikyoku zenshū*. Shun'yōdō, 1928.

Avila Girón, Bernardino de. *Nihon ōkokuki* (A Record of the Kingdom of Japan). Iwanami Shoten, 1965. (Japanese translation of *Relación del reino de Nippon a que llaman corruptante Japon.*)

De Bary, William Theodore, ed. *Sources of Japanese Tradition.* 2 vols. New York: Columbia University Press, 2001.

Berry, Mary Elizabeth. *Hideyoshi.* Cambridge, MA: Harvard University Press, 1982.

Bitō Masahide. *Genroku jidai* (The Genroku Period). Vol. 19 of *Nihon no rekishi*. Shōgakukan, 1983.

Blusse, J. L., and W. G. J. Remmelink, eds., trans. *Deshima Diaries.* Vol. 2. Tokyo: The Japan-Netherlands Institute, 2004.

Caron, François. *A True Description of the Mighty Kingdoms of Japan and Siam.* Translated by Capt. Roger Manley. London: Roger Boulter, 1671.

Cassius Dio. *Roman History.* Vols. 1–8. Books 61–70, Loeb Classical Library. Cambridge, MA: Harvard University Press, 1925.

Chamberlain, Basil Hall. *Things Japanese: Being Notes on Various Subjects Connected with Japan for the Use of Travellers and Others.* London: John Murray, 1905.

Chiba Tokuji. *Seppuku no hanashi* (On Seppuku). Kōdansha, 1972.

Cioran, Emile. *On the Heights of Despair.* Chicago: University of Chicago Press, 1992.

———. *The Temptation to Exist.* Chicago: University of Chicago Press, 1998.

Cortazzi, Hugh. *Dr. Willis in Japan, 1862–1877*. London: Athlone Press, 1985.

Daidōji Yūzan. *Budō shoshinshū* (Basics of the Martial Way). Tokuma Shoten, 1982.

Dai Nihon shiryō (Chronological Source Books of Japanese History). No. 12, vol. 16. Tōkyō Teikoku Daigaku Bunka Daigaku Shiryō Hensangakari, 1913.

Dickens, Frederick. *The Life of Sir Harry Parkes, Minister Plenipotentiary to Japan*. London: Macmillan, 1894.

Di Nunno, N., et al. "Suicide by Hara-kiri: A Series of Four Cases." *The American Journal of Forensic Medicine and Pathology* (March 2001): 68–72.

Du Petit-Thouars, Bergasse. *Furansu kanchō no mita Sakai jiken* (The Sakai Incident As Seen by the French Captain). Shinjinbutsu Ōraisha, 1993. (Japanese translation of extracts from *Le vice-admiral Bergasse du Petit-Thouars d'après ses notes et sa correspondance*. Paris: Pellan, 1906.)

Esquirol, Jean-Etienne. *Mental Maladies: A Treatise on Insanity*. New York: Hafner Publications, 1965.

Friday, Karl. "Bushidō or Bull? A Medieval Historian's Perspective on the Imperial Army and the Japanese Warrior Tradition." *The History Teacher* 27, no. 3 (May 1994).

———. *Samurai, Warfare and the State in Early Medieval Japan*. New York: Routledge, 2004.

Fuji Kimifusa. *Sengoku shōgun no jisei* (Death Poems of the Sengoku Warlords). Karuchā Shuppansha, 1973.

Fujii Shinji, ed. *Edo bakufu nikki* (Edo Government Diaries). Vol. 25. Yumani Shobō, 2004.

Fujioka Shūzō. *Matsunaga Hisahide no shinjitsu* (The Facts about Matsunaga Hisahide). Bungeisha, 2007.

Fukunaga Takehiko, ed. *Konjaku monogatari* (Tales of Times Now Past). Kawade Shobō Shinsha, 1982.

Fukushima Shirō. *Seishi chūshingura* (A True History of the Loyal League). Chūkō Bunko, 1992.

Furukawa Tesshi. *Junshi: Higeki no iseki* (Martyrdom's Tragic Relics). Jinbutsu Ōraisha, 1967.

Gianroku: Seppuku kinshi shikaru beshi no gi (Parliamentary Minutes: Motion to Ban Seppuku). March–May 1869.

Harima Mitsutoshi, ed. *Zoku-kojidan* (More Old Tales). Ōfū, 2002.

Harris, Sam. *The End of Faith: Religion, Terror, and the Future of Reason*. New York: W. W. Norton, 2005.

Harte, Richard. "A Case of Hara-Kiri which Terminated in Recovery." Vol. 27 of *Annals of Surgery*. Philadelphia, June 1898.

Hasegawa Tadashi, ed. *Taiheiki* (Record of the Great Peace). In *Shinpen Nihon koten bungaku zenshū*. Shōgakukan, 1998.

Hayakawa Kiyoji. *Shijitsu: Aizu byakkotai* (Historical Facts of the Aizu White Tigers). Shinjinbutsu Ōraisha, 1976.

Hearn, Lafcadio. *Japan: An Attempt at Interpretation*. London: MacMillan & Co., 1920.

Heki Ken, ed. *Kaga-han shiryō* (Historical Documents of the Kaga Domain). Vol. 5. Seibundō, 1970.

Hiraishi Benzō. *Aizu Boshin sensō* (The Aizu Boshin War). Fukushima: Maruhachi Shōten Shuppanbu, 1927.

Hoffmann, Yoel. *Japanese Death Poems*. Tokyo: Tuttle Publishing, 1986.

Honma Junji. *Nihontō no rekishi* (A History of the Japanese Sword). Tokuma Shoten, 1966.

Horiuchi Densaemon. *Horiuchi Densaemon oboegaki* (Memoirs). Vol. 8 of *Kaitei shiseki shūran*. Rinsen Shoten, 1985.

Hoshino Tsunetomi. *Bugaku shūsui* (Miscellany of Military Studies). Bunkyōen, 1997.

Hosokawa ryōkeki (Records of the Two Hosokawa Families). Vol. 20 of *Gunsho ryuijū*. Zoku-Gunsho Ruijū Kanseikai, 1979.

Hurst, G. Cameron. "Death, Honor, and Loyalty." *Philosophy East and West* 40 (1990): 521–27.

Inoue Takashi. *Shōbu ari: Inokuma Isao no hikari to kage* (Fight! The Light and Dark of Inokuma Isao). Kawade Shobō Shinsha, 2004.

Inoue Tetsujirō, ed. *Bushidō shū* (A Bushido Reader). Vols. 1–3. Dai Nippon Bunkokan Gyōkai, 1940.

Ise Sadatake. *Anzai zuihitsu* (Essays of Anzai). 2 vols. Meiji Tosho Shuppan, 1993.

———. *Kyōrei-shiki* (The Deadly Ritual). Vol. 17 of *Kaitei shiseki shūran*. Rinsen Shoten, 1984.

Ishii Shirō, ed. *Kinsei buke shisō*, (Military Thought in the Early Modern Era). Vol. 27 of *Nihon shisō ōgakari*. Iwanami Shoten, 1974.

Itiko Teiji, ed. *Heike monogatari* (The Tale of the Heike). Vol. 29 of *Nihon koten bungaku zenshū*. Shōgakukan, 1973.

Itō Makoto. *Hōreki chisui to Satsuma hanshi* (The Hōreki Water Project and the Satsuma Samurai). Tsuru Shobō, 1943.

Iwata Tokuyoshi. *Hōreki chisui kōji Satsuma gishi junsetsu-roku* (The Hōreki Water Project and the Satsuma Martyrs). Azabu Gakkan, 1919.

Jesus kaishi Nihon tsūshin (Letters of the Jesuits in Japan). 2 vols. Translated into modern Japanese by Murakami Naojirō. Yūshōdō Shoten, 1969.

Jōchō (Yamamoto Tsunetomo). *Hagakure*. Vols. 1–3, Iwanami Shoten, 2006–2009.

Kaempfer, Engelbert. *Kaempfer's Japan: Tokugawa Culture Observed*. Edited by Beatrice M. Bodart-Bailey. Hawaii: University of Hawaii Press, 1998.

Kagawa Masanori. *Intoku taiheiki* (Secret Record of the Great Peace). Kyōikusha, 1980.

Kaionji Chōgorō. *Akunin retsuden* (Lives of Evil Men). Asahi Shinbunsha, 1970.

Kaishaku narabini seppuku dōtsuki no shidai (Notes on Decapitation and Stomach-cutting). Handwritten manuscript, ca. 1720. Archive of Kanazawa City Library.

Kaishaku no shikihō (Decapitation Method). Handwritten manuscript, ca. 1830. National Archives of Japan.

Kaisōsho Kankōkai, ed. *Kōranki* (Kō Battle Records). Vol. 2 of *Kaisōsho*. Daiichi Shobō, 1974.

Kajihara Masaaki, ed. *Gikeiki* (The Tale of Yoshitsune). Vol. 31 of *Nihon koten bungaku zenshū*. Shōgakukan, 1971.

———, ed. *Soga monogatari* (The Tale of the Soga). Vol. 53 of *Shinpen Nihon koten bungaku zenshū*. Shōgakukan, 2002.

Kamo no Chōmei. *An Account of My Hut: The Hōjōki of Kamo no Chōmei*. Translated by Donald Keene. Pawlet, Vt: Banyan Press, 1976.

Kanzawa Tokō. *Okinagusa* (Pasqueflowers). Vol. 24 of *Nihon zuihitsu taisei*. Nihon Zuihitsu Taisei Kankōkai, 1975.

Kasuga Tarō. *Hana no wakamusha: Nishina Gorō Morinobu* (Glorious Young Warrior: Nishina Morinobu). Ina Mainichi Shinbunsha, 1982.

Katō Tōru. *Kairiki ranshin* (Things Supernatural). Chūō Kōron Shinsha, 2007.

Keene, Donald. *Emperor of Japan: Meiji and his World 1852–1912*. New York: Columbia University Press, 2002.

Kigoshi Osamu, ed. *Ukiyo zōshi kaidanshū* (Chilling Tales from the Floating World). Kokushokan Kōkai, 1994.

Kikuchi Kyūjirō. *Nihon ni okeru ryūketsu to shi no tetsugaku* (Philosophy of Death and Bloodshed in Japan). Kitoku Shobō, 1974.

Kipling, Rudyard. *From Sea to Sea and Other Sketches*. London: MacMillan, 1928.

Kishitani Seiichi, ed. *Hōgen monogatari* (The Tale of the Hōgen Rebellion). Iwanami Shoten, 1934.

Koike Yoshiaki. *Hagakure: Bushi to hōkō* (Hagakure: Warriors and Servitude). Kōdansha, 1999.

Koishikawa Zenji. *Autorō no kindaishi: Bakuto, yakuza, bōryokudan* (A Modern History of Outlaws: Gamblers, Yakuza, and Violent Gangs). Heibonsha, 2008.

Kondō Heijō, ed. *Kaitei shiseki shūran* (Collection of Historical Materials: Revised Edition). Vols 1–15. Rinsen Shoten, 1983–84.

Konishi Katsujirō, *Satsuma gishi-roku* (Records of the Loyal Satsuma Samurai). Gifu: Seinō Insatsu-gaisha Gifu Shuppanbu, 1915.

Kudō Yukihiro. *Jijin-roku* (Records of Suicide by Sword) in *Rekishi kōron*, 50–66, June 1937.

Kurano Kenji, ed. *Kojiki* (Records of Ancient Matters). Iwanami Shoten, 1978.

Kuroki Yūkichi. *Nogi Maresuke*. Kōdansha, 1978.

Kurose Shōjirō. *Seppuku*. Chichi Shuppansha, 1996.

Kurume jinbutsu-shi (Biographies of Famous People of Kurume). Fukuoka: Kurume Jinbutsu-shi Kankōkai, 1981.

Kuwata Tadachika, *Sen no Rikyū*. Sōgensha, 1952.

———. *Sen no Rikyū kenkyū* (Researching Sen no Rikyū). Tōkyōdō Shuppan, 1976.

Kuzū Yoshihisa. *Kōshi Yamaoka Tesshū* (Life of Yamaoka Tesshū). Ōzorasha, 1997.

Lü Buwei. *The Annals of Lü Buwei*. Translated by J. Knoblock and J. Riegel. Stanford: Stanford University Press, 2000.

Matsubayashi Yasuaki, ed. *Jōkyūki shintei* (Chronicle of the Jōkyū Disturbance: New Edition), Gendai Shinshōsha, 1982.

Matsuoka Jōji. *Takechi Hanpeita den* (Life of Takechi Hanpeita). Shinjinbutsu Ōraisha, 1997.

Miki Yasushi. *Shimazu Yoshihiro no subete* (All About Shimazu Yoshihiro). Shinjinbutsu Ōraisha, 1986.

Mishima Yukio. *Ketteiban Mishima Yukio zenshū* (Complete Works). Shinchōsha, 2005.

Mitamura Engyo. *Daimyō no onna hara-kiri* (Belly-ripping Wives of the Feudal Lords). Vol. 2 of *Mitamura Engyo zenshū*. Chūō Kōronsha, 1975.

———, ed. *Seirinki* (The Seirin Chronicles). In *Rekkō shinpi roku*. Kokusho Kankōkai, 1914.

Mitford, A. B. *A Tragedy in Stone*. London: John Lane, 1912.

———. *Tales of Old Japan*. London: Macmillan, 1903.

Miyazawa Seiichi. *Akō rōshi* (The Akō Samurai). Sanseidō, 1999.

Muramatsu Takeshi. *Shi no Nihon bungakushi* (A History of Death in Japanese Literature). Shinchōsha, 1975.

Muro Kyūsō. *Kenkaroku* (A Record of Kenka). Vol. 3 of *Nihon keizai sōsho*. Nihon Keizai Sōsho Kankōkai, 1914–1917.

———. *Sundai zatsuwa* (Sundai's Miscellany). Vol. 6 of *Nihon zuihitsu taisei*. Yoshikawa Kōbunka, 1977.

Nakai Isao. *Seppuku*. Nōberu Shoten, 1970.

Nakajima Motoyuki, *Chūgoku heiranki* (History of the Chūgoku Battles). In *Shinshaku Bicchū heiranki*. Sanyō Shinbunsha, 1994.

Nakamura Akihiko. *Byakkotai* (The White Tigers). Bungei Shunjū, 2001.

Nakamura Hirasato. *Senran seppuku no kigen* (Origins of Stomach-cutting in Battle). In *Rettō no bunkashi 11*, October 1998.

Nakayasu Hiromichi. *Seppuku: Hisōbi no sekai* (Seppuku: World of Tragic Beauty). Kubo Shoten, 1960.

———. *Seppuku: Rekishi to bungei* (Stomach-cutting in History and Literature). Kyoto: Sanninkai, 1979.

Nanzan Shiga kishō (Historical Records of the Shiga Family). Vol. 1 of *Oita-ken kyōdo shiryō shūsei*. Oita: Oita-ken Kyōdo Shiryō Kankōkai, 1938.

Naoki Sanjūgo. *Yui Kongen daisatsuki* (The Bloody History of Yui Kongen). Rippū Shobō, 1970.

Nicholson, Peter (director). *Day of the Kamikaze* (documentary movie). Smithsonian Networks, 2007.

Nihon kiryaku (History of Japan). Vol. 2. Kokushi Taikei Kankōkai, 1929.

Nitobe Inazō. *Bushido: The Soul of Japan*. London: G. P. Putnam's Sons, 1905.

Nogi Maresuke. *Nogi Maresuke zenshū* (Complete Works). 3 vols. Kokusho Kankōkai, 1994.

Noguchi Takehiko. *Akō jiken: Shijitsu no nikusei* (The Akō Incident: The Verbatim Facts). Chikuma Shobō, 1994.

Norimoto Yoshihiro. *Nihonjin no shiseikan* (Japanese Attitudes to Life and Death). Sankyō Shoin, 1943.

Ōeiki (Record of the Ōei Revolt). Vol. 7 of *Koten shiryō*. Sumiya Shobō, 1970.

Ōishi Manabu, *Shinsengumi: Saigo no bushi no jitsuzō* (The Shinsengumi: A Portrait of Japan's Last True Warriors). Shinjinbutsu Ōraisha, 2004.

Ōkuma Miyoshi. *Seppuku no rekishi* (History of Stomach-cutting). Yūzankaku Shuppan, 1973.

———. *Shinpūren kekki* (The Uprising of the League of the Divine Wind). Shinjinbutsu Ōraisha, 1975.

Ōta Gyūichi. *Shinchō kōki* (The Life of Oda Nobunaga). 2 vols. Translated into modern Japanese by Sakakiyama Jun. Shinjinbutsu Ōraisha, 1997.

———. *Taikō gunki* (Biography of Toyotomi Hideyoshi). In *Taikō shiryōshū*. Edited by Kuwata Tadachika. Shinjinbutsu Ōraisha, 1971.

Ōtomo kōhaiki (The Rise and Fall of the Ōtomo, ca. 1615). Vol. 2 of *Oita-ken kyōdo shiryōshū*. Oita: Oita-ken Kyōdo Shiryō Kankōkai, 1938.

Owada Tetsuo. *Toyotomi Hidetsugu* (Life of Toyotomi Hidetsugu). PHP Shinsho, 2002.

Oze Hoan. *Shinchōki* (Battles of Nobunaga, ca. 1630). 2 vols. Gendai Shinchōsha, 1981.

———. *Taikōki* (The Taikō Chronicles, 1626). Iwanami Shoten, 1996.

Pinguet, Maurice. *Voluntary Death in Japan*. Translated by Rosemary Morris. Cambridge: Polity Press, 1993.

Saeki Ariyoshi, ed. *Bushidō zensho* (Complete Writings on Bushido). Jidaisha, 1943.

Saikaku (Ihara Saikaku). *Namagimo wa myōyaku no yoshi* ("Raw Livers Make a Most Unusual Medicine"). Vol. 5 of Ebara Taizō, ed. *Saikaku zenshū*. Chuo Koronsha, 1975.

———. *Nanshoku ōgakami* (The Great Mirror of Male Love). In *Ihara Saikaku shū*. Chikuma Shobō, 1959.

Sakamoto Tarō, ed. *Nihon shoki* (Chronicles of Japan). 2 vols. Iwanami Shoten, 1967.

Sakanoue Nobuo. *Seppuku-kei* (Stomach-cutting as Punishment). In *Hanzai kagaku*. February 1931.

Sanada Zōyo. *Meiryō kōhan* (Bakufu Histories, ca. 1704). Kokusho Kankōkai, 1912.

Sasaki Hideaki. *Nogi Maresuke*. Kyoto: Minerva Shobō, 2005.

Sasaki Kaizō. *Senshū Sakai-to hanshi rekkyo jikki* (A True Account of the Sakai Samurai). Kōchi: Tosa Shidankai, 1979.

Satō Kanzan. *The Japanese Sword*. Tokyo: Kodansha International, 1983.

Satō Masahide, ed. *Kōyō gunkan* (Kōyō Military Chronicles). Chikuma Shōbō, 2006.

Satow, Sir Ernest. *A Diplomat in Japan*. Oxford: Oxford University Press, 1968.

Segawa Hideo, comp. *Kikkawa Tsuneie-kō jiseki* (Contemporary Documents Pertaining to the Life of Lord Kikkawa Tsuneie). Private publication, 1931.

Seki Atsuo. *Hitosuji no hotarubi—Yoshida Shōin: Hito to kotoba* (Yoshida Shōin: Man and Words). Bunju Shinsho 2007.

Sendō gunki (Sendō War Chronicles). In *Sendō gunki ganban gunki shū*. Rekishi Toshosha, 1979.

Seppuku kaishaku no shidai (Concerning Stomach-cutting and Decapitation). Undated manuscript ca. 1725. University of Waseda Library.

Seppuku mokuroku (Main Points of Stomach-cutting). Unpublished manuscript ca. 1749. Private collection.

Shimamura Arihiro, ed. *Ōninki* (The Ōnin War). Vol. 2 of *Nihon gassen sōdō sōsho*. Benseisha, 1994.

Shimazu yorokki (History of the Shimazu Family). Unpublished manuscript dated 1648. Archives of the Kyushu University Museum.

Shimizu Katsuyuki. *Kenka ryōseihai no tanjō* (The Birth of Dual Blame). Kodansha, 2006.

Shiraishi Ichirō. *Seppuku*. Bungei Shunju, 1996.

Sima Qian. *The First Emperor: Selections from the Historical Records*. Translated by R. S. Dawson. Oxford: Oxford University Press, 2007.

Sobue Tsunetsugu. *Seppuku kaishaku den* (Remarks on Stomach-cutting and Decapitation). Facsimile of 1633 manuscript; afterword ca. 1815. Archives of Tokyo Metropolitan Tama Library.

Sōseki (Natsume Sōseki). *Kokoro*. Translated by Edwin McClellan. London: Peter Owen, 1957.

Spence, Jonathan D., and John E. Wills, eds. *From Ming to Ch'ing: Conquest, Region, and Continuity in Seventeenth-Century China*. New Haven: Yale University Press, 1979.

Suzuki Ryōichi. *Toyotomi Hideyoshi*. Iwanami Shoten, 1960.

Tacitus. *The Histories*. Vols. 1–3. Loeb Classical Library. Cambridge, MA: Harvard University Press, 1925.

Takahashi Yoshitaka. *Shi to nihonjin* (Death and the Japanese). Shinchōsha, 1959.

Takayama Hikokurō. *Takayama Hikokurō zenshū* (Complete Works). 4 vols. Edited by Hagiwara Susumu. Takayama Hikokurō Ikō Kankōkai, 1954.

Takayanagi, Mitsutoshi. *Takayanagi Mitsutoshi shigaku ronbunshū* (Historical Essays). Yoshikawa Kōbunkan, 1970.

Takeda Izumo. *Chūshingura: The Treasury of Loyal Retainers.* Translated by Donald Keene. New York: Columbia University Press, 1971.

Tomikura Tokujirō, ed. *Meitokuki* (Record of the Meitoku Rebellion). Iwanami Shoten, 1941.

Uegaki Setsuya, ed. *Harima fudoki* (Winds and Earth of Harima). Vol. 5 of *Shinpen Nihon koten bungaku zenshū.* Shōgakukan 1997.

Ujiie Mikito. *Bushidō to Eros* (Bushido and Eros). Kōdansha Gendai Shinsho, 1995.

———. *Ō-edo shitai-kō: Hitokiri Asaemon no jidai* (Dead Bodies in Edo: The Era of Asaemon the Chopper). Heibonsha, 1999.

———. *Ō-edo zankoku monogatari* (Cruel Tales of Edo). Yōsensha, 2002.

Usami Tomoharu. *Seppuku kuketsu: Sudata-ryū seppuku kaishaku den* (Rules for Stomach-cutting: The Sudata Method of Stomach-cutting and Decapitation). Fascimile of handwritten manuscript, ca. 1840. Tokyo Historiographical Insitute.

Wada Katsunori. *Seppuku.* Aoba Shobō, 1943.

———. *Seppuku tetsugaku* (Philosophy of Stomach-cutting). Shūbunsha, 1927.

Washburn, Stanley. *Nogi: A Great Man Against a Background of War.* London: Andrew Melrose, 1913.

Watanabe Kyōji. *Shinpūren to sono jidai* (The League of the Divine Wind and Its Times). Yōsensha, 2006.

Watanabe T., et al. "Hara-kiri and Suicide by Sharp Instruments in Japan." In *Forensic Science,* May 1973.

Watanabe Yosuke, ed. *Akō gishi shiryō* (Historical Papers Concerning the Akō Incident). Vols. 1–3. 1931. Reprint, Yūzankaku, 1999.

———. *Seishi Akō gishi* (True History of the Akō Samurai). Kōwadō, 1998.

Williams, Harold S., and Naitō Hiroshi. *The Kamakura Murders of 1864: Major Baldwin and Lieutenant Bird.* Tokyo, 1971.

Wilson, William, trans. *Tale of the Disorder in Hōgen.* Tokyo: Sophia University, 1971.

Wittermans, Elizabeth P., and John Z. Bowers, trans. *Doctor on Desima: Selected chapters from J.L.C. Pompe van Meerdervoort's Vijf jaren in Japan [Five Years in Japan] (1857-1863).* Tokyo: Sophia University *Monumenta Nipponica* monograph, 1970.

Yagiri Tomeo. *Seppuku no bigaku* (Aesthetics of Stomach-cutting). Akita Shoten, 1971.

———. *Seppuku ronkō* (Thoughts on Stomach-cutting). Chūō Kōronsha, 1979.

Yagyū Munenori. *Heihō kadensho* (Book of Traditional Tactics). Iwanami Shoten, 1985.

Yamada Tadao. "Sano Masakoto seppuku yowa" (Some Details Concerning the Seppuku of Sano Masakoto). *Shigaku* 57, no. 4. Keio University, 1988.

Yamamoto Hirofumi. *Chūshingura* (The Facts about the Loyal League). Chūkei Shuppan, 2003.

———. *Junshi no kōzō* (The Structure of Martyrdom). Kōbundō, 1994.

———. *Seppuku: Nihonjin no sekinin no torikata* (Seppuku: How the Japanese Take Responsibility). Kōbunsha Shinsho, 2003.

Yamana Shōtaro. *Nippon jisatsu jōshiki* (History of Love Suicides in Japan). Dai-dōkan Shoten, 1928.

Yamaoka Shunmei. *Hara-kiri kō* (Thoughts on Belly-ripping, 1772). *Zuihitsu bun-gaku senshū*. Shosaisha, 1927.

Yashiro Kazuo, ed. *Akamatsu monogatari, Kakitsuki* (The Tale of Akamatsu: The Chronicle of Kakitsu). Translated into modern Japanese by Yashiro Kazuo. Benseisha, 1994.

———, ed. *Baishōron* (Of Plums and Pines). Gendai Shinchōsha, 1975.

Yokoyama Kendō. *Seppuku-ron* (Theory of Stomach-cutting). Vol. 1 of *Bungei Kōenshū*. Bunrokudō, 1906.

Yoshimoto Shinji, ed. *Dankai, gyokuteki inken* (Documentary Record of the Tokugawa Period, ca.1680). Kyūko Shoin, 1985.

Yuasa Jōzan. *Jōzan kidan* (Tales of Jōzan). Osaka: Izumi Shoin, 1992.

Žižek, Slavoj. *Welcome to the Desert of the Real*. London: Verso, 2002.

INDEX

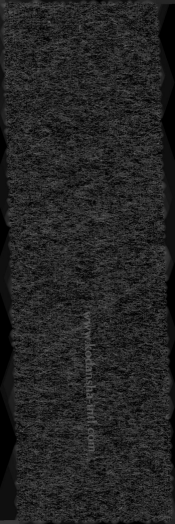

（英文版）切腹

Seppuku: A History of Samurai Suicide

2011年1月25日　第 1 刷発行

著　者　　アンドリュー・ランキン

発行者　　廣田浩二

発行所　　講談社インターナショナル株式会社

〒112–8652　東京都文京区音羽 1–17–14

電話　03–3944–6493（編集部）

　　　03–3944–6492（マーケティング部・業務部）

ホームページ　www.kodansha-intl.com

印刷・製本所　大日本印刷株式会社

落丁本・乱丁本は購入書店名を明記のうえ、講談社インターナショナル業務部宛にお送りください。送料小社負担にてお取替えします。なお、この本についてのお問い合わせは、編集部宛にお願いいたします。本書の無断複写(コピー)、転載は著作権法の例外を除き、禁じられています。

定価はカバーに表示してあります。

DATE DUE